MUSCULAR CHURCHES

Photographs by the author

Drawings by Elam Denham

The University of Arkansas Press

Fayetteville   1989   London

MUSCULAR CHURCHES

Ecclesiastical Architecture of
the High Victorian Period

C. M. Smart, Jr.

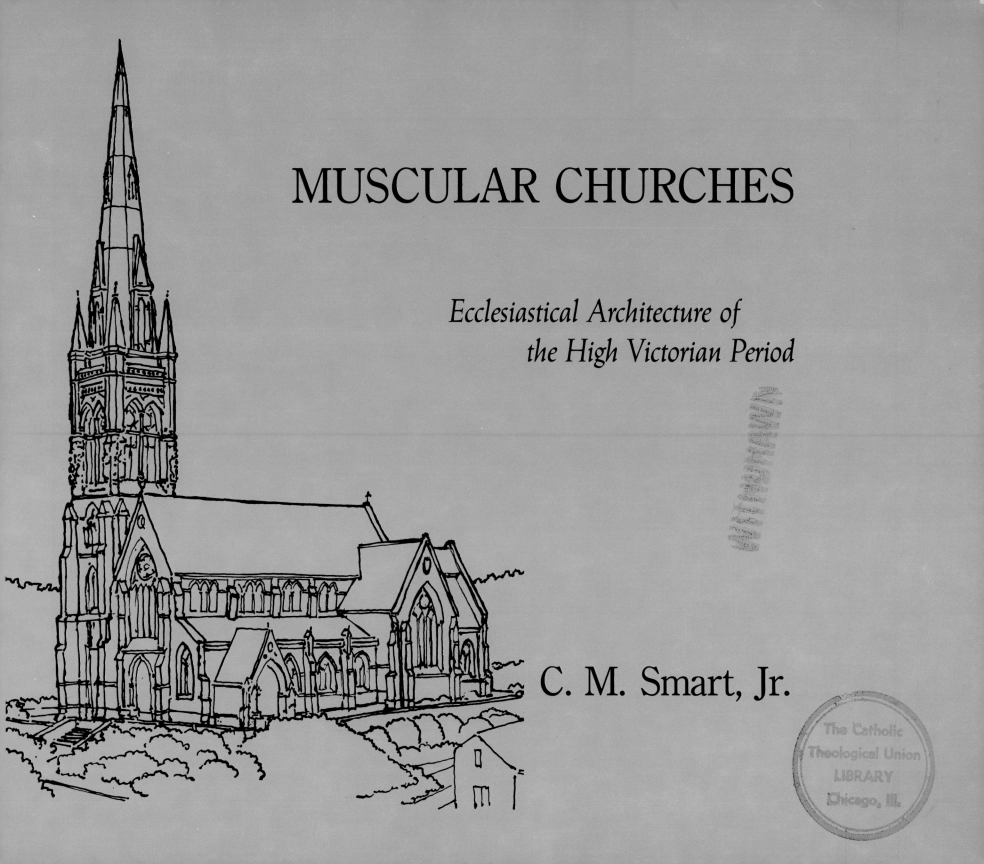

Designer: *Chang-hee H. Russell*
Typeface: *Linotron 202 Century Old Style*
Typesetter: *G&S Typesetters, Inc.*
Printer: *Dong-A Publishing & Printing Co., Ltd.*
Binder: *Dong-A Publishing & Printing Co., Ltd.*

The paper used in this publication meets the minimum
requirements of the American National Standard for
Permanence of Paper for Printed Library Materials
Z39.48-1984. ∞

Library of Congress Cataloging-in-Publication Data

Smart, C. M.
    Muscular churches : ecclesiastical architecture of the high
Victorian period / C.M. Smart, Jr. ; drawings by Elam Denham ;
photographs by the author.
        p.   cm.
    Includes index.
    Bibliography: p.
    ISBN 1-55728-088-6 (alk. paper).
    ISBN 1-55728-089-4 (pbk. : alk. paper)
(pbk. : alk. paper)
    1. Church architecture—England.   2. Architecture,
Victorian—England.   I. Title.
NA5467.S6   1989
726'.5'094209034—dc20   89-31653
                                                CIP

To *Carolyn,* in grateful appreciation

CONTENTS

ACKNOWLEDGMENTS

I am grateful to University of Arkansas Chancellor Dan Ferritor and Vice Chancellor for Academic Affairs Donald O. Pederson for allowing me time away from my administrative duties, including an off-campus-duty assignment, to complete the research for and writing of this book. I am thankful to Associate Dean Ernest Jacks and Program Director Michael Buono for the willingness they demonstrated in taking over many of my duties during the period that the manuscript was underway; I could not have completed the book without this assistance. I am also appreciative of the help provided by my secretary, Ruth Casey, and my colleagues, especially Geoffrey Baker, Graham F. Shannon, and Charles Witsell, who were kind enough to read my manuscript and offer valuable suggestions. The staff of the interlibrary loan department of Mullins Library and Joyce Clinkscales, the Fine Arts Librarian, were unfailingly helpful throughout the research stage. Most of all, however, I am grateful to my wife, who willingly helped in so many ways—map reading, keeping notes on photographs and keeping up with photographic gear, editing and proofreading, and offering encouragement throughout the seven-year period that I worked on this project.

In England, countless individuals assisted me by providing access to buildings and permission to photograph. The list of these people includes the following:

Canon Derek W. Allen, St. Saviour, Eastbourne
The Reverend R. J. Avent, St. Augustine, Kilburn Park
The Reverend W. J. Bennett, St. Peter, Daylesford
Precentor P. W. Bide, Christ Church, Oxford
Churchwarden Mary Braden, St. Mary, Thixendale
The Reverend David Brazington, St. John the Baptist, Huntley
The Provost, Lord Briggs, Worcester College Chapel, Oxford
The Reverend F. E. Brown, St. Augustine, Pendlebury
The Reverend and Mrs. Norman J. Brown, All Saints, Maidenhead
The Reverend Ian E. Burbery, All Saints, Selsley
The Reverend Keith Butterworth, Holy Cross, Clayton

The Reverend J. M. G. Carey, Dean, St. Fin Barre's Cathedral, Cork

The Reverend Dr. T. A. Chadwick, Albion Reformed Church, Ashton-under-Lyne

Churchwarden John F. Chapman, St. Mary, Fimber

The Reverend Thomas Cockburn, St. Giles, Cheadle

Canon Alan Coldwells, St. Andrew, Rugby

The Reverend N. H. Collins, St. Augustine, Penarth

Miss L. M. Dakin, St. Margaret's Convent, East Grinstead

The Very Reverend A. H. Dammers, Dean, Bristol Cathedral

The Reverend Nicholas Davis, St. Peter, Vauxhall

Archivist Frances Davey, St. Michael and All Angels, Lyndhurst

Parish Clerk Dinah Dean, Waltham Abbey

The Reverend Anthony de Vere, St. Barnabas, Horton-cum-Studley

The Reverend John H. B. Douglas, Thirkleby and Bagby Parish Churches

Mr. John Drake and his colleagues, Historic Buildings and Monuments Commission for England

The Reverend Eric Essery, Christ Church, Reading

The Reverend John Fagan, St. Editha, Amington

The Reverend Jeremy Fairhead, All Saints, Notting Hill

The Reverend Bruce Findlow, Manchester College, Oxford

Mr. C. T. Fletcher, Bursar, Keble College, Oxford

Mr. P. C. Gibbing, Administrator, Faringdon Collection Trust, Buscot Park

The Reverend M. F. Glare, All Saints, Babbacombe

The Reverend Noel Godwin, St. Michael, Croydon

The Reverend Andrew Grant, St. Peter, Vauxhall

The Reverend Robert Greaves, All Saints, Brightwalton

The Reverend Paul Green, Holy Innocents, Highnam

The Reverend C. J. Hawthorn, St. Martin on the Hill, Scarborough

The Reverend Francis Hewitt, Christ Church, Appleton-le-Moors

Director of Music Michael Hill, Manchester College, Oxford

The Reverend D. N. Hope, All Saints, Margaret Street, London

The Reverend B. Hopper, St. Michael and All Angels, Brighton

The Reverend David Hoskin, St. Leonard, Scorborough

The Reverend Prebendary John Howe, Holy Angels, Hoar Cross

The Reverend H. E. Hutchinson, St. Mary, Dalton Holme

Mr. Ivan Hutnik, Administrator, The Oxford Center for Mission Studies (St. Philip and St. James Church)

The Reverend D. H. R. Jones, St. Peter, Bournemouth

Parish Secretary Lilian M. Jones, All Hallows, Allerton

The Reverend Robert Kilvert, St. James, Clanfield

Mrs. Mary Kirk, Secretary to the Headmaster, Bradfield College

The Reverend K. Peter Lee, St. John the Divine, Frankby

The Reverend Ian Ludlow, St. Michael and All Angels, Tenbury Wells

Parish Administrator Cameron Mcintosh, St. Augustine, Queen's Gate, London

Parish Administrator and Mrs. George E. McKean, All Souls, Haley Hill, Halifax

The Reverend R. C. D. Mackenna, St. Peter, Hascombe

The Reverend Michael Markey, St. Mary Magdalene, Munster Square, London

Churchwarden A. L. Moon, St. Peter and St. Paul, Cattistock

The Very Reverend Basil Moss, Provost, Birmingham Cathedral

Churchwarden Edward C. Nash, St. John the Baptist, Lower Shuckburgh

The Reverend Peter B. Price, St. Mary Magdalene,
Addiscombe, Croydon

The Reverend Eric Rastall, All Saints, Denstone

The Reverend Peter Richards, St. Andrew, Toddington

The Reverend C. A. Rowe, St. Matthias, Stoke Newington, London

Dean Christopher Rowland, Jesus College, Cambridge

The Reverend Canon Frank Sampson, St. John the Baptist, Tuebrook

Parish Administrator Christine Sanders, All Saints, Maidenhead

Churchwarden William Shepherd, St. Martin, Gospel Oak, London

The Reverend H. B. Siviter, St. John, Knotty Ash

The Reverend C. I. McN. Smith, St. Peter, Helperthorpe

The Reverend Walter Smith, St. James, Baldersby

Dr. Janet Soskice, Ripon College, Cuddesdon

The Reverend N. Neil Steadman, St. Martin, Brampton

Mrs. Judy Stephenson, St. John, Howsham

The Reverend M. J. Stephenson, St. Mary Magdalene, Woodchester Square, London

The Reverend Peter F. Stiric, Christ the Consoler, Skelton

The Reverend Robert Sweeney, St. Frideswide, Oxford

The Reverend D. Taylor, Holy Trinity, Hastings

The Reverend J. B. Thomas, St. Mary, Holmbury St. Mary

The Reverend Christopher Tookey, St. Thomas, Wells

The Reverend A. T. E. Treherne, St. Stephen's, Gateacre

The Reverend Len Tyler, St. Michael and All Angels, Easthampstead, Bracknell

The Reverend Francis Walsh, Holy Name of Jesus, Chorlton-on-Medlock

Miss Doris Wegg, Holy Trinity, Hastings

Churchwarden John Wells, St. Mary the Virgin, Freeland

Canon D. P. Wilcox, Principal, Ripon College, Cuddesdon

The Reverend J. R. V. Woods, St. Simon and St. Jude, Englefield Green

MUSCULAR CHURCHES

INTRODUCTION

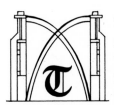he High Victorian period in English architecture began in 1849 with William Butterfield's design for the first important building in the new High Victorian Gothic style—All Saints Church, Margaret Street, London. The period lasted until the mid-1870s or longer (Butterfield, for example, never abandoned the style), although the more refined and elegant Late Victorian Queen Anne style began to supplant it as early as 1870.

Neoclassical architecture (often referred to by architectural historians as "romantic classicism") was the dominant style in Great Britain until mid-century. Early Victorian Gothic architecture co-existed with it, but the Gothic of the era either emphasized accurate imitation of medieval prototypes or applied Gothic decoration to traditional classical building plans and forms. Even the most famous Gothic building of the period, the Houses of Parliament in London, was not truly Gothic; Pugin's Gothic surface ornament camouflages Barry's rational, symmetrical, classical plan. High Victorian Gothic architecture was a new, vigorous, nineteenth-century style. It was broadly eclectic, borrowing freely from the full range of European medieval precedents but never attempting to produce literal copies of medieval buildings. The style alluded to the past; it did not seek to duplicate it. Medieval forms and details were sought, studied, revised or changed, and assimilated into new buildings that were like no others produced before. In fact, High Victorian Gothic architects saw themselves as continuing the development of the Gothic style from the point where it had been interrupted by the Renaissance, and they prided themselves on their originality. High Victorian Gothic architecture at its best had confidence, strength, and originality in startling contrast to the rarefied archaeological Gothic work of the Early Victorian period. High Victorian Gothic mirrors the confidence of the first great industrial nation at the height of its power. How vital its bold use of color, texture, and material and its strong, sculptural shapes seem when compared to the flat, gray, timid, Early Victorian stuff.

Henry-Russell Hitchcock, in his article "High Victorian Gothic," which appeared in the September 1957 issue of *Victorian Studies*, makes a persuasive case for High Victorian Gothic architecture as the most important architectural accomplishment of the third quarter of the nineteenth century. The preeminence of England's High Gothic architecture (The phenomenon was almost exclusively English; only in the United States, in the work of architects like Eidlitz, Furness, and Richardson, was High Victorian work of similar character and quality elsewhere produced.) was due to its success in reflecting the romantic characteristics of English society and thought at mid-century.

The nineteenth century was the romantic age. High Victorian Gothic architecture was as much a romantic phenomenon as was the poetry of Wordsworth or the painting of Géricault and Delacroix. The Englishman of 1850 was an antiquarian, fascinated by the heraldic past, absolutely convinced of the superiority of "happy" medieval life, nostalgic for the simplicity of a pre-industrial society. He was fiercely nationalistic, the nineteenth century being the century of Empire with a fifth of the world's surface governed by Victoria's England. He was also intensely religious; the nineteenth century produced both the Anglo-Catholic revival and the great growth of evangelical Christianity. A tremendous concern for the welfare of the souls of the urban poor was felt by the wealthy and influential. The nineteenth-century Englishman was confident, wealthy, and manly, interested in both his moral and physical well-being. He sought a dignified but non-ostentatious life and was much more interested in sport and social convention than in art. He believed himself able to accomplish almost anything if he acted forcefully and creatively, and he had a genius for organization and definition that aided him in the achievement of his goals.

High Victorian Gothic architecture was born of and nurtured by these characteristics. It satisfied the pervasive interest in the glorious past of knights and chivalry. It was an English style in contrast to the foreign classical style borrowed from Greece and Rome. It was Christian rather than pagan, and, by default, it could be considered Protestant as well since classicism was associated with St. Peter's and the Roman Church. It was flexible in plan and asymmetrical in form (therefore original and picturesque), and it was capable of producing mystical, spiritual spaces for worship (as well as for impressing and converting the urban slum dweller who had heretofore shown little interest in the church). Most characteristic of all, High Victorian Gothic was a masculine style that eschewed the dainty and the delicate in preference for the bold and impressive in form and detail.

Kerr wrote in the *Gentleman's House*:

that there is a spirited and substantial vigour in the presently prevailing revival of medieval architecture is not to be questioned—far less explained away. People may not sympathize with the demands of pre-raphaelite enthusiasm, or the affectations of sentimen-

3

tal romance; they may smile with more or less disdain, or laugh with more or less amusement, when they see common-sense unreservedly and even angrily cast overboard; they may fairly be permitted to express a doubt whether so singular an enthusiasm as this 'Gothic Mania' ever seized upon Art before, or ever will seize upon it again; they may reasonably speculate upon the questions how long it is to endure and what amount of ridicule is to be visited by posterity upon its borrowed plumage; but all this does not deprive muscularity of its muscularity.[1]

"Muscular Gothic" was an architectural style that paralleled the "Cult of Manliness" espoused by such writers as Thomas Carlyle, Charles Kingley, and Thomas Hughes. These writers and others disparaged gentleness, sensitivity, and appreciation for beauty; they glorified toughness of muscle and toughness of heart. Fighting for the right was seen as the chief duty of man. Personal and national glory was revealed by strength and power. Kingley liked to describe himself as a strong, daring, sporting, wild, man-of-the-woods. He extolled "a healthful and manly Christianity, one which does not exact the feminine virtues to the exclusion of the masculine"—his was the Church Militant.[2]

During the High Victorian period, Gothic replaced Neoclassic as the dominant architectural style for all types of buildings. Public buildings, country houses, banks, office buildings, and warehouses, as well as churches, parsonages, schools, and colleges, were built in the style. The Gothic style is most closely associated with churches, however, and it is through church design that most High Victorian architects established their reputations. Only one of the great names in High Victorian architecture, Alfred Waterhouse, became famous through secular commissions. (Waterhouse was a Quaker, a sect that was unaffected by the church building fever of the age, and consequently he had little opportunity to design buildings for either the Anglican Church or the various evangelical denominations.)

In the first half of the century Victorian Britain experienced two successive religious revivals, the Evangelical Movement, which resulted in the construction of numerous chapels and Anglican Low Church buildings, and the Oxford Movement, which led to the building of an even greater number of Anglo-Catholic High Church structures. (The latter movement produced most of the best architecture; only E. B. Lamb's Low Church buildings are of comparable quality to the High Church buildings of Butterfield, Street, and others.)

Roger Dixon and Stefan Muthesius, in their volume, *Victorian Architecture,* reveal the extent of the architectural opportunity at mid-century; they report that from 1840 until nearly the end of the century, more than one hundred new churches were constructed annually at an average cost of approximately three thousand pounds.[3] Some of these churches were estate churches built by the wealthy as adjuncts to their country homes. More of them, however, were built either in new parishes in the rapidly expanding industrial cities or in urban slums in an attempt to save the masses from atheism and revolution.

Two architectural theorists and two societies established the architectural philosophy on which the Gothic style was built. The two theorists were Augustus Welby Northmore Pugin (1812–52) and John Ruskin (1819–99), and the two societies were the Tractarians, founders of the Oxford Movement, who published *Tracts for the Times* (from whence the nickname is derived—the group's real name was the Oxford Architectural and Historical Society), and the Cambridge Camden Society (later the Ecclesiological Society), publisher of *The Ecclesiologist,* the arbiter of ecclesiastical fame during the High Victorian era.

The Oxford Movement was initiated in 1833, in response to John Keble's famous Assize Sermon, by a group of theologians and Oxford undergraduates whose goal was to combat liberalism and the "new science" that was eroding the faith and destroying the church. Their writings stressed the ancient tradition and continuity of the Anglican church and its "Catholic" medieval past.

The Tractarians were not so much interested in architecture as they were in the form of worship practiced—they insisted on adherence to the traditional *Book of Common Prayer* of the Anglican church and argued that the sacraments, not the sermon, were the most important elements of worship—but they supported the architectural positions of the Ecclesiologists who followed them. The Tractarians were interested in doctrinal reform. They wanted a return to spirituality and mystery in the church, and they believed that a high degree of ritualism was necessary to achieve this. They supported Anglo-Catholic High Church ritual and were in favor of whatever architectural forms it demanded.

The architectural prophet most admired by the Tractarians was A. W. N. Pugin. He was the author of a number of signally influential books on architectural theory. The first of these, *Contrasts or a Parallel between the Architecture of the Fourteenth and Fifteenth Centuries and Similar Buildings of the Present Day,* was published, privately, in 1836. It was followed in 1841 by *True Principles of Pointed or Christian Architecture.*

Pugin's architectural theory had a strong sociological base. Robert Macleod, in his book *Style and Society,* says:

> Pugin extracted, from Southey, Cobbett, and almost certainly Carlyle, the principles of social criticism which were current, and used them as the basis for an assault on contemporary architecture. What he produced out of this extrapolation was a distinctly new proposition: that the artistic merit of the artifacts of society was dependent on the spiritual, moral, and temporal well-being of that society.
>
> In thus concerning himself with the operations of society, Pugin was led inevitably to concern himself with buildings not as visual entities, nor even as functioning elements, but as technical *processes,* which engaged the skills and aspirations of the community in their erection. Thus his interest in construction was founded in materials and methodology, and not simply, as the Neo-Classicists, in the visual vocabulary of constructional elements.[4]

Pugin postulated two principles of architectural design in a lecture he delivered at St. Marie's College, Oscott, in 1841: first, all features must be necessary for convenience, construction, or propriety, and second, all ornament should consist of enrichment of the essential construction of the building.[5]

By "convenience," Pugin meant that form should be an expression of the functional components of a building arranged in a convenient manner. He despised classical design that sacrificed convenient arrangement to arbitrary regularization and concealment in a neat package. Although he admired picturesque composition, his wrath was also directed at the arbitrary irregularization practiced by some architects in their efforts to achieve picturesque arrangements. He believed that the plan should dictate the elevation; the elevation should not dictate the plan.

By "propriety" Pugin meant that the architect should accept and design for a hierarchy of decorum determined by the social status of the client, the social importance of the building (churches were more important than parish halls which were more important than schools, for instance), and the significance of the individual building component (In churches, chancels were more significant than naves, for example). The more important the client, building, or component, the more elaborate its decoration should be.

And by "construction," Pugin meant that building form should be derived from the way the building is constructed and the nature of materials that are employed. Pugin's appeal for truth in construction focused on the Gothic style as an honest expression of medieval masonry building techniques. Consequently, Pugin drew attention away from stylistic detail and focused that attention upon stylistic principle. He believed that every material had intrinsic qualities that dictated the manner in which it should be utilized in building. (A wall of cut stone should be very different from one of flint, which should be very different from one of brick.)

Pugin's principles are not style specific. In fact, the canons of modern architecture embrace them all to varying degrees. What makes Pugin a uniquely nineteenth-century figure is his unswerving commitment to Gothic architecture. He believed that the classical style was pagan, worldly, and especially unsuitable for church design. In contrast, the verticality of the Gothic style symbolized Christian concern for heavenly things and was more appropriate in England's rainy, sunless climate. Pugin liked his churches to be filled with "lofty arches, majestic lines of pillars, intricately carved capitals, great rood lofts, and high altars blazing with gold and jewels."[6]

Professor H. S. Goodhardt-Rendel, in a lecture delivered before the Royal Institute of British Architects in March 1924, noted that Pugin's prejudice for Gothic architecture compromised his architectural theory. Professor Goodhardt-Rendel said, wittily:

> Far stronger than any Principle in Pugin's mind was the prejudice that nothing could be comely save what was mediaeval. He therefore unconsciously worked his argument backwards. He premised that all good buildings have mediaeval elevations. But every elevation must be the inevitable outcome of the plan of the building to which it belongs. Now it may be presumed that a mediaeval elevation can be the inevitable outcome only of a mediaeval plan. Therefore, all good buildings have mediaeval plans. Again, the plan of every good building is the inevitable outcome of the habits of the man it is made to suit. And it has been seen that the plan of every good building is a mediaeval plan. Now it may be presumed that a mediaeval plan can be the inevitable outcome only of mediaeval habits. Therefore, all good plans are the inevitable outcome of mediaeval habits. Therefore again, if a man is to have a good building he must have mediaeval habits.[7]

Pugin's architecture does not reveal the absolute commitment to Gothic design to which his writings attest. His masterwork, St. Giles, Cheadle (1841–47), done at great expense for his Roman Catholic patron, the Earl of Shrewsbury, while Early Decorated English Gothic in style, is strongly neoclassical in spirit. It is axial and symmetrical; it has a strongly regular plan and three-dimensional composition. These classical characteristics were not noticed by the architects and churchmen of the day. What they saw was its Gothic style. Before Pugin, nineteenth-century Gothic churches had been well-lighted with high walls and greatly sloping roofs; they had had towers without spires; and their smooth walls had been constructed of dressed stone, stucco, or evenly colored brick. After Pugin, nineteenth-century Gothic churches were dark with low walls and extremely steep roofs; they featured dramatically tall, slender spires; and their rough walls were constructed of Kentish rag, flint, or Bath or Caen Stone.[8]

The Cambridge Camden Society, founded in 1939 by two Cambridge undergraduates—Benjamin Webb and John Mason Neal—to study Gothic architecture and ritual arrangements, dictated the architectural preferences of the High Church movement begun by the Tractarians through the publication of *The Ecclesiologist,* devoted entirely to church design and criticism. In 1845, under the leadership of Alexander Beresford-Hope, the society moved to London and changed its name to the Ecclesiological Society. The society, and the periodical it published, remained important throughout the High Victorian period. Its membership included most of the important church architects of the period.

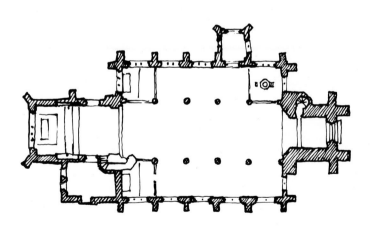

1840 Plan of the Church of St. Giles, Cheadle
The interior width of nave and aisles is forty feet; the nave is forty-five feet high. The nave bay spacing is twelve feet, and the chancel depth is twenty-seven feet.

Exterior View of the Church of St. Giles, Cheadle, from the Northeast
The height of the spire is two hundred feet.

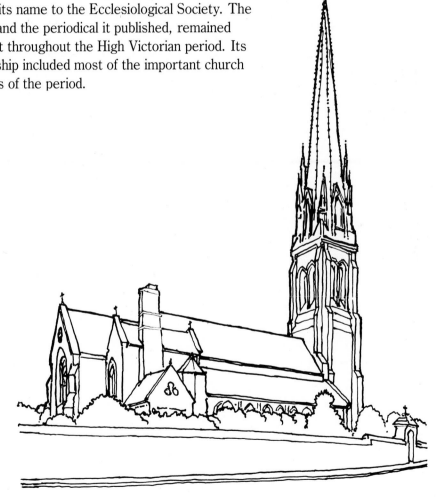

The stated purposes of the Ecclesiologists were to understand the Christian faith and the rubrics of the *Book of Common Prayer,* to develop canons for church building design that would embody these truths, and to persuade the Anglican church to follow their rules for church construction or restoration. In 1845, the Ecclesiological Society went one step further than Pugin by decreeing the only acceptable style for church building to be the Middle Pointed (Decorated) English style. (This dictum influenced the first decade of High Victorian church design very directly, even though it was counter to the writings of Pugin and the Ecclesiologists' own guru, John Ruskin.) The Ecclesiologists believed, as did most Victorians, in the law of successive rise, culmination, and fall; under this law, Early English (First Pointed) Gothic architecture was considered primitive, Middle Pointed (Decorated) architecture was perfect, and Perpendicular (Third Pointed) architecture was debased and decadent.

The Ecclesiologists accepted as their mission the revival of the Middle Pointed style, and they were very successful at their task. Soon they convinced High Churchmen that the Anglo-Catholic rite *required* Middle Pointed Gothic churches with long chancels containing stalls for the choir and clergy, elevated fonts and altars, frontals, and altar crosses. Stylistic correctness alone was not enough, however; they insisted that churches be designed by devoted Christians, not "professional architects" sullied by the design of workhouses, factories, and other crass commercial buildings.

Interior View of the Church of St. Giles, Cheadle
St. Giles is most notable for its dark, mystical interior, with all surfaces covered with intricate stenciled patterns in glowing color and gold.

Like Pugin, the Ecclesiologists argued that the administration of sacraments, rather than the sermon, was the most important part of the worship ritual. Because the sacraments were sacred, Ecclesiologists felt they should be administered in a mysterious sanctuary separated from the nave by three steps (to symbolize the Trinity), an altar rail, and a rood screen. The chancel should be richly decorated, the nave plain, and the two areas should be plainly distinguishable in plan and form, inside and outside.

The Ecclesiologists' standards were derived from meaning; they were not devices to assure beauty. In fact, they were disinterested in effect. They wanted every part of the church to be appropriate to its function in the service and to proclaim itself as part of the House of God. They looked for ways to use architecture to express meaning. A low side porch denoted humble entry; chimneys marked sacristies and gables marked altars; an apsidal chancel stood for the head of the body of Christ. Even the design of church fittings was of major concern; the model designs for church fittings published in *The Ecclesiologist* led to the establishment of numerous firms specializing in the design and manufacture of "correct" church fittings. The Morris, Minton, and Hardman firms typify this development.

The writings of John Ruskin directly influenced the attitudes of the Ecclesiologists. The impact of the writings was due as much to Ruskin's appealing, persuasive style as to their content. Michael Brooks, in *John Ruskin and Victorian Architecture,* describes Ruskin's achievement as "creating a style that not only conveyed information and crushed opponents, but also captured the emotional complexity of great architecture."[9] Ruskin was able to express the emotional, romantic appeal of Gothic architecture in his writing.

Ruskin's architectural views were accepted enthusiastically by the Ecclesiologists. His call for the construction of splendid churches that would "capture the qualities of nature in the curve of their arches and the mass of their walls"[10] struck a responsive chord in the Victorian mind. The extent to which Ruskin influenced High Victorian design is remarkable, particularly considering that he was not an architect and that he viewed architecture exclusively in terms of building ornament. He was unwilling to acknowledge that practical concerns played a part in architectural design; he thought *architecture* resulted from the addition of ornament to building. In fact, Ruskin was completely uninterested in the practical considerations of architecture; he only discussed buildings in terms of their visual characteristics.

Ruskin accepted Pugin's hierarchy as it affected decoration; he agreed that the more important the building, the greater its ornamentation should be. He was also as committed to the Gothic style as Pugin was. However, Ruskin's fascination with Gothic was not restricted to the English Middle Pointed style. His interest in ornament, particularly polychrome brickwork, led him to urge the study of the Italian Gothic style in his 1849 book, *The Seven Lamps of Architecture.* Ruskin's next two books continued to focus on lessons to be learned from Italian Gothic architecture; these were *The Stone of Venice* of 1851 and *Brick and Marble of the Middle Ages in Italy* of 1855.

Because Ruskin influenced High Victorian architecture so dramatically, and because Ruskin's theories concern the visual characteristics of architecture—composition, color, materials, mass, ornament—study of his views on these matters is necessary for an understanding of the High Victorian Gothic style.

Pattern & Color

Of all Ruskin's enthusiasms, none was greater than his love for color. He wrote in the *Stones of Venice,* "I believe [color] to be one of the essential signs of life in a school of art that loves colour; and I know it to be one of the signs of death in the Renaissance schools that they despised colour."[11]

Ruskin recommended using four techniques for adding color to buildings: stone in various natural colors, horizontal bands of stone in brick walls, zigzag and diaper brickwork patterns, and stone or stucco as a veneer surface on masonry. Ruskin was almost unique in his age in recommending the use of stucco. Most architects considered it a sham material and associated it with picturesque Regency architecture, which they despised. Ruskin liked stucco because it could be used like gesso for the application of color. Stone veneers were equally out of favor with Pugin and the Ecclesiologists, but Ruskin defended their use so long as the material of the veneer was used for its own sake. (There is an inconsistency in the attitude of the Ecclesiologists about stone veneers. It is hard to justify their disapproval of stone used in this way when they advocated the application of tile veneers.) Ruskin's justification of veneering was associated with the demand for a

special aesthetic that was based on the use of small, light, delicate, weightless, jewel-like treatment that clearly established the non-load bearing, ornamental nature of the veneer.

Ruskin's rules for the use of color were very different from those of his contemporary Owen Jones, author of *Grammar of Ornament.* Jones recommended that color be used to define and express structure; he tried to do precisely this in his painting scheme for the Crystal Palace. Jones used blue on concave surfaces because blue recedes from the eye, yellow on convex surfaces because yellow emphasizes projection, red on horizontal planes, and white on vertical planes.[12] In contrast, Ruskin believed that color should be used independently of form or structure. As justification of his color theory, he cited the use of color (and pattern) in the animal kingdom; certainly color and pattern is independent of form in the tiger, leopard, zebra, and giraffe. Ruskin developed a number of rules for the use of color. He said that columns should be striped vertically (horizontal striping of columns suggests that they are made up of drums of different colored stone; this was rarely the case in High Victorian architecture); he was opposed to picking out separate moldings through the use of color; and he preferred the use of similar colors to emphasize detail on all moldings. He did not like sculptural decoration set out by colored background; he suggested that a common color or pattern run freely over figure and ground. He thought color on simple forms should be simplified; complicated color and pattern should be saved for use on complicated forms. Finally, he advised that color should always be tempered and interlocked, not disposed in separate closed compartments. (This last rule was his justification for the use of diaper, zigzag, and checkered patterns that range freely over wall surfaces.) Ruskin believed that color is most effective when its contours are simple and it is not disturbed by conflicting patterns of light and shade.

Ruskin's appeal for color in architecture fell on fertile soil. No other period in architectural history is as noted for its use of color as is the High Victorian period. Although painted stenciled decoration was used extensively on interior surfaces of churches built during the period, High Victorian Gothic architecture is most famous for its use of constructional polychromy—colored patterns that are the result of the use of a number of materials of different natural colors. Britain's nineteenth-century commitment to a comprehensive railroad network facilitated the development of constructional polychromy; bricks or stone could easily be transported from one area to another.

The Ecclesiologists embraced color as an antidote to puritanical austerity and the cold, cheerless English climate. For them it stood for the glory of Anglo-Catholic Christianity. They said in *The Ecclesiologist* in 1845, "We would have every inch glowing, Puritans would have every inch colorless."[13]

Paul Thompson, in his biography of William Butterfield, elaborates:

> Colour, in short, was a deliberate assault not upon the senses, but on the puritan spirit which starved them. It was an assertion of Catholicism in a Protestant England, of luxury in the age of Gradgrind, of sensuous pleasures at a time of rigorous suppression. All Saints and Keble, to Evangelical Victorian England, were red rags in a moral as much as a visual sense, and this was one reason for the hostility of much contemporary criticism. It required Ruskin, knowing the

Evangelical mind from his parents, to justify constructional colour in terms which appealed to Protestant instincts. It was certainly untrue to suggest, he wrote in *The Stones of Venice*, that colour was a 'mere source of a sensual pleasure. . . . None of us enough appreciate the nobleness and sacredness of colour. . . . All good colour is in some degree pensive, the loveliest is melancholy, and the purest and most thoughtful minds are those which love colour the most.' Ruskin satisfied his own audience and helped to make constructional colour into a middle-class fashion by the 1860s; yet in retrospect it seems more significant that the denial of its sensuousness was necessary.[14]

William Butterfield is the architect who first used constructional polychromy in a uniquely High Victorian way (although almost all High Victorian architects soon followed his lead). Color and pattern are inseparable in Butterfield's work. His color combinations are restrained—red brick patterned with blue or gray, brown brick with flint and white stone, or cream and buff stone with red patterns. He used dark brown or green woodwork, and his ironwork was black. His pattern work became increasingly complex in the 1860s; in the work of this decade, wall surfaces became planes of linear pattern.

Ornament

Ruskin and his fellow Victorians regarded architecture as the art of decoration—an idea in opposition to the classicists' view of architecture as the art of proportion. (Architects did not abandon classical proportioning systems entirely, however. Burges and Teulon, in particular, used classical proportional systems in their designs, both in plan and elevation.) The Victorians equated beauty with sculpture, color, and ornament rather than with harmonious proportion. The more important the building, the greater the quantity of ornament it should receive. Ruskin made this case in the *Seven Lamps of Architecture;* sculpture and painting, he believed, created architecture—all else was mere building.

Ruskin insisted that sculptural ornament should be realistic and organic in form to contrast with flat geometric decoration on the wall planes. (Victorians preferred naturalistic decoration; they regarded nature as the outstanding testimony of God's handiwork.) Ruskin did not like conventionalized ornament, but he was willing to allow a modicum of abstraction in the design of naturalistic ornament as long as the vitality or grace of the ornament was not compromised. Stiff leaf column capitals were almost invariably used on nave arcades. As much as he liked sculptural ornament, however, Ruskin thought it should be concentrated at doors, windows, and gables, not spread evenly over a building's wall surfaces. He also argued for systems of ornament at different scales so that some would be apparent from a great distance, others from only a short distance. He believed ornament should tell a story as it had in the great medieval churches, and it should therefore be easily readable. (This constraint affected both the size and naturalism of stained glass and sculpture design particularly.)

Because architects were so committed to ornament as an integral component of their designs, they either designed the ornament themselves or supervised its design and manufacture by firms like the Morris Company. Henry-Russell Hitchcock said: "It is not the least claim to distinction of the High Victorian Gothic that it nurtured this brilliant revival of decorative art led by Morris. Many English churches of the sixties and seventies are worth visiting chiefly for their windows by Morris, Brown, and Burne-Jones, and some of their fine glass was exported to America."[15]

Material and Construction

The buzzword of the High Victorian era was "truthful," and truth was demanded of construction as well as of planning. An ethical concern for truthfulness in regard to construction methods, the expression of the intrinsic nature of materials, and the belief that different materials should be expressed in different ways prevailed. One result of this was an emphasis upon the wall and its brick or stone construction rather than upon the frame. A corollary result was a demand for simple, heavy, "honest" masses in building design. Buildings were broad and low with large, simple timber roof forms. (Open timber roofs adapted more easily to irregular places and were cheaper than vaulting.) Spires or towers provided a powerful counterpoint to the heavy, horizontal masses.

The Ecclesiologist, in 1843, proclaimed that "The essential elements [of a building] are strength, utility, and reality, which alone constitute true beauty."[16] It held that each material used in construction should be employed in a way that was consistent with its nature and that the material itself should suggest form. It is not surprising, therefore, that the typical shapes and motifs used in brick construction differ from those of stone.

The wall rather than the frame or column has traditionally been the most significant part of any English building, and so it was in the High Victorian Gothic period. The masculine character of High Victorian Gothic, plus the age's dislike of stucco, led to a new interest in texture and materials. Pugin preferred walls made up of small stones laid in an irregular, rough manner, bound at the corners and windows with larger cut stone. Ruskin, in contrast, liked the substance and surface of hard, cut stone which produced smooth, uninterrupted walls. In the *Stones of Venice,* Ruskin called for walls that had "smooth, broad, lineless, unbroken surface[s characterized by] flatness, [and] breadth of surface." [17] He also suggested that stone banding be placed in facades in such a way as to suggest the stories contained within. (Few architects used stone banding in this way, however. Butterfield's use of stone banding to organize the facade and to tie sills and string courses together is much more typical. In his work and in that of most of his contemporaries, the interior and exterior banding rarely coincide; and in contrast to stone bands, brick diapering is used as a continuous pattern to tie the various facade elements together.)

Ruskin taught that thick walls should be treated differently from thin walls. Thick walls should be decorated in a manner that reveals their stratification, while thin walls should be decorated with diapering or checkering that emphasizes their non-structural nature and minimizes their apparent weight. Butterfield accepted Ruskin's teaching. He said, "As in all well-conducted lives, the hard work, and roughing, and gaining of strength comes first, the honour or decoration in certain intervals during their course, but most of all in their close, so, in general, the base of a wall, which is the beginning of its labour, will bear least decoration, its body more, especially those epochs of rest called string courses; but its crown or cornice most of all." [18]

Ruskin's writings reveal that he did not like stone rustication and despised the utilization of cast-iron, particularly as columns carrying masonry. (There is a paradox of sorts here or, at least, an inconsistency. Ruskin was instrumental in getting the commission for the natural history museum in Oxford for his friends Deane and Woodward, and he liked the building they designed in spite of its bravura use of iron for columns and roof structure inside.) Ruskin demanded that the wall be organized vertically into clearly perceivable base, body, and cornice zones and horizontally into areas of concentrated strength such as piers and buttresses or piers he called the *wall-veil.* The term is misleading to us today; it was not intended to have a meaning parallel to the modern term *curtain-wall.* Ruskin's term simply implies a wall that veils the interior. The wall carries some suggestion as to what the interior is like. He did not intend for the wall-veil to be light-weight; in fact, Ruskin insisted that it have mass. His favorite wall-veil had horizontal bands of a strong material alternating with bands of a weaker one to tie the wall-fabric together. Ruskin suggested the use of different size masonry units for variety. He was explicit in his demand that shafts, columns, lintels, and architraves be made of massive stone pieces. He wanted the materials to convey the idea that each unit was doing its proper work. (It is important to note that Ruskin was more interested in the appearance than the reality, however.)

All High Victorian Gothic architects used brick for town churches, stone for rural ones. Ruskin and Butterfield were the first to advocate the use of brick. This preference for brick in city churches was not based on economics but on contextual factors—most city buildings were brick. In fact, economics did not affect the decision to use brick in many cases. Butterfield, for example, always worked with the best brick that he could afford, often having special shapes or special colors manufactured for his jobs. The new fascination with brick masonry was stimulated by the variety of colors, shapes, sizes, and finishes made possible by the newly mechanized brick factories. Brick also made available a wide range of color and pattern opportunities not possible with stone.

Of all the architects of the period, Butterfield embraced brick most enthusiastically. He preferred his walls to be laid in the English bond pattern (alternating courses of headers and stretchers). The brick thickness most typically employed was two and five-eighths inches; mortar joints were only one-fourth of an inch thick. Consequently, the resulting wall had a very dense texture.

No discussion of materials employed in High Victorian Gothic churches would be complete without some mention of stained glass. The best Victorian stained glass made during the second half of the nineteenth century competes in quality and effect with the best medieval glass. The sixteenth and seventeenth centuries had produced no glass of quality. During this period, pictures had simply been painted on clear glass, resulting in stained glass that deteriorated quickly and had none of the jewel-like quality of medieval stained glass. The revival of medieval architecture created a demand for stained glass that transmitted beautiful colored light in the medieval manner. Colored glass that approximated the rich colors of medieval glass began to be manufactured in quantity. The best stained glass designers, like Morris/Burne-Jones, Powell, and Hardman, produced hundreds of windows of extremely high quality. Although some details of the stained glass designs continued to be painted and fired, the windows were composed largely of colored glass pieces cut and leaded into place to make the design. (Only Tiffany and LaFarge in America entirely gave up painting details on stained glass and depended only on pieces of colored or opalescent glass to make the picture.) The best nineteenth-century stained glass utilized conventionalized figures with naturalistic or geometric background patterns around them.

Although spectacular stained glass continued to be produced throughout the Victorian era, the most architectonic stained glass was produced during the High Victorian era. This glass was designed two-dimensionally so that it would be an integral part of the wall surface; it did not feature scenes in perspective that pulled the eye out of the interior space. It balanced clear or white translucent glass with brilliantly colored glass so that an adequate supply of light would be admitted. The Morris/Burne-Jones and Weeks-Saunders glass produced for Bodley and Burges churches, respectively, is the chief glory of the buildings in which it is located.

The Victorians were convinced that dusk provided the best, most worshipful light, and efforts were made to design windows that would admit a golden twilight to the space during daylight hours.

In addition, the windows were often lighted by exterior gas lights so that the window designs would not go black but would continue to glow for nighttime services.

During the 1850s, the glass was typically placed in the exterior wall plane, thereby creating deep interior reveals. During the 1860s and 1870s this placement was reversed; the windows were placed in the plane of the interior wall surface, creating deep outside reveals.

Mass and Composition

Mass vies with color as the most important characteristic of High Victorian Gothic architecture. Ruskin maintained that "the relative majesty of buildings depends more on the weight and vigour of their masses than on any other attribute of their design."[19]

The Victorians wanted everything substantial and solid. The apparent heaviness and the great volume of High Victorian churches is consistent with this desire. Michael Brooks, in his definitive study of the effect of Ruskin's theories upon Victorian architecture, discusses Ruskin's desire for mass. He quotes Ruskin: "Mass of everything, of bulk, of light, or darkness of colour, not mere use of any of these, but breadth of them: not broken light nor scattered darkness nor divided weight, but solid stone, broad sunshine, starless shade."[20] Ruskin meant that a building should reflect the quantity, strength, and weight of its materials. Brooks goes on to say that

this doctrine is an updating of the doctrine of the sublime, replacing terror with a stress on strength and power—*muscularity*. He says, "Ruskin's sublime is triumphantly calm rather than darkly menacing."[21]

Related to Ruskin's desire for mass was his desire for monumental *scale* rather than monumental *size*. Brooks quotes Ruskin as saying, "Sublimity begins when any form reaches the degree of magnitude that will make a living figure look less than life size beside it."[22]

Ruskin characterized sublime buildings as having "angular and broken lines, vigorous oppositions of light and shadow, and grave, deep, or boldly contrasted color."[23] He went on to include size and simplicity of outline as contributing to sublimity. He recommended church design featuring "vast flat surfaces gathered up into a mighty square, bounded by continuous lines as much as possible and crowned by a vigorous cornice."[24] Ruskin and the High Victorian architects turned the tide away from the Picturesque toward massive uniformity.

Related to the Victorians' love of mass is an abhorrence of line. They disliked curvilinear or perpendicular tracery, for example, preferring instead simple geometrical plate tracery into which lights are inserted in apertures which look as if they were punched out of the stone. The only linear element they advocated was a single continuous bounding line that revealed the size and majesty of the composition.

A concern for breadth of surface rather than elegance of line led High Victorian architects to prefer forms that approach simple geometric shapes. They associated the mass of the wall with broad areas of light and shadow. Ruskin says, "No building is truly great unless it has mighty masses, vigorous and deep, of shadow mingled with its surface."[25] High Victorian architects liked their building compositions to feature diagonal lines, blank walls, and large, dominant roof forms.

In spite of their concern for mass and sublimity, the architects of the period continued to strive for a picturesque skyline. In their buildings they tried for a tight composition built-up of triangles into a pyramidal composition. They invariably softened their forms, however, with spiky or knobby details. Although Ruskin was convinced that all beauty was intuitive and that rules of composition were meaningless, others, particularly White and Pearson, wanted to combine intuitive details, refinements, and variations with a system of proportion based on geometrical or arithmetical ratios.

New Style

The architects of the High Victorian period wanted to develop a new nineteenth-century style that would be to their century what the Renaissance had been to the fifteenth century or the Baroque to the sixteenth and early seventeenth centuries.

Exterior View of Manchester Assize Courts
This is an example of High Victorian Neo-Gothic applied to the design of a major public building.

Interior View of Manchester Town Hall
The medieval baronial hall was regarded as an appropriate
model for the great civic spaces of the era.

Two schools of thought as to what would generate the new style existed. Joseph Paxton, Coventry Patmore, and Matthew Digby Wyatt were convinced that the new style would evolve through the utilization of the new iron and glass technology. They had seen the Crystal Palace and had marveled at it as an example of iron and glass construction without peer.

Ruskin and the High Victorian architects discussed in this book disagreed. They saw the new style as a development of the Gothic style. Their task was to demonstrate to the nation that Gothic architecture was not only beautiful but also expressive of a progressive age. The faithful replication of medieval forms that had characterized the Early Victorian period could not accommodate the design of a wide range of new building types—hotels, train stations, warehouses, government office buildings, and commodious homes for the wealthy. Gothic had to be enlarged to meet this need. In the process of development and expansion of the Gothic style, forms, proportions, and materials changed. Because there was no academy to dictate style, High Victorian architects felt free to mine the entire inventory of European medieval buildings in their quest for design prototypes which were both appropriate to the age and reminiscent of the past. Their architecture, consequently, alludes to the architecture of the past, never copying it directly.

Alfred Waterhouse was identified earlier in the chapter as the only major High Victorian Gothic architect whose work was largely secular. His work was extremely important because it demonstrated that the High Victorian Gothic style had universal applicability and could absorb the developments of modern technology—gas lighting, sash windows, large expanses of plate glass, etc.—while retaining a strong connection to the medieval past. Waterhouse's Manchester Assize Courts Building of 1859 and Town Hall of 1868 testify to the ability of the style to accommodate modern technology and functions.

Sir George Gilbert Scott is another architect of the period that is remembered primarily for his secular work as well as for being the most successful architect of the period. His office produced designs for over 150 buildings during his career. Although he had designed numerous churches and was

17

Interior View of All Souls Church, Halifax
In its lightness, spaciousness, and verticality, All Souls is a link between Pugin's St. Giles and the work of the Late Victorian era; it has little of the muscularity of the High Victorian style.

Exterior View of All Souls Church, Haley Hill, Halifax
This is Scott's best parish church, now redundant, vacant, and falling into disrepair, although its 236 foot spire remains a significant element in the Halifax skyline.

the restorer of seventeen cathedrals and Westminster and St. Albans abbeys, his ecclesiastical work remained archaeological and Early Victorian Gothic in style. It is only in their massing that his churches reflect the bold new muscular High Victorian style. This is not to say that his church designs are mean or unsuccessful. His church of All Souls at Haley Hill in Halifax, which he regarded as one of his very best designs, is a handsome structure, well-proportioned, rich in detail and decoration. It was long held as a model Victorian church. Its design shows a much greater kinship to Pugin's work—St. Giles, Cheadle, for instance—than to the works of Butterfield, Street, and the other architects whose work is discussed here.

Scott's secular works, in contrast, were boldly High Victorian in style, and these were what brought him great fame. They include the Home and Foreign Offices building in Whitehall, London, the St. Pancras Hotel, London, and most important of all, the Albert Memorial in Kensington Park, London.

As Barry and Pugin's Houses of Parliament are symbolic of Early Victorian Gothic, Scott's Albert Memorial stands for the Gothic architecture of the High Victorian period. Construction of the memorial began in 1863 and lasted nearly ten years. The monument is colossal, over 140 feet tall. It is brash and hard; its silhouette, cusps, and pointed arches are explicitly Gothic. The materials are shiny and cold—polished granites and marbles of various colors, gilded details, and brilliantly colored glass mosaics. Its base splays out at the four corners to support white marble sculpture groups representing Europe, Africa, Asia, and America. White marble friezes portray figures from all the professions. The sculpture is realistic and romantic; it is classical rather than Gothic in feeling. The iconography in its sentiment, excess, pathos, and imperial nationalism is uniquely High Victorian.

The Albert Memorial, Kensington Park, London
The Albert Memorial has come to symbolize the High Victorian Neo-Gothic style. Its form, a vaulted canopy over a seated bronze figure of the prince, is based in part on fourteenth-century English Eleanor crosses and in part on the Gothic Scaligere tombs in Verona; it is a ciborium executed at monumental scale.

Stylistic Development

High Victorian Gothic began in the late 1840s and early 1850s as a movement away from delicate and pretty Early Victorian Gothic churches toward bold, chunky, massive church buildings. The churches of the new style were extremely heavy in appearance. They abandoned Early Victorian pier clusters and delicate moldings for squat massive columns and plain chamfers. Roofs became more prominent and silhouettes much simpler. The Early Victorian delicate patterns and soft colors were replaced by larger patterns and strong primary colors. All that was dainty or feminine disappeared. The new architecture was bold and masculine. It alluded to earlier and earlier medieval prototypes; early French and Italian Gothic forms were much admired, although Middle Pointed precedents were used almost exclusively.

In 1850 the typical church group was like a small village; it was dominated by the church rather than a country house, and the church was surrounded by buildings that housed the parsonage, the school, and various workers. As the period progressed, church groupings became tighter and more urbane. The urban church was invariably constructed of brick, the rural one of stone or stone and brick.

The Albert Memorial

G. E. Street, in an article that appeared in *The Ecclesiologist* in 1850, described the town church as needing to be a massive "citadel fortress" with high, smooth walls, flatish roofs, colored bands of stone, set-backs, panels, thin projections, large windows, and high clerestories.[26] One of the earliest High Victorian Gothic urban churches was Carpenter's St. Mary Magdalene, Munster Square, London, of 1849. It follows Street's prescription almost exactly, but because it was built of rough, irregular Kentish rag, it seems to be a primitive, rural intruder in its London context. It remained for Butterfield, in his All Saints, Margaret Street, to design a church that had an urbane quality; Butterfield created urbanity by the use of brick rather than stone and by the introduction of constructional polychromy.

The 1850s was a decade of conflict between the Liberals who embraced the classical and Italianate styles and the Tories who insisted on Gothic structures. By 1860 the Tories had won the battle; Gothic reigned supreme and it looked as if High Victorian Gothic might well become a universal style. In the 1860s, however, a number of architects—Burges, John Pollard Seddon, E. W. Godwin, and others—challenged Butterfieldian Gothic. These new prophets of architecture were not as tied to Early and Middle Pointed English precedent as their predecessors had been during the previous decade; they were much more eclectic, borrowing freely from French, German, and Italian Gothic tradition. They placed maximum emphasis on simple massing, balanced composition, continuous horizontal lines, and bold unchamfered corners, creating particularly masculine buildings. Their polychromy was less strident in color than that of Butterfield's and Street's churches of the 1850s, and they preferred flat, con-

The Church of St. Mary Magdalene, Munster Square, London Carpenter's design complete with the spire, which was never built.

21

ventional, unobtrusive patterns. Figure carving was strongly naturalistic. All of the characteristics of the High Victorian Gothic style were fully developed; these included relatively simple plans and three-dimensional composition, simple decoration except in chancels and on gables and around openings, details based on simple geometric forms, flat wall surfaces, polychrome materials, and naturalistic sculptural decoration that had religious meaning.

By the 1870s many of the characteristics that had given High Victorian Gothic architecture its special appeal became unfashionable. Late Victorians equated massiveness with absence of grace; they regarded polychromatic decoration as vulgar, and they decided, imperiously, that the style's copious ornament did nothing more than camouflage feebleness of form. Interest shifted away from the aesthetic theories of Ruskin and Morris and focused upon their social theories instead. England was ripe for the Queen Anne and Old English styles. Henry-Russell Hitchcock summed up the importance of the High Victorian Gothic period in his 1957 article "High Victorian Gothic." He said:

> The High Victorian Gothic had been one of the boldest of all nineteenth-century attempts to create an architecture for the present within a broadly historical frame of stylistic reference. In its most typical monuments, such as the Albert Memorial, the High Victorian Gothic created something never seen before, an epitome of many of the most typical aspirations of the day; in its finest monuments, Butterfield's churches and Webb's houses, it left a legacy that was as worthy as that left by any other quarter of the nineteenth century, irrelevant though many of their virtues must seem to the problems of our own period a hundred years later. To ignore, or worse to laugh at, Victorian

The Church of St. Mary Magdalene
The church as constructed. Although the rough informality of the Kentish rag construction makes the church a rural intruder in its urban setting, *The Ecclesiologist* praised it enthusiastically, calling it the "most artistically correct new church yet consecrated in London."

architecture is to miss one of the age's characteristic and vital contributions, a contribution whose very ambiguities may well throw revealing light on other critical problems of the age. It is futile to study the critical writings of Ruskin on architecture without examining carefully the buildings that were designed by his close associates; to detach the achievement of Morris as a decorator from the buildings of Woodward, of Webb, and of Bodley which his decoration completed is equally willful and arbitrary. The creative vitality of the Victorian age is hardly more notable in any field than in the Gothic of the fifties and sixties. To call it "High" is not just a bad joke but rather a justifiable recognition of its relative position among the artistic manifestations of the period.[27]

NOTES

1. Mark Girouard, *The Victorian Country House* (New Haven and London: Yale University Press, 1979), 54.

2. Girouard, 56.

3. Roger Dixon and Stefan Muthesius, *Victorian Architecture* (New York: Oxford University Press, 1978), 193.

4. Robert Macleod, *Style and Society* (London: RIBA Publications Limited, 1971), 9, 10.

5. Kenneth Clark, *The Gothic Revival* (New York: Harper and Row, 1962), 140.

6. Michael W. Brooks, *John Ruskin and Victorian Architecture* (New Brunswick and London: Rutgers University Press, 1987), 37.

7. H. S. Goodhardt-Rendel, "English Gothic Architecture of the Nineteenth Century," *Journal of the Royal Institute of British Architects*, Volume XXXI, Number 11 (April 5, 1924): 328.

8. H. S. Goodhardt-Rendel, *English Architecture Since the Regency* (London: Constable, 1953), 93, 94.

9. Brooks, 61.

10. Brooks, 2.

11. Brooks, 82.

12. Brooks, 85.

13. Paul Thompson, *William Butterfield* (Cambridge: M.I.T. Press, 1971), 229.

14. Thompson, 229.

15. Henry-Russell Hitchcock, "High Victorian Gothic," *Victorian Studies* (September 19, 1957): 56.

16. *The Ecclesiologist* II (1843): 118–21.

17. Brooks, 32.

18. Thompson, 138.

19. Thompson, 275.

20. Brooks, 78.

21. Brooks, 78.

22. Brooks, 78.

23. Thompson, 323.

24. Dixon and Muthesius, 202.

25. Brooks, 50.

26. Street, "On the Proper Characteristics of a Town Church," *The Ecclesiologist* II (1850): 227–33.

27. Hitchcock, 71.

PART I

The Form Givers

WILLIAM BUTTERFIELD
GEORGE EDMUND STREET
JOHN LOUGHBOROUGH PEARSON
WILLIAM BURGES

WILLIAM BUTTERFIELD

**illiam** Butterfield (1814–1900) was the son of a prosperous London chemist, druggist, and non-conformist churchman. He was first apprenticed at age sixteen to a builder, Thomas Arber of Pimlico. Two years later, his family's increasing wealth—his father had added coal merchant and wharfinger to his business titles—made it possible for Butterfield to abandon the building trades he was then involved with and pursue a more socially acceptable career as an architect. From 1833 to 1837 he was articled to E. L. Blackburn, a restorer of ancient churches and an antiquarian scholar. After finishing his indenture with Blackburn, Butterfield was employed for a short time in the office of William and Henry Inwood, architects who specialized in the design of classical buildings. But classical work did not suit Butterfield, and he remained in the Inwood office for only a few months before accepting a position as assistant in the office of a Worcester architect, probably Harvey Eginton. (The records are not complete on this score.) In 1840 he set up his own office at 38 Lincoln's Inn Fields, moving two years later to 4 Adam Street in the Adelphi Terrace where his office remained until his death in 1900.

Butterfield's practice was devoted almost completely to church architecture. During his lifetime he designed nearly one hundred churches. His secular practice, except for the schools and parsonages that often accompanied his church commissions, was negligible; this work was limited to two large houses, buildings for Keble College, Oxford, and Rugby School, and the Royal Hampshire County Hospital.

Butterfield left his evangelical background behind

early on, becoming a champion of the Anglo-Catholic movement to which he gave his total loyalty. He was elected to membership in the Ecclesiological Society in 1848. His friends were limited to his fellow members in the Athenaeum, a club dominated by aristocratic High Churchmen. These men became his patrons. Through them he secured a number of commissions (including his first major work—the rebuilding of St. Augustine, Canterbury, as a missionary college in 1844) and an honorary position as supervisor for the production of sacred vessels and church furniture from designs approved by the Ecclesiological Society. In this capacity, he contributed extensively to *Instrumenta Ecclesiastica,* a book of approved designs for all sorts of things from stools to cemetery chapels.

Butterfield's only professional friends were Philip Webb and Henry Woodyer. (Woodyer was one of only two or three pupils Butterfield accepted during his career.) He was really close only to his family. He never married, but he adored his nieces and nephews as if they were his own children. For his sister Ann Starey and her family, he designed one of his two large houses, Milton Ernest Hall. This house became his own home as well.

Butterfield was as much a loner in work as he was in life. He handled all client contacts, inspected sites, programed all work, and prepared preliminary designs that took the form of fairly small, crude sketches which he would work out using only a pair of folding compasses and a two-foot ruler. He would turn these drawings over to his draftsmen to draw up and return to him for revision. Although he left the production of working drawings and design details to his draftsmen, he supervised and corrected all work meticulously. Each of his buildings is clearly his own. He did not take part in competitions or submit his work for publication. He prepared no elegant perspective drawings of his buildings. He wrote no articles for the architectural press. He was, however, the consummate professional; he controlled every facet of design, cost estimate, and building execution precisely. His client and friend Lord E. H. Coleridge wrote of him, "Architects and contractors are an unstable lot of fellows in general, though I have been spoiled by old Butterfield, who kept his time to an hour, never exceeded his estimate by a shilling, and whose work, some of which I have known for forty years, seems as if it would last for ages."[1]

Butterfield's work was never popular, and it was often attacked, even by his friends. He suffered in silence, withdrawing into himself, becoming increasingly remote. He tried to convince himself that true genius is rarely appreciated in its own time. He became such a recluse that he even refused to attend the 1884 ceremony at which he was awarded the gold medal of the Royal Institute of British Architects.

Paul Thompson, in his definitive biography of Butterfield, says, "Butterfield is remembered as a narrow relentless bachelor, insular in his ideas, savage to his staff, crochety with his clients, allowing himself but one personal pleasure, a daily walk from his office to the Athenaeum; a volcano of constricted passion who spoke only in the pent-up power of his architecture." Thompson contends: "In short, [Butterfield] was caught in a vicious cycle; not a hard, cold man, but a man full of unexpected emotion, needing more intense, more frequent human contact, but for lack of it driven more and more to an obstinacy and ill temper which left him still more isolated. No wonder, as he grew older, he became increasingly pessimistic, railing against the world, his voice hysterical."[2]

Throughout his life, Butterfield, like Pugin, was faithful to the Gothic Revival style. Butterfield was not a conventional Gothic Revivalist, however. Basil Clarke described him as a builder who had absorbed Pugin's True Principles.[3] (He was much more concerned with the principles of medieval design than he was with the archaeological correctness of details.) It is true that Butterfield always began his designs with historical precedents, but he invariably transformed these prototypes into something uniquely his own. Butterfield preferred simple forms, smooth planar surfaces, and geometric decoration; he simplified florid Gothic ornament to make it conform to his own taste. He combined features from a variety of sources, and he adapted historical precedents to the social customs and industrial technology of his day. He never allowed precedent to become a barrier to convenience. When no appropriate medieval precedent existed for a particular design, he allowed Victorian concepts of proportion and harmony to prevail. W. R. Lethaby says of Butterfield, "Gothic was to him an essence and a logic rather than a magazine of 'cribs' for designers, where they might borrow attractive, unexploited features. . . . His mind was set on structural results, not on paper schemes."[4]

Lethaby categorized Victorian architects as "Softs" and "Hards." The Softs made beautiful drawings and produced correct but synthetic Gothic churches. The Hards understood building and materials and took into account common modes of construction. Lethaby put Butterfield squarely in the Hard column; he says Pugin talked Hard but produced Soft buildings. Goodhardt-Rendel summed it up well when he said, "Butterfield reversed Pugin's aim of forcing his age to conform to the necessities of Gothic, and succeeded in forcing Gothic to conform with the necessities of his age . . . Butterfield showed that Gothic was a living language, having words for racket-court, operating theater, and latrine."[5]

In a similar vein, John Summerson said in his essay on Butterfield:

> . . . Butterfield was not a medievalist and . . . All Saints [Margaret Street] shows not the slightest nostalgia for the Middle Ages. In a Pugin church the nostalgia is—nearly—everything; in a Butterfield church it is conspicuously absent. . . . He was a Victorian builder, accepting with a queer literal-mindedness the conditions of his own time. He habitually used common red and black bricks or . . . London stocks. His rafters are pit-sawn timbers of ordinary scantling. He used luscious marbles when he had the chance, but he was perfectly happy with ordinary Birmingham tiles. . . . On the practical side he was most painstaking; Halsey Ricardo has recorded that he even liked to have the curves of chimney flues set out full-size on the site.[6]

Eastlake had a similar view of Butterfield. In his *A History of the Gothic Revival,* he said:

> There is a sober earnestness of purpose in his work widely different from that of some designers, who seem to be tossed about on the sea of popular taste, unable, apparently, to decide what style they will adopt, and trying their hands in turn at French, at Italian, and what not, with no more reason than a love of change or a restless striving after effect. He does not care to produce showy buildings at a sacrifice—even a justifiable sacrifice—of constructive strength. To the

pretty superficial school of Gothic, busy with pinnacles, chamfers, and fussy carving, he has never condescended. He has his own (somewhat stern) notions of architectural beauty, and he holds to them whether he is planning a cottage or a cathedral. His work gives one the idea of a man who has designed not so much to please his clients as to please himself. In estimating the value of his skill, posterity may find something to smile at as eccentric, something to deplore as ill-judged, and much that will astonish as daring, but they will find nothing to despise as commonplace or mean.[7]

Butterfield's architecture has a modern quality not shared by the works of his contemporaries. It comes from an emphasis upon powerful forms bound by simple flat wall planes, enlivened by color used (in Butterfield's case, built-in) in a very contemporary way. His buildings are not picturesque; they strive for the sublime. His interior spaces lack the complexity of Pearson's best work. He has none of Burges' humor. He avoids small scale, spiky effects. He neither sculpts his forms nor uses sculptural decoration. His buildings are powerful, hard, experimental, and deeply felt, but they were strange and inexplicable to the nineteenth-century world, which found them ugly.

Like Dickens in literature, Butterfield was a realist in a romantic age. E. A. Freeman described his work as hideous. The *Building News* in 1857 referred to "prodigalities of ugliness" in his work. Even his champion, *The Ecclesiologist,* in reviewing the design of All Saints, Margaret Street, observed "the same dread of beauty, not to say the same deliberate preference for ugliness" that characterized Millais' painting.[8]

Twentieth-century viewers, schooled by the architecture of the modern and post-modern move-ments, are able to understand, appreciate, and find beauty in Butterfield's buildings in a way nineteenth-century viewers never could. Paul Thompson sums up the reasons for both Butterfield's appeal and his importance in his comment, "No other architect so consistently explored both the material expressiveness of wall architecture, and its discipline through wall planes; and, at the same time, through colour, the triumphant joy of faith, and through line and pattern, the insecurity of an age of doubt and change."[9]

Butterfield's fame as an architect is associated with the use of brick and with colored decoration built into the fabric of his buildings—sheer brick walls and constructional polychromy. Actually Butterfield worked in both brick and stone and did not invariably use constructional polychromy in his buildings. Butterfield preferred local stone facing for country churches; he saw brick as primarily an urban building material. He shared the view of his contemporaries that structure should be "real" or "truthful." For him this meant that stone should be rough and massive and that it should have a continuous masonry texture. To emphasize the intrinsic characteristics of stone he de-emphasized the mortar joints, holding them back from the face of the wall; he gave walls a rough face even if it had to be achieved by hammering; and he emphasized the roughness of stone masonry by contrasting it with bands and dressings of smooth stone.

Butterfield insisted on brick for his urban churches. He saw brick as the ideal material for city use. As compared to stone, brick lasted indefinitely and was a better protection against fire. Brick was also the traditional building material, so brick buildings were always compatible with the urban context. More important, brick's smooth surfaces made possible powerful urbane forms, and its range of colors facilitated the addition of color and pattern that would add an element of gaiety to the drab urban scene. (Butterfield did not use brick because it was cheap. He always insisted on the use of the best materials available locally, and the brick he chose was sometimes more expensive than the best local stone.)

Butterfield also liked brick because it allowed him to achieve the pure, simple geometries he preferred. His forms are not molded; they look like they are cut by a knife. His planes are smooth and crisp and his decoration is linear. His design begins with emphatic horizontal and vertical lines; it is enriched by asymmetrical composition, lively silhouette, and the acceptance of duality. Like Venturi, Butterfield was willing to accommodate contradiction; sometimes it seems as if he deliberately sought it. (Because structure and decoration have their own organizational systems, Butterfield often featured collisions between them instead of making one subservient to the other.) Summerson pointed out that to Butterfield "truthfulness to nature" meant more than utilization of natural materials and organic ornament; it also meant that "if the convenient arrangement of a building suggested a violent duality or a format discord, the duality and the discord could be accepted as right."[10]

Truthfulness to nature also affected church planning, the expression of functional units, and decoration; Butterfield used a hierarchy based upon physical, social, or symbolic importance in planning, shaping, and decorating space. He believed that major volumes should express their function and organize the composition; minor elements should be subservient to major ones. All should be tied to-gether, if at all possible, with a long unbroken roofline. Nave and chancel were often undifferentiated in form; interior decoration was concentrated in the sanctuary; gables almost always expressed an altar; aisles invariably had a lean-to structure; even mundane practical elements like chimneys were articulated; and the tower, as symbolic connection to heaven, dominated and anchored the whole.

The ritualistic demands of the Ecclesiological Society were embraced by Butterfield; he also shared its preference for the Decorated Style. He was unwilling to accept all Ecclesiological dicta, however. He refused to obstruct the view of the sanctuaries in his churches with rood screens, and he ignored the Society's theory of symbolism in churches. He also sought out idiosyncratic Decorated prototypes to vary the smooth perfection of the preferred Middle Pointed style. Summerson believes that Butterfield was, at heart, a primitive with a wonderful childish inventiveness. As proof he points to his naive sense of composition, the crudely colored zigzags and circles of his decoration, and his painted roofs like "huge, ingenious toys from a giant's nursery."[11]

In a letter, Butterfield described his work as "largely dependent on, and connected with, coloured material."[12] This is an interesting comment, particularly considering that in two-thirds of Butterfield's churches interior color is restricted to floors and sanctuary walls and that constructional polychromy is an important design element only in his major urban commissions. Away from London, Butterfield's patterns were often small in scale and soft in color. Butterfield's fascination with color began as an aspect of his appreciation for the intrinsic characteristics of natural building materials, but by the late 1850s color had grown into an overwhelming concern for him. (Paul Thompson suggests that for Butterfield, constructional polychromy was fundamentally a reaction against the bonds of historicism.[13] I think not. Butterfield agreed with Ruskin that unadorned buildings have little to do with art and that ornamentation is what separates architecture from building. I believe that Butterfield's constructional polychromy is simply consistent with his preference for pure geometries and sleek, unsculptured, planar forms.)

Butterfield's polychromy is different inside from outside. Outside patterns penetrate the walls only at the window jambs; a completely different system of decoration is used in the interior. Patterns, particularly the exterior ones, contribute directly to the compositional whole. Diapers are used to make horizontal links between shadow-casting architectural features and to lengthen the shadows under the eaves; bands link sills and cornices and stress the layers of construction; checkers and diapers visually lighten the mass of the upper wall. Invariably, color and pattern serve to unite architectural features and to emphasize the unity and planar quality of the wall. (Incidentally, Butterfield never extended his decorative patterns to the roofs of his buildings; he felt that because they were unbroken planes with no features needing organization, surface patterns would be superfluous.)

Color in the interiors of Butterfield's buildings is bright and clear; he turned his back on romantic gloom. He used floor tiles of yellow, red, and dark green and applied patterned tiles (either glazed or terra-cotta inlaid with colored mastic) to the walls. He preferred warm colors; red, pink, and yellow predominate. Ceilings were decorated with delicate foliate patterns. He tried to restrict the use of stained glass so that the colors of his decoration would appear natural and bright; he always wanted clear glass in clerestory windows. (Unfortunately, Butterfield's clear glass was usually replaced by colored memorial glass over time.)

As brick became more uniform due to improved manufacturing techniques, Butterfield increased his use of pattern and color constructional decoration. His most individual work—with polychrome patterns of surpassing splendor—dates from the 1860s and early 1870s and includes the churches at Penarth and Babbacombe and the chapels at Rugby School and Keble College, Oxford.

Butterfield's Early Victorian work of the 1840s is picturesque, although the individual building parts seem to be composed in a classical way. The parts convey no feeling of organic unity; they are placed informally in the landscape; their silhouettes are irregular; and each elevation is distinctly different from every other. There is little variation in color or texture. During this period, Butterfield's designs are exclusively based on Middle Pointed precedents.

The next decade, the 1850s, saw the emergence of Butterfield's mature High Victorian style. With All Saints, Margaret Street, in London, Butterfield began his experiments with constructional color. His forms became simpler and bolder with the uninterrupted wall-plane and the continuous roof-line becoming important organizational devices. He broadened his catalog of design precedents to include Early English, Perpendicular, and continental Gothic sources as well as Middle Pointed ones. His interiors achieved a new spatial unity that is uniquely High Victorian.

All Saints Church, Margaret Street, London

The building generally credited with beginning the High Victorian period is Butterfield's Church of All Saints, Margaret Street, London, built during the years from 1850 to 1853, although its decoration continued until the end of the decade.

The church was designed as a model church for the Ecclesiological Society. It was intended to be an example of the way a church should be built in order to accommodate ritualistic High Church worship. In selecting Butterfield to be the architect, the Society chose one of their own. Two members of the Society, A. J. Beresford-Hope and Sir Stephen Glynne, were charged to supervise the project, but, as Glynne's avocations took so much of his time, the task really fell to Beresford-Hope, who was a generous contributor and a highly knowledgeable student of church architecture.

Butterfield's task was not an easy one. Not only did he have to please an authoritarian client and the society he represented, but he had to produce a work that would be a missionary in brick and mortar for High Church attitudes about church form and planning. Additional difficulties were imposed by the very small site, 98 feet by 108 feet, upon which were to be fitted in, jig-saw puzzle style, a large church; a

Exterior View of All Saints Church, Margaret Street, London
In its massing, plan arrangement, patterned brick construction, and extreme verticality, All Saints was new and unorthodox.

choir school with dormitory, dining room, class-rooms, and kitchen; and a clergy house for the vicar, two curates, and servants. To make matters worse, other properties were contiguous to the site on the west, north, and east; the only street frontage was on the south. The building had to be very tall to get light from either the north or west; windows on the east were impossible.

The difficulties imposed by the site were handled brilliantly by Butterfield's compact planning scheme. The north two-thirds of the lot was devoted to the church; the south one-third was divided between the choir school on the west, the clergy house on the east, and a courtyard in the center that provided access to all three major components of the plan. All components share a common basement. The clergy house and choir school accept the height limitations imposed by the Georgian Street; the church and tower rise dramatically behind them.

The nave and aisles of the church occupy a space that is approximately sixty feet square and seventy feet high at the ridge. Four piers composed of clusters of polished red granite shafts carry arcades that divide the square almost equally into a three-bay nave with flanking aisles. The arcade bays are very wide, giving the interior an open spatial character. The aisles are low; the nave is very high, especially in relationship to its twenty-four foot width. The deep (thirty-eight feet, six inches), square-ended chancel is an extension of the nave; the nave arcades continue into the choir bay. The chancel's vaulted ceiling is much lower inside than the timber roof of the nave, although its exterior form is actually slightly higher.

All Saints' impact upon the architectural world came more from its exterior appearance than from

its plan. First, it was constructed of brick rather than stone—the first of countless brick urban churches that would be constructed over the next two decades. The brick was not just any brick but an exorbitantly expensive soft-pink blend, banded and diapered all over with flat black patterns unrelated to the organization of the three-dimensional architectural forms. These patterns emphasize surface continuity rather than the thickness of the walls or the architectural masses. Masses are simplified;

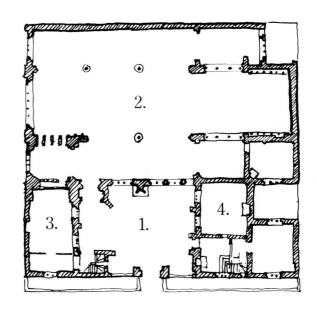

Plan of All Saints Church, Margaret Street
1. Courtyard
2. Church
3. Choir School
4. Clergy House

Entrance Porch of All Saints Church, Margaret Street
Brick striping and diapering emphasizes wall continuity and the
bold collision of three-dimensional masses.

buttresses are reduced; window tracery is installed
flush with the exterior wall.

Second, the church is extremely vertical in its
composition. It has no strong horizontal forms, and
the various masses are allowed to interpenetrate or
collide in extremely complicated ways. The entrance
porch seems to disappear into the mass of the tower
and choir school. The great buttress anchors and or-
ganizes the elements of the entrance courtyard.
Windows are not organized into bands horizontally
or vertically; they occur where they are needed;
they are integrated into the overall composition by
the connecting bands of brick pattern-work.

Third, the church is a fascinating blend of ancient
and modern. The windows of the choir school and
clergy house are modern double-hung sash instead
of Gothic casements, and iron beams are used in the
structural frames of these units. Moreover, there is
not much that is Gothic about the street facades of
the choir school and clergy house. No historic precedent can be found for the total composition—it is
uniquely Victorian—but many precedents affected
the design of individual elements. The tall square
tower with its broached wood spire covered with
lead and slate is based upon the spire of St. Mary's
Church, Lubeck (at over 210 feet, it is the tallest
church spire in London); the high exterior form of
the sanctuary is borrowed from Freiburg in Breisgau;
and the vaulted interior form of the chancel is based
upon the upper Church of St. Francis, at Assisi.
German precedent legitimized the brick construction, Italian precedent the constructional color. All
other details come from English Decorated sources,
but in each case Butterfield simplifies and trans-
forms the prototype into something original.

Interior View of All Saints Church, Margaret Street

The nave and aisle walls are completely covered with geometric flat patterns (the aisles also have glazed tile murals) made from red, black, and white bricks and tiles, green, yellow, and gray glazed bricks, and pale stone and terra-cotta inlaid with red and black mastic.

Diagonal View of Nave, Aisle, and Chancel at All Saints Church, Margaret Street
The richness of the decoration and the darkness of the interior camouflage the elegant verticality of the space.

London had seen nothing like this before. George Hersey put it colorfully and succinctly when he said, "Into this world, not greatly disturbed by Pugin, All Saints burst like a Congo chieftain into a performance of *Les Sylphides*."[14] A new era of muscular power in architectural design, in dramatic contrast to the restraint of the previous decades, had been initiated; the High Victorian era was underway.

All Saints, at seventy thousand pounds, was one of the most expensive churches built during the Victorian era. A major part of this enormous sum went into the interior decoration of the church. All Saints' interior was Butterfield's richest interior ever. The chancel is paneled with tiers of alabaster canopies which contain blue and red figures on gold grounds. (The original painted figures were done by William Dyce. They faded badly and were replaced with new ones of similar spirit by Ninian Comper in 1895.) No roodscreen separates the chancel from the nave; only a bold alabaster and granite altar rail is used. The most conspicuous single feature is the abstract intarsia decoration of the chancel wall above its fairly low arch. How much more successful is Butterfield's decoration here than the fresco Watts painted above the chancel arch in Street's great Church of Saint James the Less. Butterfield's interior patterns, unlike his exterior ones, are clearly determined by architectural surfaces and structure; like his exterior patterns, they diminish the weight of the wall and emphasize its smooth surface character.

In its review of All Saints, *The Guardian* contrasted the virility of Butterfield's decoration with the "weak" (painted) patternings of Pugin and Owen Jones and described the church as masculine and strong. *The Ecclesiologist* described it as "manly and austere, almost sublime." Surely this decoration is decidedly more muscular than Pugin's painted plaster patterns even though Pugin used many of the same decorative figures. John Summerson paid All Saints its supreme compliment when he said, "From the hardness and ruthlessness of All Saints emerges the noble elegance which makes it, in some ways, the most moving building of the century." George Edmund Street would undoubtedly agree. In 1859 he wrote, "I cannot hesitate for an instance in allowing that this church is not only the most beautiful, but the most vigorous, thoughtful, and original among them all."[15]

John Ruskin summed up the importance of All Saints, Margaret Street, in his book *Stones of Venice III* of 1853. He said, "It is the first piece of architecture I have seen, built in modern days, which is free from all signs of timidity or incapacity. In general proportion of parts, in refinement and piquancy of

All Saints Church, Margaret Street
The wide aisles and tall arcades create a very open, unified interior space.

mouldings, above all in force, vitality, and grace of floral ornament, worked in a broad and masculine manner, it challenges fearless comparison with the noblest work of any time."[16]

The Church of St. Matthias, Stoke Newington, London

At the same time that All Saints, Margaret Street, was under construction, another great London church by Butterfield was being built—the Church of St. Matthias, Stoke Newington. Butterfield received the commission from Dr. Robert Brett, who also commissioned Brooks' slightly later series of East End churches. St. Matthias was begun in 1851, a year after All Saints, but was completed in 1853, long before All Saints was finished.

Like All Saints, St. Matthias was a town church. Both churches are constructed primarily of brick; both were designed to stand well above the houses that surrounded them; both emphasize the vertical in their composition; both are flooded with light from clerestory windows; both have chancels that are extensions of the nave, marked only by changes in floor and ceiling; both are built up of solids that emphasize wall rather than mass.

St. Matthias is a slightly larger church than All Saints; the two churches are similar in width and height, but St. Matthias is about one-third longer. It

was built for only seven thousand pounds, approximately ten percent of the cost of All Saints. The difference in cost is attributable to the lesser cost of materials and decoration. St. Matthias' exterior is light gray-brown stock brick with minimal, rather crude, stone dressing; red brick is used inside. It has none of All Saints' rich interior (surface) decoration. Color, either constructional or applied, is not a factor here.

Unlike All Saints, St. Matthias stands free from encroachment of surrounding buildings; it was designed to be seen in the round. Its tower is not a separate, tall, slim, vertical structure, but an integral part of the larger mass. Its size, placement, and design are all unusual. It rises above the choir of the church and is the full width of the nave and chancel. It is carried on two great brick arches which are the dominant feature of the interior. It rises about forty feet above the ridge line of the nave, but it seems much taller. Its upper, belfry portion echoes the composition of the west front—an equilateral triangle above a square conjoined by a huge arched window with its base on the base of the square and its head penetrating the gable above. When approached from the west, the tower gives the church an extremely tall, slender proportion that is distinctly continental.

The buttresses that define the edges of the facade composition are extensions of the north and south clerestory walls. Similarly, the tower buttresses are extensions of the tower east and west walls. The tower is wider north to south than it is east to west, so its east and west walls are its dominant ones. These buttress/wall extensions reinforce the importance of the walls, rather than the mass, in the composition of the church.

Exterior View of the Church of St. Matthias, Stoke Newington, London, from the West

The west facade is a masterful composition. Its center is an expression of the nave. Gabled porches leading to the narthex from north to south establish a strong horizontal base for the composition. Lean-to aisle roofs pass through these porches, linking their horizontal forms with the tall vertical mass of the nave.

St. Matthias is firmly anchored to the ground by the very low, lean-to aisle forms (the sheer clerestory walls rise dramatically tall above the very low aisles), by the transept-like projections of the narthex on either side of the entrance facade, and by the extremely heavy, grossly overscaled, squat corner buttresses on all the porches.

The centerpiece of the facade composition is one of Butterfield's more bizarre borrowings from medieval precedent, this time from Dorchester Abbey, which Butterfield restored. A huge central buttress rises from the apex of the porch gable to bisect the west window and support the large rose in the window arch. The buttress is a double-functioning element; it both bisects and connects. It bisects the window but connects the porch and portal with the window rose and facade wall. The composition is powerful but ungainly. In its weight, mass, and detail, it seems out of character with the planar emphasis of the rest of the composition; yet it adds drama and interest to the facade.

Other windows are equally perverse. Clerestory windows are so tall and aisle windows so short that they constitute a reversal of normal proportion. None of the tracery has the flowing character of the Decorated Style which is the basis for their design; Butterfield did not like the double curve, so his tracery avoids it. St. Matthias' tracery features the pure geometries that Butterfield preferred—the square, the circle, the equilateral triangle—and seems tight, strange, and ungainly in consequence.

St. Matthias was badly damaged during World War II. It was rebuilt but is in sad repair. Its exterior remains intact, however, and is one of Butterfield's most powerful, urbane compositions.

The Church of St. James, Baldersby, North Yorkshire

In 1853 Butterfield began an association with Viscount Downe of Baldersby Park for whom he designed a number of churches, vicarages, and schools characterized by neat contours, few buttresses, and simple tracery. Butterfield's experiments with simply shaped forms which feature squareness and surface manipulation continued through this period. Polychrome decoration became increasingly important as Butterfield's design philosophy developed. The polychrome of these buildings is more restrained than at All Saints, however. Interior veneer has been abandoned and patterns are smaller and more evenly distributed. Arch profiles are simpler and more delicate but window tracery is more elaborate.

The most important work that resulted from Butterfield's association with Viscount Downe was the small village group of church, vicarage, school, and cottages for Baldersby. (The secular buildings at Baldersby represent an important architectural development that foreshadowed the development of arts and crafts housing. They were a conscious return to honest, unpretentious domestic architecture with little historical dressing, similar in style to Philip Webb's Red House done for William Morris.) The Church of St. James, Baldersby, is Butterfield's outstanding country church of the late 1850s. As it served the Viscount's estate village, Baldersby Park, it is the largest and most lavish of Butterfield's country churches of this period.

St. James' composition is very simple. It has a tall nave flanked on either side by very low aisles. The nave roof pitch is very steep (sixty degrees) and the pitch of the aisle lean-to roofs is very shallow. The nave is extended, full width, to create a sanctuary with a slightly lower roof than the nave; the south aisle stops at the chancel wall but the north aisle continues to form a vestry. A tall square tower with a slender pyramidal spire is attached to the south aisle wall so that its west facade is in the same plane as the west facade of the church. Entry to the church is through the tower.

In the masses of the church, all plan elements, even the vestry chimney, are expressed directly and simply. Buttresses are minimal; as at St. Matthias, they generally extend a major wall past a minor, intersecting one. The tower is buttressed only at its base; in its upper stages buttresses diminish and become no more than raised binding elements like quoins. Buttresses that diminish to slightly projecting vertical panels mark the bay divisions of the aisle and clerestory walls. Buttresses, tracery, regular horizontal bands, and other wall dressings are made of smooth, precisely-dressed stone. Buttresses and wall bands establish a rugged linear framework which is filled with panels of soft, rubble-faced ashlar stone; soft irregular stone is shaped and restrained by the hard, crisp armature. Window and door frames often take a very different shape from the actual openings; the tympanum of the main portal is unpierced and the windows at the west end of the aisles are circular openings in elliptical tracery, for example.

There is considerable textural contrast but little color variation on the exterior. Constructional polychromy as a major design feature is reserved for the

Exterior View of the Church of St. James, Baldersby, North Yorkshire, from the Southwest
The simple masses that comprise the church have crisp, square edges; the planes look as if they have been cut with a knife.

41

interior and is subtle and restrained in contrast to the riotous display of color at All Saints. Butterfield changes the major wall material inside from stone to brick. The aisle and clerestory walls and the spandrels above the five-bay nave arcade are made of soft pink brick set off by broad bands of white stone, some of which are decorated by small, inlaid, mastic, geometric designs. The brick above the chancel arch is gray. The piers are all white stone; the stone arcade arches have alternating gray and white voussoirs. Dark wood roof collars and rafters with arched cross-bracing contrast with white plaster ceilings.

The chancel, though more elaborately decorated, is equally restrained. Its wainscot is richly veined alabaster carved with quatrefoils in rondels; its upper wall continues the pink and white stripes of the nave; above the arch of the east window the pink brick changes to gray to match the brick above the chancel arch. The white stone frame of the window is inlaid with a delicate scroll pattern. The nave arcades continue one bay into the chancel establishing a division between choir and sanctuary. The floor is elaborately tiled. The interior effect of the church is restful, almost pastoral, in deliberate contrast to the lively vitality of urban All Saints. St. James shows Butterfield in his most mellow mood and dramatically illustrates the different approach taken by Butterfield, and most of his peers, when designing country as opposed to city churches.

Interior View of the Church of St. James, Baldersby
Pink brick and gray and white stone produce an interior of restrained constructional polychromy.

The Church of St. Alban,
Holborn, London

Butterfield had the opportunity to design a third major London church, St. Alban, Holborn, built from 1859 to 1862. In form it had much in common with St. Matthias, but in its constructional polychromy it was quite different from anything that had preceded it. (St. Alban was badly damaged in World War II; only Butterfield's great west front with its colossal tower construction was left standing. The nave, aisles, and transepts were rebuilt by Sir Giles and Adrian Scott, but not to the original design. It is a shame that its interior was lost; all surfaces were covered with constructional pattern work using the same family of abstract patterns employed on All Saints' veneered surfaces. The materials used included red and yellow brick, Portland stone, terracotta, and incised mastic. The character of the original interior can be imagined by combining the memory of All Saints' color with an examination of the drawing of the interior that appeared in the 1862 *Builder.* The drawing indicates that the patterns here continued to emphasize the flat, smooth nature of the wall.)

The plan was much like the plan of All Saints; it was almost completely surrounded by other buildings. Entry could only be provided from a narrow passage on the south side; the church had to reach very high for clerestory light; aisle windows on the north side and an east, sanctuary, window were impossible. The nave space (and arcade) extended into the chancel with only a very slight diminution in

Exterior View of the Church of St. Alban, Holborn, London
Only this great west-end narthex and tower construction survived the bombing of World War II.

width, as at All Saints, St. Matthias, and St. James—this was Butterfield's favorite nave/chancel relationship. The congregational space at All Saints is nearly square; here it was strongly longitudinal. Moreover, the aisle width was reduced to little more than a passage; almost all worshippers had an unobstructed view into the sanctuary. St. Alban had a more typically interior space than did All Saints.

Butterfield created a wide narthex to accommodate entrance from the south and north. He then raised this feature vertically, creating a tower the width of the nave with tall gabled transepts perpendicular to it on each side over the north and south portals. (The arch from this dramatic narthex into the nave was actually taller than the chancel arch. Street had used a similar form earlier at St. Peter, Bournemouth.) The tower has a double-pitched gable roof that echoes the aisle and nave roof pitches. It is regularly banded with white Portland stone. A square stair turret is thrust up the center of the facade; it has its own gable from which an arcaded octagonal element with its own pyramidal roof cap rises. Its west wall is almost completely opened by an attenuated two-lancet window which is flanked on the main tower wall by three-lancet windows of the same height. The north transept portal has a central buttress which engages the apex of the porch gable in a manner similar in feeling to the composition of the west facade at St. Matthias. The tower is loosely based on the tower of St. Cunibert, Cologne; the proportions and style of the interior were based on Tintern Abbey. Butterfield, as others did during the 1850s, combined English and continental elements freely.

George Hersey, when discussing St. Alban, said that he had the impression that all elements were either squelched (the doors, buttresses, and aisles) or arbitrarily stretched upward (the windows, tower, transepts, and clerestory).[17] Butterfield's proportions are certainly unusual, and St. Alban is a powerful, masculine building. In its exterior effect and urbanity, it is similar to St. Matthias. Both churches display Butterfield's fascination with planar surfaces, neat contours, and square, blocky, but visually lightweight form. St. Alban also reveals Butterfield's increased fascination with constructional pattern and color, a fascination that would dominate his work during the next decade.

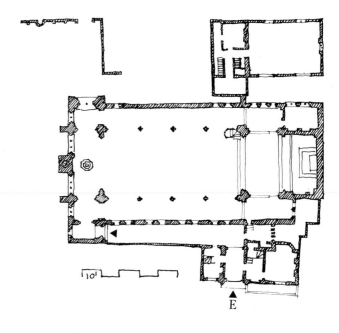

Plan of the Church of St. Alban, Holborn
Entry was provided through a long, corridor-like court on the south side that led to a narthex portal.

Interior View of the Church of St. Alban,
Holborn
Drawing published in the 1861 *Builder*.
Credit: Courtesy of the Library of Congress

45

The Church of the Holy Cross, Ashton New Road, Clayton, Manchester

A comparable church to St. Alban, in much the same style with a very similar plan, was built in the Manchester suburb of Clayton during the years 1863 through 1866—Butterfield's Church of the Holy Cross. Like St. Alban, Holy Cross was built as part of a campaign on the part of the Oxford Movement to convert the urban working class, only about twenty percent of whom ever went to church.

In its form, Holy Cross is much more traditional than any of the churches discussed above. The tower is reminiscent of the tower of Baldersby except that its proportions are different (the square tower is taller; the pyramidal spire is reduced to a cap), it snugs up closer to the nave because of its position in the west bay of the south aisle, and it is made of brick.

The west facade has an asymmetrical character; the slope of the north aisle roof carries the eye to the slope of the nave gable which in turn leads to the cap of the spire. However, the continuous tall, slender,

West Facade of the Church of the Holy Cross, Ashton New Road, Clayton, Manchester
Entry is from a central door in a shed-roofed narthex bound on either side by buttresses that are extensions of the clerestory walls (as at St. Matthias) or from the south porch attached to the tower.

Exterior View of the Church of the Holy
Cross, Clayton, from the Southeast
The massing at the east end of Holy Cross
balances powerful horizontal and vertical
forms much as in the composition of the
west facade of St. Matthias.

nave/chancel block is the dominant mass of the
church; every other form, including the tower, is
subservient to it. Its low ridge line is broken only by
the expression of a parapet at the location of the
chancel wall. Aisles end in transepts located perpendicular to the choir bay of the chancel; the transepts
receive double gables and double windows and were
obviously inspired by the transepts of Street's
Church of St. James the Less of 1859.

What is new and different about the exterior of
Holy Cross is its polychrome pattern decoration.
(Butterfield had used polychrome brick patterns in
the exterior wall of All Saints, but he had abandoned
them in St. Matthias, St. James, and St. Alban.)

The entire dark yellow-brown brick building is
striped with horizontal bands of blue brick and white
stone. Panels below the sill lines of the major east
and west windows and above the south porch arch
and the clerestory windows are filled with blue diapers. Buttresses, except on the south porch where
they splay to invite entry, are insignificant; banding
continues through them with no interruption. The
forms are austere and simple but are inseparably
joined by the bands which tie all the forms together.
The building's forms are dramatically vertical; the
polychrome decoration is emphatically horizontal. A
handsome equilibrium is achieved.

47

Detail of Exterior Wall Brick Polychromy at the Church of the Holy Cross, Clayton

The interior of Holy Cross shows us how St. Alban must have looked before its destruction. The walls are red-brown brick, striped and diapered with black brick. Arcade piers and arches are built up of alternating beige and dark gray stone. Beige and dark gray stone bands alternate with brick bands in the aisle, clerestory, and chancel walls. The lower chancel wall is covered with red and black tile laid diagonally and inlaid with gold fleurs-de-lis; the tile is framed with carved white stone. A blind arcade of stone cusped arches supported on black shafts is superimposed on the middle stage of the striped brick chancel wall; its cornice establishes a sill for the chancel windows. A carved alabaster reredos with cusped-arch panels filled with red, black, white, and yellow tile patterns complements the altar.

The patterned surfaces diminish the weight of the structure at the same time that they establish the primacy of the wall. The treatment of the bay of the arcade located in the chancel is instructive. The brick diaper pattern on the spandrels above the large arch dies abruptly into the adjacent banded chancel wall but continues, uninterrupted, in the spandrels above the nave arches. It is clear that the wall is continuous and that the arches have been cut from it; the spandrel pattern is not designed to fit the wall shapes above the arches. It is equally clear that the spandrel above the double arches set into the larger arch is a tympanum panel specifically designed to fill the space. It is not part of the wall above it; both its pattern and its plane are different, and it is carefully bound on all sides by an architectural frame. Differences of this sort create a hierarchy of importance of the various surfaces and establish order and legibility. The continuity of the clerestory fenestration through nave and chancel, and the continuous sill lines and decorative bands, reinforce the order and logic of the noble space.

Chancel Detail at the Church of the Holy Cross, Clayton
Constructional patterns are used to emphasize wall layering; they are shaped by the function of the wall surface in which they are located.

Interior View of the Church of the Holy Cross, Clayton
The simplicity of spatial forms and interior surfaces is enriched and enlivened with constructional polychrome patterns.

The Church of
St. Augustine,
Penarth, Glamorgan

Butterfield's best churches of the mid-1860s are the churches of St. Augustine, Penarth, built from 1864 to 1866, and All Saints, Babbacombe, begun slightly later. Both churches reflect Butterfield's tendency to move to simpler masses such as those that characterize the Church of the Holy Cross in Manchester and to abandon continental precedents in favor of exclusively English forms. As the shapes of the forms become simpler, Butterfield softens them with projecting moldings; he abandons the planar volumes of the late 1850s and early 1860s for sculpted three-dimensional wall faces enlivened with buttresses, sunken panels, and recessed windows. Buttresses continue to be more symbolic than structural; they mark entrance or orientation or the division of space by function. Paul Thompson says, "Line is the essence of the new style of the 1860s as surface and volume had been of the previous decade."[18] Butterfield moved from the addition of volumes and spaces to their subdivision, and from unqualified mass to a complex linear texture.

Exterior View of the Church of St. Augustine, Penarth, Glamorgan, from the West
The asymmetrical massing of this church, balancing the powerful vertical tower form with the equally strong horizontal form of the north porch of the narthex, is one of Butterfield's most successful compositions.

Exterior View of the Church of St. Augustine, Penarth, from the Northeast This view shows Butterfield's preference for bracketing long, low forms like the aisle with strongly projecting, usually vertical, forms like the transept wing and the narthex porch.

The design of detail and decoration also changes in the mid-1860s. Smaller, more intricate forms and patterns appear with increasing frequency. Color is variable, sometimes soft, sometimes strident with dramatic contrasts.

Thompson describes St. Augustine, Penarth, as "crouched gray-white on a hill above Cardiff harbour, concealing an interior of yellowish ashlar and pink sandstone and raw, red brick with harsh white and black diapering which is only held together by the tough simplicity of its architecture."[19]

At Penarth, Butterfield retains the strong diagonal emphasis and asymmetrical composition of Holy Cross. The diagonal line of the north aisle and nave gable roofs is resolved in the gable of the saddleback tower, approximately ninety feet tall, attached in front of the west facade as an extension of the south aisle. Entry is from the west rather than the south. This is Butterfield's boldest asymmetrical composition to date. If Butterfield had designed no other churches, his competence as a High Victorian architect would have been established by St. Augustine. All forms are interactive, interdependent. The west facade is instructive; the tower overlaps the nave which overlaps the north entrance porch. The north entrance porch is elongated to establish a horizontal

Interior Detail of the Nave Arcade at the Church of St. Augustine, Penarth
The simple circular and polygonal piers and the splayed arcade intrados emphasize weight and mass.

line equal to the vertical line of the tower. Secondary, lower, forms are either bracketed by or incorporated into tall major ones. The south aisle is contained between the tower and south transept, and the north aisle is bracketed by the north transept and the north porch. The vestry is incorporated into the north transept by the extension of the east roof plane. Individual functions are articulated, but the unity of the total composition is never compromised.

The sober exterior conceals a magnificent interior of multicolored brick and stone. The spatial volumes are simple; the nave is broad, the aisles are narrow, and the choir is unusually short. Architectural details are simple and strong. Nave arcades feature stumpy stone columns in alternating round and octagonal shapes. The intrados of the arcade arches are shaped as simple chamfers rather than as curved moldings. Sunken cinquefoil rondels decorate the spandrels. A projecting notched molding band separates the arcade from the clerestory. The columns and arch surrounds are constructed of yellow Bath stone and pink sandstone; walls are of red brick, interspersed with orange and pink, decorated with stone bands and insistent (John Hilling uses the adjective *arrogant*)[20] black and white diapering. The clerestory window reveals are deeply splayed; they echo the chamfers of the arcade intrados and emphasize the thickness and weight of the wall. Butterfield is moving away from an architecture of *surface* toward an architecture of *mass*.

The separation of wall and ceiling planes that was a feature of earlier works is diminished at Penarth. St. Augustine has a barrel roof formed of six planes; it is a continuation of the wall planes to which it is strongly connected by long wall posts. The ceiling is decorated with closely spaced rafters that impart a strong linear pattern to the roof surfaces similar to that given to the wall by the diapering. Both linear patterns function to de-emphasize particular architectural features and to bring unity and continuity to the larger spaces.

John Hilling says, "At St. Augustine's, Butterfield expunged all medieval details and at the same time built more in the spirit of the medieval mastermasons, which gives the building a unity and an integrity lacking in some of his other churches."[21] There is no question that St. Augustine belongs uniquely to the High Victorian era. Paul Thompson suggests that at Penarth the design of form and details has caught up with color and pattern; he hypothesizes that it took a decade for Butterfield to reach an understanding of the impact of High Victorian color and pattern upon architectural design.

All Saints Church, Babbacombe, Torquay, Devon

All Saints, like St. Augustine, Penarth, hides a brilliant polychromatic interior behind a long, low, gray stone exterior. But Babbacombe has a gentler exterior aspect than Penarth. For one thing, the church is located in a park filled with the lush vegetation of the Devon coast. For another, Babbacombe abandons the strong diagonal facade composition and stark geometric volumes of Penarth for a traditional symmetrical composition and softer, decorated volumes.

Exterior View of All Saints Church, Babbacombe, Torquay, Devon, from the Southeast
All Saints is unusual in that, with the exception of the tower, its forms are horizontal rather than vertical in character. North and south transepts located on either side of the choir bay of the chancel were intended; only the south transept containing the Lady Chapel, and visible in this view, was built.

At All Saints, the tower is located on the longitudinal axis in the center of the west facade. A west portal, located in the base of the tower, leads to a wide, long nave which is almost undifferentiated, on the exterior at least, from the chancel. Only a very slight projection of the chancel wall through the roof marks the internal division of the space. The low roof pitch (forty-five degrees) emphasizes the length of the form; so does the absence of a clerestory. (The dormers were not added until early in this century; originally only a narrow strip of wall divided aisle and nave roofs.) Bay divisions of the nave and aisles are marked by buttresses which have gable heads that project past the eave of the aisle roofs— an unusual detail for Butterfield. Only the open porch with its pyramidal roof, designed to resemble a lich gate, breaks the symmetry of the composition; the porch is attached to the south wall of the west bay of the aisle.

The tower consists of two square stages and a broached spire. The tall lower stage is buttressed at all corners; it is penetrated by a tall, slender two-light lancet window above the portal. The portion that projects above the nave ridge is decorated on all sides with wide panels of buff tiles; the tiles are incised with quatrefoils filled with steel blue and gray-green mastic. The panels give the effect of grills instead of solid wall. The second, belfry, stage has a similar patterned band that runs from the springline of the large arched openings to the top of the stage. Strong projecting moldings establish a cornice; chamfered corners extend past the cornice as spirelets. Corners and buttresses of dressed stone form frames for the "grill" panels at both stages, as well as at the corners of the south porch where the tiles are perforated and a true grill results. The grill is also layered over the gable of the chancel east wall above the arch of the east window. The grills perform much as checkers or diapers do at other churches; they visually lighten the weight of the upper wall. The gray stone walls are banded and dressed with stone of the same buff color as the grillwork.

Some exterior details seem peculiarly idiosyncratic even for an architect of Butterfield's originality. Notable among these are the disparity in shape between the arch of the east window and the arch in the grillwork above it and the nimbus shape of the side windows of the chancel with their eight-cusp openings.

Because exterior decoration seems either to be recessed into and contained by the basic structure (as is the case in the tower or porch) or to be superimposed upon the wall (as in the case with the chancel gable), the decoration serves to emphasize mass rather than surface and is substantially different in effect from earlier churches. The character of the tower seems to parody Pugin's tower at St. Giles, Cheadle.

The interior of the Babbacombe church is as innovative, and difficult, as the exterior. It reveals Butterfield at his most original and creative. Paul Thompson said of All Saints, "In his defiance of traditional harmony Butterfield is a modern, an Expressionist, and as such he has appealed profoundly to modern critics. It is certainly hard to forget his church at Babbacombe seen perhaps in the gloom of a winter afternoon, the nave held tightly horizontal by a long, low raftered roof, the severe nave arcades on brown marble cylinder-columns, the wall-space above patterned with bold diagonal ribs on grey-black and red brick walls, the nave floor of

Exterior Detail of the East Facade of All Saints Church, Babbacombe
This drawing shows the disparity in shape between the window panel and the actual window opening.

harsh wasp-yellow, red and black tiles; and beyond this the soft colours of the chancel, a wide floor marbled in broad patterns, pinks, grey-blues, a little black, sea-green, veined yellow, much buff; open in effect, but two great double side-arches thrusting sharply upwards beside the vertical columns of the sanctuary, reaching up into the arched vaulted roof—the whole spatial effect intensely contrary and victorious . . ."[22]

The decoration of the walls above the nave arcades is particularly interesting. It reveals Butterfield's new interest in *layered* decoration. The wall itself is made of red and dark gray sandstone laid in

Interior View of All Saints Church, Babbacombe
The interior proportions of All Saints seem much lower and longer than in earlier churches; the horizontal movement axis is strongly stressed.

Interior Detail of the Nave Arcade Spandrel Decoration at All Saints Church, Babbacombe

stripes. Applied to the inner surface is a diagonal lattice of widely spaced, extremely slender, molded members that connect the wall cornice with the boldly shaped projecting moldings of the arcade arches. The two systems—wall and lattice—are reconciled by diagonal patterns inlaid in the striped wall surface in the center of each lattice panel. Strongly directional seven-foiled recessed medallion panels in the spandrels also help to relate wall and lattice while adding a third, recessed plane to the wall system. How different this is from the completely smooth surface decoration in earlier churches.

The chancel decoration is as elaborate as any Butterfield designed. The lower walls are paneled in stripes of richly veined beige and brown marble. The red and gray banded stone of the nave spandrels continues on the upper chancel walls above an elaborately designed, deeply cut, stiff-leaf frieze; recessed rondels inlaid with dark stone are set into the upper walls. Window and niche reveals are decorated with sculpted geometric patterns. The reredos is a layered tracery arcade with cusped panels filled with Salviati mosaics—figures on gold grounds. The chancel wall above the east window is decorated with an applied diagonal lattice similar to that used on the nave spandrels, but more regular and more elaborate. Absurdly slender polished black marble shafts divide the chancel into bays—the shafts are doubled at the division between choir and sanctuary; they run the full height of the wall and are continued across the faceted wood barrel vault as projecting beams. The ceiling is paneled with diagonal ribs; panels are painted to simulate a recessed intarsia pattern. Unlike the decoration at All Saints, Margaret Street, the decoration of All Saints,

Interior Detail of the Sanctuary Decoration of All Saints Church, Babbacombe

Babbacombe, seems to be intrinsic to the basic constructional system of the building.

The contrast Butterfield intended between a brilliantly lighted chancel and a dark nave has been altered, probably fortuitously, by the insertion of small dormer windows into the nave roof. Butterfield intended for all light in the nave to come from aisle windows. (The aisles are narrow and the aisle windows are reasonably large and located in widely splayed recesses; nevertheless, an inadequate amount of light entered the nave space.) Butterfield wanted a heavy, dark, dynamic space that would sweep the viewer on to the sanctuary but the effect he achieved was too dark to suit the parishioners. The aisle walls are connected with the nave arcade by arched buttresses that not only carry the thrust of the roof but emphasize the mass and weight of the construction. The nave roof is a trussed rafter system with narrowly spaced dark bottom chords relentlessly, rhythmically moving forward toward the chancel, uninterrupted by bay divisions. Even today, after the introduction of clerestory light, the nave is dramatically darker than the chancel. (Butterfield must have been displeased with the strangely dynamic space and the strong contrasts of dark and light that he employed at Babbacombe. He abandoned these devices, never using them in his later churches.)

The Church of St. Augustine, Queen's Gate, South Kensington, London

The Church of St. Augustine, Queen's Gate, was built during the years 1871 to 1875 to serve the rapidly increasing population brought to South Kensington by the Great Exhibition of 1851 and the subsequent building of the museums and the Imperial College. The church is similar in plan and size to St. Alban, Holborn, except that its major entrance is on axis in the center of the west facade like at St. Matthias.

St. Augustine, Queen's Gate, has no tower or spire. Its west front is its most remarkable feature; the nave gable is not expressed in the west facade, which is a rectangular composition tightly constrained within octagonal stair towers which mark the width of the nave and bracket a porch with a lean-to roof. Each stair tower is capped by an octagonal pyramidal roof. The center portion of the facade is extended above the rectangle to form a massive gabled bellcote pierced for two bells. (Thompson says that the precedent Butterfield used in the design of this facade is the westwork of the German church of Chorin; it may also have been inspired by the brick belfries of French churches in the neighborhood of Toulouse.)

As at St. Matthias, the predominantly vertical facade composition is anchored to the ground by a broad base formed by the extension of the narthex to create one-story porches at either side of the church. The lean-to aisle roofs penetrate rather than die into these porches creating diagonal lines that lead the eye upward from the horizontal base form to the tall vertical central facade element. Butterfield explores duality in the facade composition. Although an arched two-lancet window is placed on axis above the portal, the thickness of the center division is exaggerated and is made of brick to match the wall rather than stone to match the tracery. This window is flanked by lancet windows of equal height and width. The effect is of four tall, slender individual lancets rather than a large central window with smaller flanking windows. (This effect is reversed inside where the central mullion is part of the tracery rather than the wall.) Above the apex of the center window arch, a buttress corbels out to become the center of the composition of the belfry; the buttress is flanked by the belfry openings. Duality is finally resolved by the belfry gable with its rondel. The facade is anti-classical and anti-picturesque in its organization.

    The church is constructed of buff stone and brick. The brick used included London stocks, blue Staffordshire brick, red Suffolk Brick, and a boldly patterned patented brick, pale buff in color moulded with fleurs-de-lis. Molded terra-cotta bands and richly carved stone moldings enrich the exterior surfaces, as do carved stone grill panels through which red brick can be seen.

The West Facade of the Church of St. Augustine, Queen's Gate, South Kensington, London
This most interesting of Butterfield's facades is an exercise in the reconciliation of odd-numbered and even-numbered elements. For example, four identical lancet windows are contained within only three arched frames.

Interior View Looking toward the West
Entrance of the Church of St. Augustine,
Queen's Gate
St. Augustine is much taller than the country
churches at Penarth and Babbacombe; it
rises high to admit copious quantities of
light—a reaction to its smoky London en-
vironment. Its interior color scheme is also
much lighter in value than those Butterfield
had used in his earlier churches.

The interior of St. Augustine, Queen's Gate, is a development of the interior of St. Augustine, Penarth. The central space is extremely vertical; it has the tall clerestory windows considered essential to bring light into urban churches. Arcades are carried on simple, stumpy columns made of alternating buff and dark gray stone drums. The arcade arches are strongly molded buff stone. Spandrel walls are constructed of the patented patterned brick; in the spandrels tracery arches surround quatrefoil panels filled with mosaic figures. Clerestory walls alternate broad bands of buff stone, yellow brick, and red brick. Black and buff stone shafts extend the roof braces down the walls to the arcade spandrels. Red diapering on a yellow brick ground fills the upper portion of the chancel wall; below it are horizontal bands like those on the clerestory walls with red, buff, and black diapering made using the patented bricks as background. Although similar patterns exist on the clerestory walls and the chancel wall, they are not continuous from one surface to another; Butterfield wants us to understand that the chancel wall is an insertion that is not part of the basic constructional system of the space.

The chancel of St. Augustine, Queen's Gate, is much less successful than those in the churches described above. A gilded baroque altar and baldachin have been inserted that are not sympathetic to Butterfield's crisp geometric forms. Moreover, the bottom half of the large east window recess is filled with banded brickwork; only the upper portions of the tracery have lights. The resulting proportion is very awkward, and the sanctuary is dark in contrast to the bright, happy, colorful nave. The chancel's darkness is exacerbated by the use of gray and mauve marble veneer on its lower walls. It depends

Interior Showing the Chancel Wall Treatment at the Church of St. Augustine, Queen's Gate
The most unusual detail in the church is the design of the chancel wall. The upper portion of the chancel (which is as tall as the nave) is visible through an unglazed window placed in the wall above the rather low, heavy chancel arch.

upon artificial light to compensate for diminished natural light.

(The ceramic tile murals were added in the 1890s; they were not part of Butterfield's original scheme and were done long after the tile murals at Keble College Chapel.)

The color at St. Augustine, Queen's Gate, is as fresh and bright today as it was in 1875. The church, after a period in which Butterfield's polychromatic decoration was obscured by white paint and plaster, has been restored to its original appearance. The church is also an excellent example of the balance between surface and mass that Butterfield achieved in his work of the late 1860s and 1870s.

Rugby School Chapel, Warwickshire

Butterfield's style, unlike that of Street, Pearson, Bodley, and others, never evolved into a Late Victorian phase. He remained a High Victorian architect long after the style had gone out of fashion, and his buildings of the 1870s, although different in some respects from his buildings of the 1850s and 1860s, remained truly High Victorian in style. St. Augustine, Queen's Gate, discussed above, is very much a High Victorian building. So are Butterfield's most important churches of this decade—his master-pieces, Rugby School Chapel, 1870–72, and Keble College Chapel, Oxford, 1867–83.

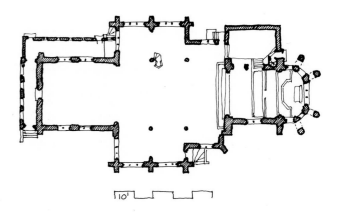

Plan of Rugby School Chapel, Warwickshire
The chapel has an "open-plan" spatial character due to the way the transepts and the easternmost bay of the nave are handled.

Rugby Chapel engages the buildings of the school's quadrangle on its west and part of its north side. Only its south side and sanctuary stand free of other buildings.

The chapel plan, because it is a school chapel and had to accommodate a large number of boys, looks more like a plan by E. B. Lamb than by Butterfield. On its major longitudinal axis, the chapel is nearly 132 feet long, forty feet of which is devoted to the chancel. Slightly east of the center of the nave, a major cross axis is introduced, sixty-seven feet wide, in the form of double transepts. The nave area between the transepts and the chancel is almost as wide as the transepts themselves. The roof structure over this wide, open portion of the plan is carried on tall, slender, circular columns of cream and pink sandstone that challenge conventional height to radius ratios. The columns support arcades in both the longitudinal direction of the nave and north to south in the transepts. Butterfield's

Exterior View of Rugby School Chapel, from the East
The chapel tower is a study in organic form resulting from the vertical manipulation of three-dimensional geometry.

Interior View toward the Chancel of Rugby School Chapel
This is the lightest, airiest, most delicate of Butterfield's interiors. The slenderness and height of the circular columns
contributes to this effect. They are decidedly out of character
for both Butterfield and the High Victorian age.

The dominant feature of the exterior is the tower
and apse construction of the chapel's east end. In its
free manipulation of form it reveals Butterfield at
war, or perhaps at play, with historicism. The tower
is placed over the square choir bay; it is strongly
buttressed at the corners. At the height of the eave
of the nave roof, the belfry stage begins. The belfry
begins as a square form with tall arched openings on
each side. At a point mid-way up, the corners of the
square towers are broached and the belfry is transformed into an octagonal form. Its windows have
their sills in the walls of the square tower and their
heads in the walls of the octagonal tower. A band of
open arcaded panels caps the belfry. Above a machicolated cornice is a short, octagonal spire. Pinnacles
and projecting downspouts complete the spiky silhouette. From the east wall of the lower stage a
five-sided apse projects; it is radially buttressed and
has a double-sloped pyramidal roof. Strongly projecting moldings and striped and diapered bands of
a brown and red brick and buff stone wrap the
composition.

The exterior of the chancel has a massive organic
quality. Forms seem to grow out of each other. The
mass is strongly sculpted. There is little of Butterfield's normal preoccupation with surface here. Expression of the sculptural form and building weight
supersede surface concerns.

A completely different aesthetic controls the design of the interior. In its lightness, height, openness, and airy delicacy, the emphasis is upon the
space contained, not the form or decoration of
the enclosing envelope. It is almost incidental that
the wall surfaces are richly polychromatic and the
roof structure is brightly decorated. If the decoration does not emphasize the integrity of the wall,

structure has a very fragile appearance in contrast
with the heavy, low timber roofs Lamb used over
plans of this type. The chapel's interior space is
amazingly open and light, and it has a strongly vertical character in spite of the absence of a clerestory
(except in the westernmost portion of the nave).
Aisle windows are very tall and slender in proportion. All pews face north or south toward the center
aisle rather than east as they would in a conventional
church.

View of the Interior Detail of the North
Transept of Rugby School Chapel
Constructional color adds warmth and
vitality to the interior space.

it does impart a richness, a glow, a warmth, to the ambience of the interior. Halsey Ricardo said, speaking of Rugby chapel's colors, "There is a give and take amongst them, especially in the matter of colour. The yellow brick borrows something of his neighbor's crimson and flushes a tender coral or recalls the almond blossom in spring. The red . . . softens into purples and russets, with a highlight of scarlet still gleaming here and there, the black headers show an iridescence of blue lustre, and in their grave way check the riot of color." [23]

Keble College Chapel, Oxford

Pevsner called Keble College "the final triumph of the Oxford Movement." He describes it as "earnest and exacting, overwhelmingly what the age called *real*." [24]

When John Keble died in 1866, an appeal was launched immediately to raise funds to build a college as a memorial to him. Funds poured in from wealthy Anglo-Catholics, and the college was begun in 1868 and completed in 1882. Butterfield was selected to be the architect; plans were developed in 1867.

The money for the chapel was given by William Gibbs of Tyntesfield; there is disagreement regarding the cost of the chapel—Pevsner says fifty thousand pounds, Thompson says forty thousand pounds—but the gift was substantial. The chapel was completed during the early 1870s, making it contemporary with St. Augustine, Queen's Gate, and the Rugby School Chapel.

Paul Thompson quotes Butterfield as saying, "Keble College Chapel was conceived as a statement of faith; as a Te Deum, strictly ordered but manifestly triumphant." Butterfield stated in a letter to the college warden dated 22 January 1873 that his design intention was "to give the restfulness and strength, and sense of communion that come of quiet order, completeness and proportion, must be our aim." [25] Although Butterfield's most direct precedent for the design was the upper Church of St. Francis at Assisi, *The Architect* in 1870 described its style as "Early Decorated, for the purity of which the name of Mr. Butterfield is ample security." [26] To modern viewers the chapel, and the entire college, hardly seems Gothic at all, it is so completely High Victorian in appearance.

The chapel occupies the northeast corner of the large block on which the two quadrangles of the college are built. The quadrangle ranges are three stories tall with entry and end features of four stories. The chapel is equivalent to an eight-storied block. It is extremely tall and vertical in character. Its mass is divided into tall, slender bays by strongly projecting buttresses whose pinnacles project past the roof eave, in the manner of the great single buttress at All Saints, Margaret Street. Here the buttresses establish a rhythm of powerful vertical lines.

Exterior (Courtyard) View of Keble College Chapel, Oxford, from the Southwest
This is the chapel's most interesting facade because of the rhythm, proportion, and projection and recession of the tall narrow bays.

The chapel has no aisles and the only windows are placed high in the walls adding to the impression of great height.

The south quadrangle facade is more elaborate than the other facades. It is an interesting composition of tall, slender panels that project and recede in space. From left to right, the sequence of the composition is as follows: VN (a very narrow, gabled, projecting bay that includes a south entrance portal), W, W (wider receding nave bays with three-lancet clerestory windows), VW (a very wide, gabled, shallowly projecting transept bay which holds the organ chamber), N, and N (narrow receding choir bays with two-lancet clerestory windows). The north street side has the same rhythm without the transept projections, so it is less interesting. East and west facades and all projecting bays are gabled. Receding bays are capped with a deep, strongly sculptural, stone cornice band carved with a series of delicate, tangent circles. The cornice continues across the east and west facades to establish a base line for the gables. It does not, however, continue across the entrance and transept gables because it would compromise their tower-like appearance.

The wall panels between the buttresses are composed of a base and four upper stages, all divided by strongly projecting stone moldings. The lower three wall stages are red brick banded with buff stone at regular intervals. The banding increases in width and frequency as it rises, becoming more stone and less brick. The fourth stage begins at the springline of the clerestory arches; it is half brick and half stone in a checkered pattern. Buttresses are banded throughout their height; they function as frames for the checkered panels. Clerestory windows connect wall stages three and four. The first stage has a

Detail of the Entrance Portal of Keble College Chapel
At Keble, Butterfield employed all the constructional polychrome devices he had experimented with in his earlier churches— banding, diapering, checkering, and the addition of figurative sculpture.

Interior View toward the Chancel at Keble College Chapel
The chapel has no significant division between its chancel and
its nave, and it has no aisles. It is one great soaring, vaulted
space. It is, in fact, Butterfield's only completely vaulted work.

layer of blind arcading appliqued over the brick. Diapering is used on the east and west facades and in the gables. Incised tiles filled with sea green mastic like those at Babbacombe fill the spandrel above the portal in the south entrance recess. Buttress niches and the entrance tympanum are decorated with figural sculpture.

The walls appear to diminish in weight as they rise. Not only are they opened in the upper stages by the large clerestory windows, but the increased quantity of light colored stone and the grill-like checkering visually lighten the wall. Butterfield's early preference for smooth surfaces and planar volumes has obviously been replaced with concern for sculptured form, weight, and mass.

The interior, as at Assisi, is one great, tall, vaulted, rectangular space. The concentration of decorative effort upon the sheer enclosing walls is similar to Assisi, too. Space—great soaring space— is everything. Nothing in the church competes with the space, or even seems to occupy it. All furniture is kept very low and the choir and sanctuary have only minimal elevation. The altar is simple and its reredos is very much a part of the wall envelope, not an element in its own right. Side wall bay divisions are marked with tall, slender, full-height shafts that are hardly more than lines; their luxuriantly carved stone capitals receive the slender, linear ribs of the quadripartite vaulting system.

The interior walls are divided into stages much like the exterior walls, except there are only three stages instead of four. The wainscot is a strongly projecting plinth that supports the upper wall. The first stage is glazed plum-colored brick with thin stripes of sea-green brick and broader bands of buff stone inlaid with mastic patterns; as on the exterior, a stone arcade of cusped arches on simple round shafts is layered over the brick. Above the arcade a boldly cut, stiff-leaf frieze serves as cornice for stage one and base for stage two. The second stage is devoted to a series of glazed-tile mosaic scenes that culminate in the Christ Enthroned in a quatrefoil above the altar. Each wall bay is treated as a triptych; a large rectangular center scene is flanked by smaller scenes in arched panels. The mosaic scenes are rendered in soft colors—green, pink, pale blue, soft yellow, red and white. The mosaic tile is in the plane of the brick below; the scenes are framed by stone in the plane of the first stage arcading. The stone veneer of the second stage continues into the third stage as the frames of the clerestory windows. The wall that surrounds the windows is banded, checkered, and diapered brick; the predominant color of the brick is vermilion with the pattern worked in gray and buff.

The ribs of the vaulting are pink and terra-cotta in color. The entire vault surface is painted with formalized jointing patterns in broad bands of buff, sea-green, and gray. The patterns and colors of the nave continue into the chancel. (In the chancel, the tile and stone patterns of the floor and the inlaid decoration in the arcade are more elaborate than in the nave, and the central panel is treated as a reredos with a pointed canopy above a great quatrefoil rather than a rectangular panel. Otherwise the decoration is the same.)

Color gives the space a special warm glow, an ambience, that is enhanced by the great series of Gibbs windows which are predominantly light but glow with bits of scarlet, mauve, yellow, and blue-green. Unlike the color in Butterfield's buildings of the previous decade, the color is soft and the color scheme carefully controlled. Butterfield described this work as "largely dependent on, and connected with coloured material." He said, "I should be sorry to see such works published unless that treatment could be done justice to."[27]

Butterfield's use of color and pattern was already out of style when Keble College was built. Early on, Butterfield's work at the chapel was christened "the holy zebra" style. Even those who had in the past most admired his work now found it to be insensitive, startling, and restless.

Paul Thompson, in his biography on Butterfield, comments on the Oxford reaction:

Clearly Oxford had not found "the restfulness and strength, and sense of communion that come of quiet order, completeness and proportion," which Butterfield had intended in the chapel. On the contrary, it became a habit of undergraduates and younger dons "to break off on their afternoon walks in order to have a good laugh at the quadrangle"; and so loud was their laughter that when Sir Kenneth Clark wrote his pioneering reappraisal of the Gothic Revival in 1927, he could not find the confidence to write a chapter on Butterfield. It would have indeed required some nerve to refer with any respect to what Oxford opinion considered "the ugliest building in the world," and at that time attributed to Ruskin with such confidence that Clark was called a liar at a public meeting for disagreeing. Yet even in the revised edition of 1950, his respect took a backhanded form: Butterfield was "the first master of discordant polyphony." Such responses reveal the continuing hold, even in criticism of the Gothic Revival, of classical instincts; the divinity of whiteness proclaimed by Alberti, Palladio and the theorists of the Renaissance. Their belief in colourlessness was none the less powerful for being in conflict with most previous architectural tradition; so much so that in the mid–

Interior Detail of the Layered Wall Treatment
at Keble College Chapel

71

nineteenth century not merely construction poly-chromy, but even pure red brick was thought a bold gesture.[28]

Not all nineteenth-century critics reacted so negatively to Butterfield, however. He had his admirers. One of them was the poet Gerard Manley Hopkins. He wrote to Butterfield, "I hope you will long continue to work out your beautiful and original style. I do not think this generation will ever much admire it. They do not understand how to look at a Pointed building as a whole having a single form governing it throughout, which they *would* perhaps see in a Greek temple; they like it to be a sort of farmyard and medley of ricks and roofs and dovecots."[29]

Sir John Summerson, in his essay on William Butterfield in *Heavenly Mansions,* makes the case that Butterfield is to architecture what Dickens and Emily Bronte were to literature. He says, "In architecture, Butterfield is the great symbol of that sense of revulsion and liberation which permeated English art and letters in those years [1845–65] . . . [Butterfield's way] was to drag the Gothic Revival from its pedestal of scholarship and gentility and re-create it in a builder's yard. . . . Butterfield attacks architecture not as building, but as Gothic-Architecture-as-building."[30]

Today's architects and critics, liberated from the dogma of both the academic tradition and the modern movement, again find pleasure, intellectual stimulation, and beauty in Butterfield's powerful but unorthodox work. Butterfield is at last receiving his due as one of the most gifted, original architects of the nineteenth century.

NOTES

1. Paul Thompson, *William Butterfield* (Cambridge: M.I.T. Press, 1971), 19.
2. Thompson, 22, 167.
3. Basil F. L. Clarke, *Church Builders of the Nineteenth Century* (London: Society for Promoting Christian Knowledge; New York: Macmillan, 1938), 124–25.
4. W. R. Lethaby, *Philip Webb and His Work* (1935; London: Raven Oak Press, 1979), 67.
5. H. S. Goodhardt-Rendel, *English Architecture Since the Regency* (London: Constable, 1953), 134–35.
6. John Summerson, *Heavenly Mansions* (New York: Scribner's, 1948), 169.
7. Charles L. Eastlake, *A History of the Gothic Revival* (1872; New York: Humanities Press; Leicester: Leicester University Press, 1970), 262–63.
8. John Summerson, "Pugin and Butterfield," *Architectural Review* (August 1972): 97–99.
9. Thompson, 377.
10. Summerson, *Heavenly Mansions,* 172.
11. Summerson, *Heavenly Mansions,* 175.
12. Thompson, 226.
13. Paul Thompson, "William Butterfield," *Victorian Architecture,* ed. Peter Ferriday (Philadelphia, New York: Lippincott, 1964), 173.
14. George L. Hersey, *High Victorian Gothic* (Baltimore, London: Johns Hopkins University Press, 1972), 117.
15. Gavin Stamp, and Colin Amery, *Victorian Buildings of London 1837–1887* (London: Architectural Press, 1980), 38.
16. Hersey, 187–88.
17. Hersey, 124.
18. Thompson, *William Butterfield,* 326.
19. Thompson, "William Butterfield," 167.
20. John B. Hilling, *Cardiff and the Valleys* (London: Lund Humphries, 1973), 122.
21. Hilling, 122.
22. Thompson, "William Butterfield," 167.

23. Halsey Ricardo, Obituary of William Butterfield, *Architectural Review 7* (1900): 260.

24. Jennifer Sherwood and Nikolaus Pevsner, *Oxfordshire,* Buildings of England Series (Harmondsworth: Penguin, 1974), 225.

25. Thompson, *William Butterfield,* 32–33.

26. Thompson, *William Butterfield,* 82.

27. Thompson, *William Butterfield,* 226–27.

28. Thompson, *William Butterfield,* 226–27.

29. Thompson, *William Butterfield,* 305.

30. Summerson, *Heavenly Mansions,* 171.

GEORGE EDMUND STREET

George Edmund Street (1824–81) was the youngest of three sons of a Woodford, Essex, solicitor. Street's older brother, Thomas Henry, was chiefly responsible for the younger Street's interest in architecture. Thomas Henry Street was intensely interested in medieval architecture. He spent his holidays back-packing around the country, studying and sketching England's medieval parish churches. He often took his brother George Edmund with him. George Edmund was fascinated by the churches they visited, and his sketches soon outstripped his brother's in quality.

The Street family assumed that George Edmund's interest in architecture would be like his brother's, an avocation, and that he would follow his father into the practice of law. As a teenager, Street tried a clerkship in his father's office, but it was quickly apparent to Street and to his family that law was not his calling, so in 1840, when Street was eighteen, he was sent to his uncle, Thomas Haseler, a painter in Exeter, to take lessons in perspective. Haseler recognized Street's talent and arranged for him to be articled to a Winchester architect, Owen Browne Carter, in 1841.

Street spent three years in Carter's office. Apparently the office was not particularly busy, because Street seems to have spent most of his time doing measured drawings and sketches of Winchester Cathedral.

His apprenticeship completed, Street left Carter in 1844 to go to work in the London office of Scott and Moffatt, where he remained until 1849. Sir George Gilbert Scott was the most successful Neo-Gothic architect in England in the 1840s. His office was a veritable factory in which the employees were given much responsibility for the design of the countless projects in hand. Scott also allowed his employees to "moonlight," and Street began his own practice in 1847 with the commission for a small parish church in Biscovey, Cornwall. Street's client was pleased and assisted him in securing a number of other commissions in the Southwest. These commissions made it possible for Street to leave Scott's office in 1849 to establish his own practice.

Even in the early years of his practice, Street was fortunate in attracting clients who could help him establish his reputation and secure other commissions. His most important early commission was for the restoration of the Hadleigh Church, because through it he gained the patronage of Mr. William Butler of Wantage (later dean of Lincoln) and met his future wife, the vicar's niece. Through the influence of Mr. Butler, he was commissioned to design a vicarage, schools, and several other works in Wantage, and in 1850 Street moved his office there. In the same year, he was appointed diocesan architect of Oxford and took his first foreign trip. The appointment was instrumental in changing his practice from a small to a large one; the trip was responsible for his view that foreign as well as English Gothic architecture could provide inspiration for design.

In May of 1852 Street moved his office to Oxford, where he employed Edmund Sedding and Philip Webb as his assistants. The move to Oxford marked the beginning of Street's maturity as an architect, architectural critic, and philosopher. His early work had consisted primarily of unremarkable, massive, simple churches. His work of the mid-1850s integrated constructional polychromy and foreign influences into original, graceful Gothic designs. The first important works of his maturity were the parish churches of St. Peter, Bournemouth, and All Saints, Boyne Hill; the theological college at Cuddlesdon; and the convent for the East Grinstead Sisterhood. Like William Burges, Street's fame was established by his entries in the competitions for the design of the Lille Cathedral in 1855 and the Crimea Memorial church in Constantinople in 1856. Street placed second to Burges and Clutton and to Burges alone in these competitions, but his drawings were published and widely praised. (Street actually received the commission for the Church in Constantinople some years later when Burges' design proved too costly and was deemed unsuitable for the site provided by the Sultan.)

In 1853 Street revisited northern Italy, collecting material for his first important publication, *Brick and Marble Architecture*, published in 1855. He gave six lectures on architecture at the Royal Academy during the early 1850s; he also published more than twenty papers in *The Ecclesiologist* and wrote the section on Gothic architecture for the ninth edition of the *Encyclopaedia Britannica*.

In 1856 Street moved his office to London. The following year he received his first London commission–the church and schools of St. James the Less, Westminster. St. James the Less was followed, in quick succession, by commissions for important churches throughout the country including SS. Philip and James, Oxford, 1859–62; All Saints, Denstone, Staffordshire, 1860–62; St. John, Torquay, 1864–65; St. Saviour, Eastbourne, 1865–72; St. Mary Magdalen, Paddington, 1871–74; and the nave and west front for Bristol Cathedral, 1868–88.

During the early 1860s, Street made three trips to Spain, collecting material for his book, *Gothic Architecture in Spain*, published 1865. This book, although filled with beautiful drawings, did not have the impact on the course of development of High Victorian architecture that *Brick and Marble Architecture* had had. The earlier book was a "how to" book for architects; it suggested ways in which Italian Gothic forms and details might be used to bring life and vitality to High Victorian Gothic design. The Spain book was more a travelogue than a philosophical treatise.

In 1865 Street was elected associate of the Royal Academy; he became a full member in 1871. He was an active member of the Church of All Saints, Margaret Street (Butterfield's great church), for which he became church warden in 1866. At this time he began an association with Sir Tatton Sykes, for whom he designed a number of fine parish churches in the late 1860s and early 1870s. The event of the greatest importance to Street's career and reputation occurred in 1868 when he was selected to be the architect of the Royal Courts of Justice. A significant portion of Street's time from 1868 to his death in 1881 was devoted to the law courts; he personally prepared over three thousand drawings for this building. The completed building received mixed reviews from the architectural press but was a great hit with the public.

In 1874 Street was awarded the gold medal of the Royal Institute of British Architects, and in 1878 he received the knighthood of the Legion of Honour. In 1881, the last year of his life, he was appointed professor of architecture at the Royal Academy and was elected president of the Royal Institute of British Architects. He died as a result of two paralyzing strokes on December 18, 1881; he was buried in Westminster Abbey on December 29 of that year.

Throughout his life Street was an indefatigable worker. Today we would call him a workaholic. Unlike his early master, Scott, Street made all design decisions himself, even down to preparing scale drawings in pencil, which he would then turn over to draftsmen for inking. His pupils and employees, who included Norman Shaw in addition to Sedding and Webb, liked, admired, and respected him. He was essentially a simple man; he ate simple food and took no wine. He was active in church, sang in the choir, and preferred the High Church ritual. He was an active member of the Ecclesiological Society and a friend and supporter of members of the pre-Raphaelite Brotherhood. He was the great delineator, the master draftsman, of his era; he admonished his students over and over to draw more, saying, "Sketch! Sketch! Sketch!"

Henry-Russell Hitchcock, in his book *Early Victorian Architecture,* says, "Street was destined to be, after Butterfield and Ruskin, the most important architect and archaeologist critic of the High Victorian period. . . . Street was as single-minded an artist as Butterfield and a more careful student of medieval architecture than Ruskin."[1] Butterfield maintained a greater consistency of quality in his work than did Street, but Street's best work is as good as Butterfield's best work. Street's work is less startling and less original than Butterfield's; it is softer and more scholarly. Street, at his best, produced wonderfully tough, strong churches with vigorous, careful detail. He was not afraid to combine French, Italian, and even German forms and details with the Early English and Decorated styles. He held that Gothic was the style of the pointed arch, not the style of the nation or the age. He wanted his architecture to be the development and continuation of Gothic architecture, not the replication of earlier buildings. Street did not see Gothic as a frozen, finished style. He saw it instead as a style left in suspended animation, now ready to be picked up again, to grow, evolve and change to meet modern needs and demands. He accepted all Gothic precedent, not just English Decorated precedent.

Street's writings reveal his architectural philosophy. A. E. Street, in his *Memoir of George Edmund Street,* quotes his father as saying, "If architecture is only an affair of outside display no one will take any real interest in it; for, from the first, it is the evidence of the architect's love for his work which has given the human interest which is all in all to it. It is this truthfulness only, in every line and every detail of every part of a building, which can ever make great architecture. It is this only which one would wish to extract from the works of our forefathers."[2]

Truthfulness is the key word here. Street preferred dignity and restraint and obviousness of purpose (we would call it functional articulation today) to meaningless ornament which does not emphasize basic architectural forms or functions. Yet he thought detail was extremely important, and he insisted on design control over every item in his buildings. He said, "Three-fourths of the poetry of a building lies in its minor details; and it is easier to design a cathedral with academical accuracy than to devise and work out a really fine idea in stained glass, or a true, vigorous, and beautiful treatment of a story or even of foliage, in the tympanum of a doorway."[3]

He believed that the intrinsic nature of material—brick, stone, marble, iron, glass—dictated the manner in which it should be used and designed. He felt that timber needed to be overscaled to develop the visual strength required, that it was a mistake to settle for the "meanest" section. In contrast, he felt

that masonry should not be heavier than necessary, for it had "built-in" solidity and strength. He discouraged the use of iron except in engineering works because he believed it encouraged structural "virtuosity," which does not seem natural to the eye. Although he often used stone, he preferred brick because of "its superior smoothness and evenness of surface."[4]

Like contemporary architects, Street was a great believer in contextual design. He felt that a town church should be different in form and materials from a country church, for example. In his article of 1850, "On the Proper Characteristics of a Town Church," in *The Ecclesiologist,* Street developed his ideas on the differences in design that different contexts dictate—smooth stone or brick in town versus rough stone in the country, for example. As a High Church architect, he believed town churches should have higher spaces, longer chancels, and more elaborate interior decoration than country churches. He pleaded for long unbroken roof lines, even at the expense of differentiation between nave and chancel. He felt that architects should attempt to achieve a happy balance between the horizontal and the vertical, at least in town church design.

Street consistently expounded the aesthetic of the sublime; he believed that horizontality, mass, regularity, grandeur, and simple features should prevail. Muthesius says that Street grasped the "hollowness" of three-dimensional space better than any architect or critic of the period, meaning that Street used architecture to mold or sculpt space in a manner similar to baroque architects like Hawksmoor or Vanbrugh.[5] Street disliked extremes of dark and light; he preferred spaces to be dappled with alternations of light and shade like woods in sunlight. He recommended that light be admitted at critical points to illumine important features and that windows be balanced by unbroken walls; he felt there should be perceivable tension between blank wall and opening. He placed great importance on the emphasis of the expression of the horizontal line because buildings are built that way—layer by layer, course by course.

Street is unusual in that his buildings, in the main, are visible demonstrations of the beliefs about architecture expressed in his writing. Eastlake says that Street's "inventive power is only equalled by the sagacious tact which guides its application."[6] Street's great talent was that he could discern perceptively just what would seem to be absolutely right for whatever design problem was at hand, and he could make simplicity or sumptuous display equally attractive.

The Church of St. Peter, Bournemouth, Hampshire

Street's first major church commission came in 1853 when he was engaged by the Reverend Alexander Morden Bennett to remodel the small parish church

Exterior View of Tower and Narthex Transept at the Church of St. Peter, Bournemouth, Hampshire, from the South Street's unusual design of transepts at the west end of the nave provides a strong horizontal form, which counterbalances the vigorous verticality of the tower and spire.

of 1841–43, to which had already been added a new south aisle in 1851 by Edmund Pearce. Bennett was the first vicar of St. Peter, and he remained vicar throughout the various building campaigns. He died in 1880, just one month after the church was finally completed. One must admire the Reverend Bennett's vision. When the first building was begun in 1841, the City of Bournemouth was a brand new village of about two thousand souls, yet the church he envisaged, and the one built from Street's plans, was a great church large enough to accommodate twelve hundred worshippers.

When the 1841 church was torn down to make way for the new building, only the 1851 aisle was incorporated into the Street church. (It is a pity that Street had to retain the south aisle; it is the weakest part of the composition.) Financing was done from small donations—the church had no great benefactor—so it could only be built in fits and starts as funds were available. The nave and north aisle date from 1854 to 1849; the east end was added in 1860 through 1864; the tower and spire were constructed during the period from 1869 to 1879. Perhaps because the church was built in pieces and a fragment of an existing building had to be incorporated, the exterior composition of forms is chaotic. The west facade with its central tower and spire, 202 feet tall, is impressive, but the east end is a strange jumble of carelessly intersecting gabled, lean-to, and flat-roofed forms.

The axis of the church is very long; on it is an entry in the base of the tower, a west set of transepts that form a narthex, a nave of five bays, the east transepts with the choir located in the crossing, and a vaulted sanctuary. The south transept is a chapel dedicated to John Keble; this sumptuously deco-

Interior View of the Church of St. Peter, Bournemouth
The interior gives the impression of great spaciousness. The arcade arches are wide and tall and are supported on tall, slender, octagonal piers. The height of the clerestory wall adds to the effect.

rated chapel has superseded in importance the fine Lady Chapel at the end of the south aisle.

There is little about St. Peter that would indicate that its architect would become one of the most original and most gifted architects of the High and Late Victorian eras. St. Peter could well be a design

79

Interior View toward the West Entrance
at the Church of St. Peter, Bournemouth
Note the narthex transept.

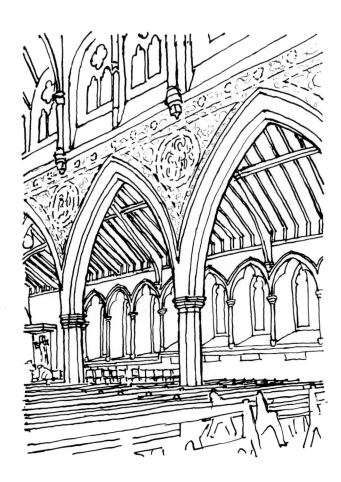

Interior View of the North Aisle at the Church of St. Peter, Bournemouth
The cloister-like character of Street's north aisle is infinitely superior to the more traditional design of Pearce's south aisle.

of Sir G. G. Scott. Its parts are more slender than massive, and archaeological accuracy to historical precedents seems to have been much more important than creativity.

The most interesting features at St. Peter are the tower and spire, the western transepts and the arch that separates them from the nave, the fenestration of the north aisle, and the sumptuous polychrome decoration of the interior, especially the chapel.

St. Peter's west facade is a striking, if flawed, composition. It is situated on high ground on a curving street opposite a busy shopping precinct in the town center. The very tall stone tower and spire are supported handsomely by the cross axis formed by the narthex transepts to either side. The tower and spire is not as elegant as Pugin's at Cheadle, which undoubtedly influenced it, but it is bolder, more muscular, in its design. It is powerfully buttressed as is the entire church. The tower is designed in two parts, each having a low stage as support for a tall one. The base stage of the upper, belfry, part is particularly handsome; it features an unusual tracery arcade of slender pointed arches with rondels between their heads. The spire seems too small for the tower; the two elements do not make a unified composition. The spire looks like an afterthought, and it is redeemed only by its impressive size and height.

Inside, one is conscious of great length and great spaciousness. The eye moves freely through the arches into the generous aisle and narthex spaces. The arches between tower and narthex and narthex and nave are taller and slenderer than the chancel arch. Particularly interesting is the second of these; its spandrels feature open tracery similar to that in the aisles of Bristol Cathedral. (This arch dates from 1874, six years after Street's work at Bristol was begun, and is clearly influenced by it.)

Street treats the fenestration of the north aisle as a continuous arcade of cusped-arch niches containing small lancet windows. The sill of the arcade steps up mid-way in its range for no discernible reason. The clerestory fenestration is equally interesting. Each major bay is given two clerestory windows (each window consists of two cusped-arch lancets and a quatrefoil in plate tracery) recessed in arches decorated with the insertion of intermittent black voussoirs and supported on polished black shafts. Larger black shafts support the posts of the trusses and define the bays. The stonework of the clerestory wall also has intermittent dark stones inserted into the predominantly gray-beige stone. The entire lower portion of the clerestory wall is treated as a steeply sloping window sill, making the upper arcade more prominent.

In contrast to the constructional polychromy of the clerestory, the nave arcades are decorated with elaborate painted patterns of cream, rose, and blue. These decorations are late (they were painted by Claydon and Bell beginning 1886) and are not in character with the bolder High Victorian style of Street's building. In contrast, the 1873 chancel arch fresco of the Crucifixion by the same artists is much more in character with its architectural setting. (Its design was carefully supervised by Street, and the result was a fresco with a bold, High Victorian feeling.)

The chancel is raised and given sumptuous decoration. A pair of arches taller, but much narrower, than the arches of the nave arcade open the space of the choir to the transepts on either side. The arches are elaborately carved with a continuous crocketed molding. A deeply carved rondel with a sculptured bas-relief is fitted into the central spandrel of each choir arcade. The arches are supported by circular columns surrounded with red and brown polished marble shafts. The capitals of the nave piers are made of simple moldings; the capitals of the choir arcades are decorated with elaborate naturalistic foliage. Street's characteristically handsome ironwork is used to form railings and screens.

The sanctuary (the only vaulted portion of the church) is a square space the same size as the choir. The ceiling is divided into two quadripartite vaults, decorated in 1891 by Bodley with angels against a starry sky. The sanctuary opens visually to the aisles on either side through sedilia arcades that are like the choir arcades at much smaller scale. Street is at his most inventive in the design of these small arcades. He layers two arcades in each opening so that the columns of one are centered in the openings of the other. These arcades are made of polished alabaster; they are the same height as the wainscot that wraps the altar platform. The lower portion of the wainscot is checkered alabaster inlay; it supports an elegant mosaic frieze of angels designed by Edward Burne-Jones. The angelic frieze brackets Earp's heavily carved alabaster reredos that features Christ Enthroned. The effect of the chancel is gorgeous. The design is bold; the colors and materials are rich. The chancel is far and away the best example of High Victorian design in this church that also contains Early and Late Victorian features.

Interior View of the Chancel at the Church of St. Peter, Bournemouth
The sumptuous decoration is particularly effective in the chancel due to Street's combination of figurative and geometric motifs executed in rich colors and materials.

All Saints Church
Boyne Hill,
Maidenhead, Berkshire

All Saints Church, Boyne Hill, Maidenhead, Berkshire
This drawing of the original ensemble shows the freestanding
tower and spire as it existed before the extension of the nave.

The Church of All Saints, Boyne Hill, is a much better introduction to George Edmund Street as a High Victorian architect than is St. Peter, Bournemouth. Its commission came a year later, 1854, but it was completed within three years, so it is entirely a work of Street's early High Victorian manner, and, unlike St. Peter, it is entirely in the High Victorian style. Its forms are simple, massive, and bold; it is built of red brick boldly striped with cream stone; and it features sumptuous constructional polychrome decoration in its interior.

All Saints is part of a larger ecclesiastical group. It occupies the north range of a quadrangle that also includes (or included) parsonage, stables, school, and schoolmaster's house. The handsome secular buildings are designed in a simplified Gothic manner that is very similar to that employed by Webb and Butterfield. There are also similarities to the work of Butterfield in the design of the church which was strongly influenced by Butterfield's All Saints, Margaret Street.

The forms of the church are very simple. It consists of a six-bay nave with aisles, a lower chancel block, and a tall square tower with a broached octagonal spire. Entry to the church is from the north through the base of the tower. (Originally, the nave only had four bays, the tower was freestanding, and entry to the church was from a south porch. Street's architect son, A. E. Street, added two additional bays in 1907 through 1911, rebuilding the original west facade in a new location. Some of the drama of the original composition was lost, but not much. Because of its position north of the north aisle, the tower still reads as an independent entity, and the character, style, and details of the original building were copied in the addition.)

The forms are crisp and planar. Connections between planes are de-emphasized rather than featured. Few buttresses are used; the ones that do exist are extensions of major walls. No elaborate cornices or parapets are used. Stone and brick banding emphasizes the simple shapes of the major masses. Clerestory windows are treated as full-height panels in the clerestory walls. Window tracery is placed almost flush with the exterior wall surface. The nave and chancel have steeply pitched roofs; the aisles are roofed at a lower pitch. Interior functions are clearly and simply expressed, yet the composition has an eminently satisfying picturesque unity. The style is the favored Middle Pointed style.

Only the tower/spire is treated as a sculptural object. Fenestration other than the entrance portal is limited to tiny slit windows. All corners are buttressed with simple, shallow buttresses. The west tower face is decorated with a semi-circular stair tower whose conical white stone roof projects into the belfry stage, the top third of the square tower. Pairs of small belfry grills are located in lancets in five stage recessed arches in square panels. The upper corners of the walls have small blind arcaded panels. All this looks extremely Italian. Above the Italian belfry rises a simple, uniquely English, cream stone broached spire with three rows of lucarnes. The composition of simple but boldly decorated forms is stunning.

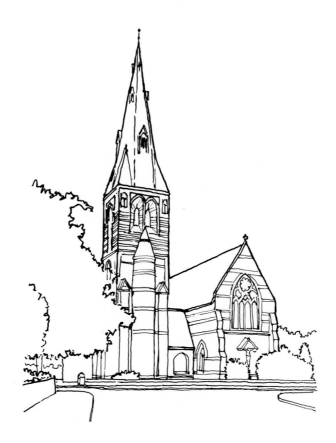

Exterior View of All Saints Church, Boyne Hill
This drawing shows the relationship of the tower to the church after the nave was extended to the west.

The interior of All Saints, Boyne Hill, is equally pleasing. The proportion of the nave arcades is much the same as at Bournemouth, but the effect is completely different. Only the piers—alternating round and octagonal made by clustering four round shafts—and the center moldings of the arch intrados are stone. The rest of the wall, excepting the sculpted rondels in the spandrels, is brick. The brick arches, in two stages, feature red, black, and

cream notched voussoirs. (This is among the first examples of brickwork cut to give a spiky appearance; it would later become a trademark of White and Teulon.) Black brick bands mark the spring lines of the clerestory and aisle windows, rising over the openings to form arches. Tracery is simple plate tracery. Street has contrived to feature a decorated wall seen through another decorated wall, not a number of individual Gothic elements.

Street's walls do not have the massive character that Butterfield achieved; his walls seem thinner, more delicate. His roof structure is also more refined. The roofs are a series of closely spaced, small-scale, scissored rafters. The ceiling spaces between them are alternately decorated in red and blue stenciled patterns. The roof is prominent because the clerestory wall is low. (Clerestory windows are unusual cinquefoil openings in tracery as broad as it is tall.)

The nave opens to the chancel through a chancel arch similar in design to the arches of the nave arcade but wider and taller. (The square-ended chancel is almost as wide as the nave; another similarity to All Saints, Margaret Street.) Above the chancel arch is a fresco of Christ Enthroned surrounded by the saved and the motto, "Blessed are the pure in spirit for they shall see God," painted by Street himself.

Exterior View of the West Facade of All Saints Church, Boyne Hill
A great deal of All Saints' charm comes from its constructional polychromy. The bottom two-thirds of the tower is predominantly red brick; black brick and stone bands are used sparingly. In contrast, the belfry is equally banded in brick and cream stone which acts to lighten the apparent weight of the mass.

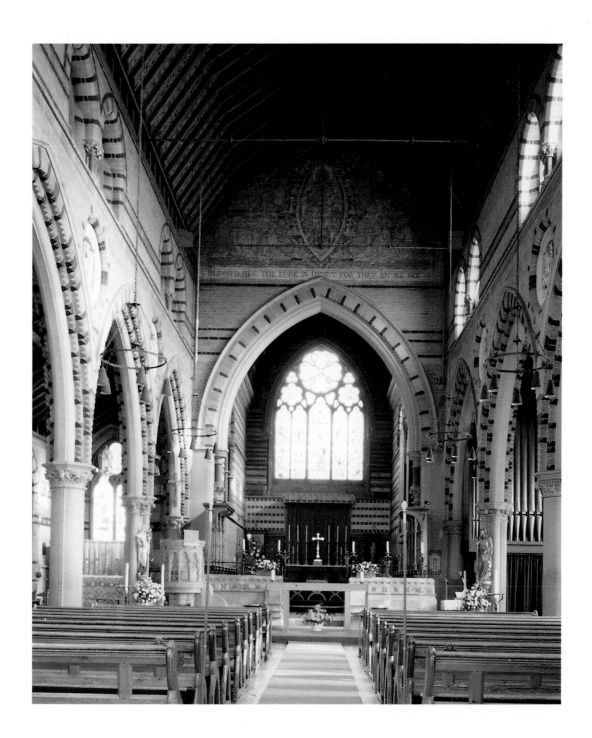

Interior View toward the Chancel at All
Saints Church, Boyne Hill
The interior, like the exterior, achieves its
effectiveness through the sensitive use of
color and pattern.

The decoration in the chancel is much more ornate than the nave. The floor is decorated with multi-colored encaustic tile. The wainscot is stone inlaid with mastic in elaborate patterns. The upper walls are red brick banded with cream stone and yellow, gray-green, and black glazed brick. The east wall has a band of patterned glazed tiles between the stone wainscot and the sill of the large east window. A sedilia is built into the south wall of the sanctuary. The emphasis remains upon the plane of the wall surface; all decoration is planar in character. The one exception is the rail that divides nave from choir; it is solid cream stone richly grooved and chamfered; inlaid with red and green intarsia patterns. It has an extremely muscular three-dimensional character in contrast to the planar character of other features.

The Church of St. John, Howsham, Yorkshire

The Church of St. John, Howsham, was built from 1859 to 1860. It is a small, two-celled church with many idiosyncrasies. Entry is from a west porch. The nave is a simple rectangle twice as long as it is wide. (It would seem to be a two bay space—the two north windows confirm this—but three south windows confuse its geometry.) The chancel is slightly narrower and lower than the nave; it is composed of a square choir bay with a vestry opening

off of it to the north through a large arch and a semi-circular sanctuary apse.

All ceilings are framed in wood. The nave ceiling is composed of a series of arched beams inserted into the steeply pitched roof; these make the nave ceiling appear to have a barrel shape. The choir ceiling abandons the curved forms in favor of scissors trusses; a wooden five-cusped arch separates it from the elaborately painted, ceiled, apse vault. These changes in ceiling construction, more than anything else, define the functional divisions of the plan.

St. John features stone masonry that is as bold and muscular as any of the period. The church seems to be carved from a mighty block of striated stone; courses of yellow stone are laid at irregular intervals in the beige stone walls. The position of these contrasting courses seems arbitrary; on the outside they do not coincide with critical features such as window sills or arch spring lines. Inside, the placement of the yellow courses is more orthodox.

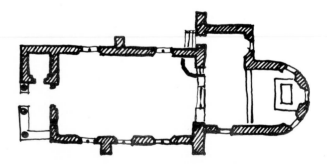

Plan of the Church of St. John, Howsham, Yorkshire
The spatial simplicity is complicated by the different treatment of the north and south walls. Form interest is also provided by the asymmetrical treatment of the west facade.

Interior View of the Church of St. John, Howsham
The functional divisions of the plan are emphasized by the
change in roof framing.

Their function is to stress the horizontal construction of the masonry and to carry the eye continuously around the mass outside or the space inside to
minimize the interruption of the wall by the windows. Placement of the windows with almost no recession from the exterior plane also emphasizes the
three-dimensional geometry of the exterior form.

(The tracery of the apse windows is curved to conform to the curve of the mass.) The walls are extremely thick for such a small church; since the
windows are placed in the outer wall face on the inside, the window reveals are very deep. The splay
of the window reveals, the massiveness of their
arches, and the relatively small size of the windows
themselves emphasize the heaviness of the masonry
construction.

The west facade is an interesting, highly original,
asymmetrical composition. The left, north third of
the facade is devoted to the tower. A porch with a
hipped roof occupies the right, south two-thirds. A
portion of the nave gable rises behind the porch. All
seem to be sliced from the larger mass by bold,
sheer knife-cuts.

The porch roof is carried by three stumpy columns with elaborately carved capitals. (Street intended for these columns to be black polished
marble; unfortunately they were cut from the same
gray stone as used in the walls.) They support impost blocks and flat lintels that have no projection
from the larger wall surface; they are supported on
a plinth that is also part of the wall. *The Ecclesiologist* did not like these flat-headed openings. In its
1859 discussion of the church it said, "Surely arches
would have been better, though, or because, less
novel."[7] The west wall of the porch becomes, on
the left, the west wall of the tower. The porch
seems to be carved out of the block rather than appended to it.

The square tower, in its middle zone, has its corners shaved away diagonally. Out of these faceted
surfaces rises a second tower, octagonal this time.
The octagonal tower has a belfry zone made of columns similar to those on the porch; these columns

carry an octagonal spire that is interrupted on every side by boldly projecting lucarnes. An amazing composition.

Inside, one is struck immediately by the massive five-cusped chancel arch that is more powerful than graceful in its outline. The low screen railings are extensions of the chancel wall. The brightly colored, intricately patterned, encaustic tile path to the altar seems to break through the chancel wall. The cusped form of the chancel arch is repeated in the inner arches of the sanctuary and choir windows (and in the wood roof structure as mentioned above). The apse arches are supported by polished marble shafts, the only detail other than the painted apse ceiling that Street employed to make the chancel area lighter or more elaborate than the nave.

Only one detail mars what is otherwise a wonderfully powerful, simple, unified interior design. The altar sits before a heavily carved and inlaid reredos built into the curved section of the apse wall. This reredos breaks up into the corners of the left and right apse windows and cuts off the bottom of the center window. It calls attention to the altar as the special feature of the space in a bold, dramatic way, but it seems to be fighting the architectural envelope in which it is placed. It looks as if it were a piece of furniture that didn't quite fit shoved up against the sanctuary wall.

Exterior View of the Church of St. John, Howsham
The entire church seems carved from a mighty block of beige and yellow stone.

The Church of
St. James the Less,
Vauxhall Bridge Road,
Westminster, London

St. James the Less was Street's first London church. It dates from 1859 to 1861, so it is contemporary with St. John, Howsham. It is vastly different from the Howsham church; it illustrates Street's views as to how city churches should differ from country churches. It was built for the three wealthy daughters of the Right Reverend James Henry Monk, Bishop of Gloucester and Bristol and former Canon of Westminster, as a memorial to their father. It cost between five and six thousand pounds.

By 1858, when Street began the design of the church, he had published his book on Italian Gothic architecture and had forcefully made the point in his lectures and articles that all Gothic building could provide inspiration for modern Gothic designers. By this time Butterfield had convinced the Cambridge Camden Society that it was legitimate to use foreign detail in English high church structures, so Street felt free to use whatever Gothic details he fancied in the design of St. James the Less. The result was a church that is picturesque, strongly influenced by Butterfield, and in a style that is a blend of English, Norman French, and Italian Gothic.

Exterior View of the Church of St. James the Less, Vauxhall Bridge Road, Westminster, London, from the North Entry is through the freestanding tower.

St. James the Less, with its schools, was a successful effort to create an oasis of charm in the drab, gray, slum environs of Pimlico. Street made the church of red brick laced with black brick and some white stone as a colorful counterpart to the gray stucco slum buildings around it. (London was after all a red brick city and was becoming increasingly so in the 1850s following the abolishment of the brick tax in 1850.) Street had accepted wholeheartedly Pugin's and Ruskin's pleas for "truthful" use of materials, color in architecture, and "functional" picturesque composition. Street was a faithful member of Butterfield's All Saints Church, Margaret Street; many decorative details at St. James the Less are based on that church. Street had also accepted Butterfield's view that proportion could depart from Gothic prototypes. (All Saints, because of its cramped site, had to reach high for light and air in a decidedly non-medieval way.) Street also accepted Butterfield's use of constructional polychromy.

Italy provided the inspiration for the tall, freestanding tower of St. James the Less; only its spire and spirelets are not Italian. (They are Norman French.) Summerson says in his article "Two London Churches" that the remainder of the church is a unique blending of "Butterfieldian, early French, and North Italian crossing and materials, lighting, detached tower, semi-circular apse, quasi-transepts, plate tracery, dormers in the clerestory, the 'quaint' treatment of the nave arcade, bold carving, and chromatic roofing, [making] St. James the Less decidedly un-English." He saw a new style emerging, but he regretted the church's "restless notching of edges, dazzling distribution of stripes, multiplicity of pattern forms, and exuberance of sculpture detail."[9]

Exterior View of the Church of St. James the Less, Westminster
This drawing shows the church's semi-circular apse and freestanding tower.

St. James the Less has a very tall nave of three bays with a clerestory and a steeply pitched roof. The nave ceiling is a beautifully painted, faceted, wood cradle roof, painted with the ancestors of Christ by Claydon and Bell from Street's designs. The nave is twenty-five and one-half feet wide and fifty-eight feet long by forty-four feet high. The nave continues through a tall pointed chancel arch into a chancel with an apsidal end. The chancel is composed of a square bay and a semi-circular apse and is vaulted. Its roof is only slightly lower than the nave roof. (Street has abandoned the idea of a single roof structure over nave and chancel, but he keeps the two roofs close to the same height to maintain a strong horizontal emphasis.) The tall exterior roof form camouflages, from the exterior, the very low chancel space (thirty-seven feet by twenty feet by only thirty-one feet high). Hitchcock feels that the lowness of the chancel spoils the interior effect.[10] This view is debatable; it is more likely that Street intended the chancel to be seen as an alcove off the main nave space.

The nave is flanked on either side by wide aisles with shed roofs of a considerably lower pitch than the nave and chancel roofs. The most interesting feature of the plan is the creation of double transepts opening off of the square bay of the chancel choir. The east ends of the aisles open into these transept spaces. The square transepts are each divided by a pair of arches into two rectangular spaces perpendicular to the chancel. Each transept subspace has its own gabled roof. These paired gables contribute to the church's picturesque exterior appearance.

The 134 foot tall tower is the dominant feature of the exterior ensemble. Street is said to have ex-

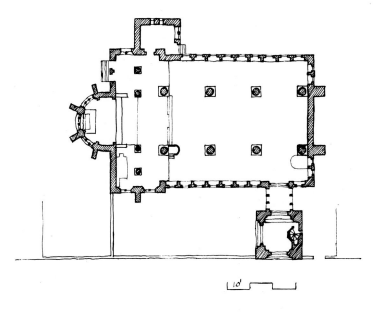

Plan of the Church of St. James the Less, Westminster

pressed the view that London needed no new spires; he wanted something different. The tower is detached from the church much like an Italian campanile. Entry to the church is by means of an arch in the tower's base, through the tower and a short cloister, to a door in the westernmost bay of the north aisle. The first stage of the tower has arches on three sides; the fourth side contains a stair. These arches are tall, pointed Sicilian arches with low spring lines; they have five recessed orders of alternating red and black brick and stone. Brick edges are notched, giving the arches a very spiky appearance. Each side of the second zone of the tower has paired flat-heated windows under pointed arches with a herringbone patterned tympanum. (These windows were intended to receive balconies in the Venetian manner.) The third tower stage has

The modern eye is struck by the boldness of form and color, the interesting 1:3:2 fenestration pattern, and the manner in which the tower completes and anchors the total picturesque ensemble.

The perceptive ways in which the polychrome patterns are handled—simple bands in lower wall zones and diapers, lozenges, and other complex patterns in upper wall zones—certainly contribute to the exterior effect. So does the sinuous elegance of the cast iron fences and the iron hardware. A particularly surprising but effective detail is the insertion of a large gabled dormer that breaks up into the nave roof above and to the west of the paired transept gables, repeating their form, and tying them into the total composition of the church. Only one of Street's exterior details seems to be unsatisfactory—the apse buttresses. These are so large and muscular that they destroy the simple apsidal resolution of the larger mass. How much more effective is Pearson's apse at his church of St. Peter, Vauxhall, with its tall, sheer, unbuttressed walls. Otherwise, the balance between detail and mass is singularly complimentary.

The interior retains much the same character as the outside. The materials and colors are the same; so are the notched brick, the red and black constructional pattern work, and the careful attention to design detail. However, the interior adds materials and patterns not found outside—white stone with patterned intarsia inlay, colonnettes of polished Devonshire marble, column shafts of polished red Aberdeen granite, deeply and elaborately carved Box stone column capitals and bases (the capitals are carved with the parables and miracles of Christ), brightly colored and patterned tile wainscot and floors, and stenciled brickwork in the chancel.

Interior View toward the Chancel of the Church of St. James the Less, Westminster

three needle lancets on each face; each lancet has a large arched head. On the fourth stage, the belfry, grandiose pairs of deeply recessed louvered windows are placed under triangular panels. The belfry stage is crowned with a corbeled, machicolated cornice which supports four small pyramidal spires which have stubby octagonal spikes rising from their centers. Eastlake remarked about the tower, "In form, proportion of parts, decorative detail, and use of color, it seems to leave little to be desired." [11]

Interior View toward the Chancel of the
Church of St. James the Less, Westminster
With the exception of the fresco, the decoration of the chancel is strongly constructional
in character.

Interior Detail of the Pier Separating the Nave from the Chancel at St. James the Less, Westminster
Street's sensitive use of constructional polychromy is particularly apparent here.

In spite of the dark colors of all its surfaces, the nave is very light and bright. Hersey describes the interior as having the general effect of "a translucent pink cave resting on mushroomy supports."[12] The bright spaces of the transepts extend the space of the nave in a manner similar to that used so often and so effectively by Pearson. The dark, low, vaulted, mysterious chancel contrasts dramatically with the higher, lighter nave. (This is an interesting reversal of the norm on Street's part; normally the nave is dark and the sanctuary is flooded with light.)

A feature of the interior is G. F. Watts' painting of Christ at Judgment that fills the chancel wall above the arch. (Street provided the large clerestory dormers to light this painting.) The painting is the one really disastrous element in the interior; it is totally out of character in drawing style and color with all other decoration. It also camouflages the character of the brick wall on which it is painted.

Although the chancel wall painting is unsuccessful here, the design of the reredos is a dramatic improvement over the Howsham design. A carved inlaid screen with a spiky, filigreed cornice is layered behind the shafts that support the apse vault; this screen fills the lower wall of the five facets of the apse and is a rich background for the altar that works with, rather than against, the architecture of the space.

St. John, Howsham, is a small, simple, rough, powerful piece of architectural sculpture intended to be viewed in the round in a verdant setting. St. James the Less, Westminster, is a large urbane assemblage of parts designed to relate to, and enrich, a complex, drab urban slum. The two churches are as different in design approach as we would expect them to be considering the differences in size and context. However, both are powerful; both reveal Street at his High Victorian best.

When times changed and Street moved into his late Victorian phase in the late 1860s, he became somewhat disenchanted with the gutsy quality of St. James the Less. His son, undoubtedly reflecting his father's views, wrote these remarks about St. James the Less in his biography of his father, "Its originality and spirit are beyond all question; the massing and outline of the whole block of building are most satisfactory, and much of the detail is very good . . . ; but at the same time there is in some of the masonry and brick work details, in the carving, and in the proportion of the nave arcade, a want of that grace which was so characteristic of all his [subsequent] work . . . ; [there is] something a little outre and overbold, which seems to speak of a strong and masterful imagination not as yet adequately restrained by a sense of purity and beauty in form."[13]

Today, when strength and power are valued more highly than purity and grace, we are inclined to disagree. John Summerson expressed a contradictory view. In discussing St. James the Less, Summerson says, "Street's artistry, his handling, does seem to me to transcend the limited interest of the style game and to speak nearly as eloquently now as it did a hundred years ago."[14]

The Church of St. Philip and St. James, Oxford, Oxfordshire

Contemporary with St. James the Less, although its construction took four years longer, is the large parish church built for Gothic north Oxford, St. Philip and St. James, popularly called Pip and Jim's by Oxfordians. Although equally powerful and original, the church is less successful than the Church of St. James the Less.

St. Philip and St. James has a particularly muscular exterior. It is constructed, inside and out, of hammer-dressed, beige Bath stone, inlaid with bands of smooth, dark, red-brown sandstone (plus bands of smooth cream stone on the interior). The nave is tall and steeply roofed, the north and south aisles less steeply so. The church has a west portal located in a very modest porch. Buttressing is also modest. Visual interest is concentrated on the east end. A powerful tower rises above the choir, from which north and south transepts and a semi-circular apse, as at St. James the Less, also project. Here the transepts are not double-gabled but are single-gabled forms, taller than the aisles but lower than the nave. Most windows are single lancets; exceptions are the rather small clerestory windows (alternating stumpy two-lancet arched and circular forms), the three large three-lancet arched apse windows, and the roses that adorn the gables of the west front and the transepts.

The tower is quite unusual. It is not square but is rectangular in plan; its east and west walls are wider

than its north and south walls. It has, engaged at its southeast corner, a stair tower with its own independent spire; this tower, too bold and tall to be called a turret, is octagonal in form. The larger main tower has two visible stories plus a rather stumpy broached spire with boldly projecting lucarnes. The first stage is solid except for needle lancets; the second—the belfry—has very large paired lancets, recessed in three stages. The spire sits on a machicolated cornice. All these motifs were used in the tower at St. James the Less, but the changes in color, material, and placement of the tower camouflage the similarities in design detail.

Critics have described St. Philip and St. James as being in a "shadowless style" because the emphasis is upon the flat planes of the forms. Street has sheared away unnecessary projections and sculptural detail, has provided the church with buttresses without nosings, has used plate tracery exclusively, and has eliminated plinths and bases from the forms. The result is a clean, powerful explication of the forms that make up the church. The impression given by the church is one of great weight and solidity, but the mass seems to have a plasticity that suggests it has been carefully molded and shaped.

The fenestration pattern of the nave and aisles is very strange; the spacing of the clerestory windows of the nave does not correspond either to the arcade geometry or to the spacing of the aisle windows. It is surprising that this modular discontinuity is not more jarring visually than it is. Perhaps the viewer

Exterior View of the Church of St. Philip and St. James, Oxford, Oxfordshire, from the East
Street's resolution of longitudinal, vertical, and cross axes in "Pip and Jim's" east end is perhaps his most powerful three-dimensional composition.

is too startled by the manner in which the nave arcades converge toward the chancel arch to notice the irregularities in the window spacings.

The altar, not the pulpit or lectern, was of paramount importance to Tractarians. Moreover, High Church ritual demanded a deep chancel. The view of the altar would be obscured in the aisles or to the sides of the nave if the chancel opening were to be made significantly more narrow than the width of the nave. Street attempted to address this concern at St. Philip and St. James by shaping the nave as if it were a modern proscenium theater auditorium. He narrowed the nave by canting the sides of its easternmost bay in toward the chancel arch. He also attempted to minimize the structure at the chancel wall by allowing the arcades that divide nave from aisles to intersect the chancel wall in such a way that the last bay of the arcade is incomplete. The incomplete arches do open up the view of the chancel, but they do so at considerable sacrifice to the logic of the structure and its organizing geometry.

Inside, the church appears as heavy and muscular as it does outside. The arcade walls are extremely thick. The arches are carried, as they are at St. James the Less, by polished red granite columns with huge, deeply carved, Early French capitals. Stone arches similar to those in the arcades span the aisles to carry wood roof purlins. The upper clerestory wall seems to be double; the arcaded inner surface appears to be a thin layer applied as dressing to the heavy stone wall behind. All arches are made of smoothly-dressed beige stone with dark-red sandstone voussoirs inserted at regular intervals. Spandrels are constructed of the same rough hammer-dressed stone that is used on the exterior. The effect is one of great weight.

Exterior Detail of South Transept Fenestration at the Church of St. Philip and St. James, Oxford
The composition of door, lancet windows in and out of plate tracery frames, and rose is extremely novel and effective.

Interior View toward the Chancel at the
Church of St. Philip and St. James, Oxford
The interior impression is one of great
weight; it features thick stone walls and low,
stumpy columns.

The proportion of the chancel arch is pleasant. It rises to the height of the clerestory walls on either side and is echoed by the shape of the wood cradle roof above. Beyond the chancel arch, the polychromed stone vaults of the choir and sanctuary are visible. The striped surfaces echo the colors of the arches in the nave. The massiveness of the masonry construction of the choir attests to the fact that it supports the tower above it. The chancel arch has a rood beam rather than a rood screen. The beam and the crucifix it supports are brightly painted. So is the carved triptych of the reredos, which is seen against a handsome patterned wall of encaustic tiles.

The chancel is the most successful part of the interior; it is powerful, yet graceful. The remainder of the interior is less satisfying, partly because of the design innovation discussed above, and partly because Street used square profiles that emphasize mass at the expense of line.

Street undoubtedly intended for the chancel wall above the arch to receive painted decoration, as is the case at St. James the Less. None was applied; simple undecorated rough stone fills the area. This stone is much grayer in color than the stone used elsewhere. Something is plainly missing and the church seems incomplete.

St. Philip and St. James has nothing of the urbanity of St. James the Less. When it was built Oxford was still a relatively small city, and Street approached its design as he might approach the design of a rural church; its materials are rough and its decoration is simple. Most important is its non-urban form. St. Philip and St. James is designed as a piece of sculptural architecture intended to be seen in the round. St. James the Less is composed as a series of picturesque elevations to be seen from London's busy streets.

In spite of its design problems, the Church of St. Philip and St. James is an extremely powerful, innovative example of High Victorian design. Unfortunately, its future is in doubt. It has been declared redundant and has been given to a missionary organization for use as offices.

All Saints Church, Denstone, Staffordshire

Only slightly later than St. Philip and St. James is another country parish church of great power and charm, All Saints, Denstone, built from 1860 to 1862. All Saints is similar in many respects to St. Philip and St. James. Both are built of the same materials—hammer-dressed Bath stone with red sandstone bands and voussoir inserts; in both, construction polychromy is handled with sensitivity and restraint. Both are masterful compositions of simple forms arranged as architectural sculpture, intended to be viewed in the middle of a green park. Both churches have fenestration that is surprising in its shapes and variety, although the discontinuity of fenestration to structural modularity that is one of the most surprising characteristics of St. Philip and St. James does not exist at All Saints. Both are unorthodox in their massing. Yet, whereas St. Philip and St. James was unsettling and disturbing in its

Exterior View of All Saints Church, Denstone, Staffordshire from the South
All Saints, like St. Philip and St. James, is an essay in Street's "shadowless style." The emphasis here is upon surface planes rather than projection and recession of mass.

originality, the same characteristics are managed at Denstone in a way that seems uniquely right and infinitely appealing.

All Saints is composed of three major elements—a nave, a chancel with an apsidal east end, and a tower—plus a south entrance porch and a north lean-to vestry. Surprisingly, the chancel roof is higher than the nave roof; the chancel wall breaks through the roofs so that both nave and chancel roofs can die into it. The tower is located adjacent to this junction on the building's north side and is circular rather than square throughout its height. It is capped with a conical spire. Eight lancets and four oculi are carved out of the top, belfry stage. The

position of the tower marries nave, chancel, and vestry in a singularly happy composition.

As is often the case in Street's churches, the fenestration on the north and south sides is completely different. The north side is mostly wall; openings in it are meager at best. On this side, the nave wall is given only widely spaced single-lancet windows, except for a large quatrefoil window placed to light the font; the vestry wall receives closely spaced needle lancets; and the chancel clerestory gets groups of quatrefoil oculi. On the south side, the nave wall opens with very wide three-lancet arched windows; the choir has an attenuated double-lancet window and a pair of oculi like those on the

Exterior Detail of the North Tower and East
End at All Saints Church, Denstone
The marriage of forms is handled in a
wonderfully satisfying, picturesque way.

The interior of the church is as successful as the exterior. In its aisleless form and with its emphasis upon mass and weight, it is reminiscent of Street's church at Howsham. However, Denstone has a sophistication that the smaller church at Howsham lacks. Decorative details, such as the cusped wooden arches that support the wooden ceiling construction and the bands of red sandstone at sill lines, arch spring lines, and in the upper wall spandrels, are handled with consummate sensitivity and restraint. The interior gives the impression of a massive stone structure leading to a brilliant sanctuary where mass dissolves in light. (Claydon and Bell's glass here is much lighter in color than is their norm.) The effect is one of great strength and great simplicity. Street would do no better than this.

Interior View toward the Chancel at All Saints Church, Denstone
The elevated chancel roof allows the chancel arch to fill the chancel wall completely; consequently, there is a happier spatial relationship between the nave and chancel here than at any of Street's earlier churches.

The Church of St. Saviour, Eastbourne, East Sussex

north chancel wall. Each of the three sides of the apse has a window composed of two lancets and a rose of more conventional proportions than in the south choir window. All have plate tracery; all are Decorated in style. The viewer is reminded of Street's dicta that walls need to balance windows and that windows should be placed and sized in relation to what they are supposed to light.

From 1865 to 1872, Street was involved in the design and construction of a large brick "town church" for Eastbourne, St. Saviour. In it, and in all subsequent works, Street abandoned the bold, solid, muscular designs of his earlier churches in favor of a style which stresses spaciousness, verticality, and elegance and features contrasts between broad planar and slim linear forms. St. Saviour is transitional in style—part High Victorian, part Late Victorian. Butterfield's influence is waning; Street is moving away from muscular Gothic just as Pearson is. This church and its contemporary, St. Mary Magdalene, Paddington, discussed below, reflect the same shifts in attitude that are revealed in Pearson's Church of St. Augustine, Kilburn Park.

The exterior of St. Saviour is a brick example of Street's "shadowless style." It is composed of simple planes rather than sculpted forms, the only exception being the deeply recessed lancet windows of the tower. Constructional polychromy has disappeared almost entirely; the only color variation comes from the contrast of the modest stone buttress dressings, window tracery, and broached spire with the brick of the walls.

At St. Saviour, Street repeated the canted east bay of the nave that he had first employed at St. Philip and St. James, but with much happier results inside and out. Here the canted walls are an integral part of both the exterior and the interior design; they articulate the transition from a wide nave to a narrower chancel. The change of form is also reflected in the roof structures; the east end of the nave changes from a simple gable to a polygonal hipped roof, with roof planes corresponding to the canted wall planes below. The chancel roof, a gable with a conical hip over the semi-circular apse, intersects and echoes the taller hipped roof of the nave. Consequently, the forms seem to flow into each other.

Exterior View of the Church of St. Saviour, Eastbourne, East Sussex, from the West
The relationship of tower to nave is much the same as originally intended for All Saints, Boyne Hill. The tension established between the two forms because of their tenuous connection shows Street's mastery of three-dimensional composition.

Interior View of the Church of St. Saviour, Eastbourne
This drawing shows the use of a canted nave bay to make the transition from wide nave to narrow chancel.

Because of the symbiotic relationship of nave and chancel, the church seems to consist of only two major masses—the tall nave/chancel block flanked by low lean-to aisles with roofs of shallower pitch than the steep pitch of the nave and chancel and a tall square tower with a broached spire attached in a tenuous manner to the westernmost bay of the north aisle. (The west bay of the north aisle is Street's favorite location for entry; he liked the broken axis sequence of experience which allowed the worshipper to focus on the font before turning to focus on the chancel.)

All windows, except the three that light the apsidal sanctuary, are small. Even the windows of the west front seem meager; they form a triangular composition of three strangely attenuated double-lancet, pointed-arched windows arranged in a huge, otherwise blind, recessed, arched panel. Everywhere the emphasis is upon height rather than mass, elegance rather than strength.

The same characteristics are found inside. All the elements that make up the form have been regularized and lightened. Gone is the irregular placement of different shaped windows that created variable levels of light. Gone is the contrast between solid and void. Arcades are tall; arches are molded instead of square in profile and are carried by tall, slender column clusters with de-emphasized capitals rather than by stumpy circular columns with elaborately carved capitals. Constructional polychromy has been replaced by patterns and scenes painted onto the brick walls. (Incidentally, Claydon and Bell's painted decoration above the chancel arch and on the adjacent canted panels is very fine; it is too bad that work of comparable quality, rather than the dismal Watts painting, could not have decorated St. James the Less.)

Although the nave and aisles have wooden roofs, the chancel of St. Saviour is vaulted. Vault ribs are brightly colored; they extend down the walls as black shafts. The wainscot consists of a semi-circular blind arcade of canopied, cusped arches filled with mosaic figures above book-matched marble slabs. The oak reredos is carved and painted; it includes statues under canopies, the largest of which is the figure of Christ enveloped in a nimbus located in the center. The chancel is unusual in that a vaulting pier with engaged shaft, rather than a window, occupies the central position behind the altar. Consequently, the longitudinal axis of the church ends at the projecting arrize of a solid instead of a void. The chancel has four large windows instead of the more usual three or five, and seems to be filled with light in contrast to the much darker nave. (The lightness of the chancel has been exaggerated in modern times; the brick of the chancel walls has been plastered over and painted white.)

St. Saviour is successful in both its space and its form; it is pleasing to the eye and interesting to experience. However, the criteria Street used in its design are not those he followed in the design of his earlier churches.

The Church of St. Mary Magdalen, Woodchester Square, Paddington, London

Street's second great London church, St. Mary Magdalen, Paddington, is contemporary with St. Saviour, Eastbourne. Street received its commission in 1865, construction began in 1867, and work was completed in 1873. Street's client was Dr. Richard Temple West, the first Vicar, a high Churchman who had previously served the congregations at All Saints, Boyne Hill, and All Saints, Margaret Street.

The form of the church was established in large measure by the size and irregular shape of the site and by the building regulations of the city. The church extends to the property lines on all sides. The shape of the property dictated a long narrow building, so only one wide aisle was possible. The other aisle, on the north, is hardly more than a low, narrow passage; its form was established by the height limitation and set-back requirement imposed on construction at the edge of the street pavement. The irregular east and south boundaries dictated the shape of the chancel and the location and size of the south transept and tower. Street was very perceptive in the way he accommodated the building to its site.

In style, the building, like St. Saviour, Eastbourne, is transitional between the High and Late Victorian periods. The emphasis is again upon height and crisp geometry rather than upon mass and solidity. St. Mary Magdalen uses the same building materials as St. Saviour. Here, though, Street creates a more strongly polychromatic exterior effect; he bands chancel, tower, and transept and dresses the remainder of the building with cream stone that is in strong contrast to the red brick.

Because the confines of the site limited projections—porches, vestries, etc.—the building's massing is simple; nothing detracts from the powerful, crisp, vertical major forms that rise sheer and unbuttressed from the surrounding pavement. Of the major masses—nave, chancel, transept, and tower—the tower is the dominant feature. It is engaged within the southeast angle of the building, between the chancel and the transept. The first third of the tower is square with chamfered corners; it evolves into a perfect octagon at a point even with the eave of the chancel roof. The middle third of the tower divides in half; the bottom portion of this stage continues the red brick construction of the lower tower, while the upper portion—the belfry—is boldly striped with equal amount of red and cream in narrow bands. The top third is a cream stone octagonal spire. The lower half of the tower is paralleled by a smaller stair tower engaged to the south face of the larger tower. The stair tower begins as a cylinder, but its upper third evolves into an octagonal form. The main tower is very tall—more than twice the height to the ridge of the nave roof. The composition of tower, smaller tower, and south transept adds a picturesque asymmetrical element to the church; it is also a strong vertical element that balances the longitudinal mass of nave and chancel. The composition is masterful; it is a development of Street's experimentation with similar

elements in the tower of St. Philip and St. James, Oxford. At Oxford, proportion and material emphasized High Victorian weight and mass; at Paddington, the soaring height and slender proportion substitute Late Victorian preference for grace and elegance.

Inside, only the elaborate constructional polychrome continues the High Victorian tradition. Proportion and detail are Late Victorian. The aisle and chancel wainscots are covered with encaustic tiles; all of the brick upper nave walls are heavily banded with cream stone. Since the elegant arcades are stone, there is a balance between red and cream. (The arcades are different from one another and are among the most interesting design details in the church. The south arcade consists of graceful clustered columns carrying molded, decorated arches. The major arches of the north arcade are supported by plain octagonal pillars and are divided in two by sub-arches carried on slender colonnettes. The whole is unified by the large clerestories which are the same on both sides.) The vaulted roof of the chancel and the wood ceiling of the nave are completely covered with polychrome designs by Claydon and Bell.

The smooth, sheer planes of brick, the slender, molded elements of the arcades, and the attenuated vertical and horizontal axes of the space result in a church that has very little in common with the powerful buildings of Street's middle, or High Victorian, period. With the churches of St. Saviour and St. Mary Magdalen, Street has led the way into the Late Victorian period, five to ten years in advance of most of his peers.

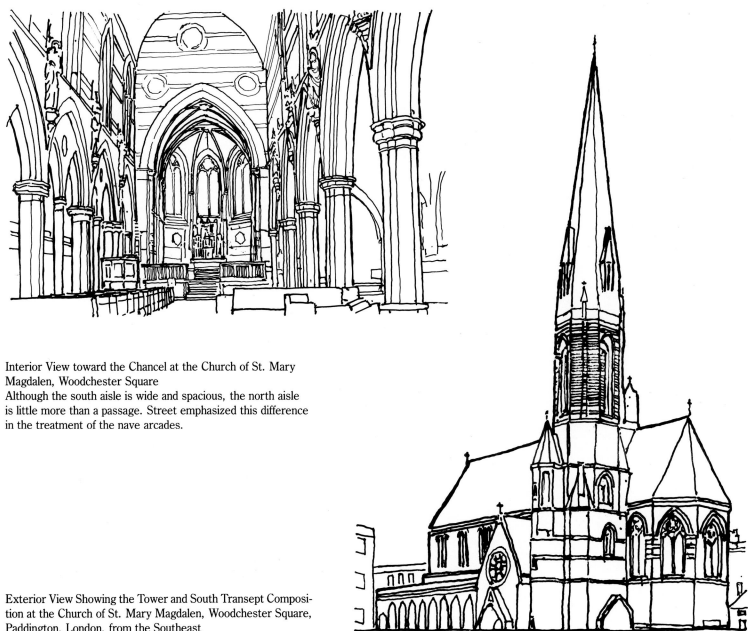

Interior View toward the Chancel at the Church of St. Mary
Magdalen, Woodchester Square
Although the south aisle is wide and spacious, the north aisle
is little more than a passage. Street emphasized this difference
in the treatment of the nave arcades.

Exterior View Showing the Tower and South Transept Composition at the Church of St. Mary Magdalen, Woodchester Square,
Paddington, London, from the Southeast

Interior Detail of the North Aisle and Clerestory Wall at the Church of St. Mary Magdalen, Woodchester Square

Street's early abandonment of High Victorian muscular Gothic forms in favor of the elegance and grace of the Late Victorian style may be a consequence of his work at Bristol Cathedral, where Street was occupied from 1866 to his death in 1881.

An Augustinian abbey was founded in Bristol in 1140, and an abbey church was consecrated about twenty-five years later. The eastern end of the church, including the choir, was reconstructed in the years 1298 to 1330 by a master mason of unusual genius. The central tower was completed about 1500 and rebuilding of the nave was begun. Nave construction was abandoned when the monasteries were dissolved by Henry VIII. More than three hundred years later, Street was given the commission to complete the church, now the cathedral of Bristol, by designing the nave and the west front.

Parts of the fourteenth-century nave foundation were found; these guided the layout of the church. The character and details of the choir were faithfully followed by Street in his design for the new nave. Only in his design for the west front was Street free to express his own creativity.

George Hersey, in his book *High Victorian Gothic,* dwells at some length upon the feminine characteristics of the fourteenth-century choir and its aisles which he describes as being sensuous, flowing, organic, and plaint. He suggests that the appreciation for things muscular and masculine in the 1860s caused Street to detail the new work in a stiffer, more abrupt and powerful manner, stressing structure rather than space.[15] Undoubtedly Hersey is correct; however, the differences between the new work and the old are insignificant when compared to the similarities between them. By replicating the tall, slender, graceful fourteenth-century forms in his new work, Street was accepting an aesthetic that would come to dominate both his own later work and the Late Victorian period. The magic of Bristol Cathedral was too potent to resist.

Interior View of Street's New South Aisle at Bristol Cathedral

NOTES

1. Henry-Russell Hitchcock, *Early Victorian Architecture in Britain,* 2 vols. (New Haven: Yale University Press, 1954), 1: 602.

2. Arthur Edmund Street, *Memoir of George Edmund Street* (1888; New York: Blom, 1972), 59.

3. Street, 87.

4. Street, 39.

5. Stefan Muthesius, *The High Victorian Movement in Architecture 1850–1870* (London and Boston: Routledge & Kegan Paul, 1972), 41.

6. Charles L. Eastlake, *A History of the Gothic Revival* (New York: Humanities Press, 1872; Leicester: Leicester University Press, 1970), 322.

7. Nikolaus Pevsner, *Yorkshire: the North Riding,* Buildings of England Series (Harmondsworth: Penguin, 1966), 265.

8. John Summerson, *Victorian Architecture: Four Studies in Evaluation* (New York: Columbia University Press, 1970), 70.

9. Eastlake, 321.

10. Hitchcock, 166.

11. Eastlake, 322.

12. George L. Hersey, *High Victorian Gothic* (Baltimore, London: John Hopkins University Press, 1972), 130.

13. Street, 54.

14. Summerson, 70.

15. Hersey, 52–53.

JOHN LOUGHBOROUGH

PEARSON

L. Pearson (1817–97) was born in Durham and lived there until he was twenty-five years old. His father was an artist—a watercolor painter—and the son early demonstrated that he had inherited his father's talent at drawing. When he was fourteen years old, he was apprenticed to Ignatius Bonomi. Bonomi's office was in Durham where Bonomi held the post of County Surveyor. In this capacity he was responsible for the design and upkeep of county buildings. Pearson remained in Bonomi's office for ten years, working on a succession of eclectic country houses and churches in both classical and medieval styles.

David Lloyd, in his fine essay on Pearson contained in the book *Seven Victorian Architects,* makes the point that Durham Cathedral undoubtedly helped shape the young architect's particular gifts for spatial manipulation and proportioning.[1] Durham Cathedral is vaulted; Pearson is the Victorian architect who consistently employed the vault wherever economics allowed. Durham Cathedral features a great unified nave/chancel space from which glimpses into lesser, more intricate spaces can be had; Pearson utilizes a similar spatial arrangement in his best buildings. Durham Cathedral is famous for its superb relationship of structure and space; Pearson achieved a similar harmonious relationship in his High and Late Victorian churches.

In 1841 Pearson left Bonomi's office. The following year he moved to London, where he found employment first in Anthony Salvin's office, then in the office of Philip Hardwick. He was dissatisfied, however; he felt that he had little to learn from these positions. Consequently, in 1844 he established his own practice. It was during this period that Pearson began a serious study of Pugin's architectural philosophy. This study led him to embrace the Gothic style enthusiastically. Interestingly, however, Pearson's Gothic is always tempered with a concern for proportion that he had developed during his mainly classical training in the Bonomi, Salvin, and Hardwick offices.

Pearson maintained his ties with the North. The early work of his new office included a number of North Yorkshire churches, as well as a few in other parts of the country. One of his Yorkshire clients, Archdeacon Bentinck of Sigglesthorne, was a Canon of Westminster. In 1849 he commissioned Pearson to design a new church, Holy Trinity, for Bessborough Gardens, a poor section of Westminster. This church is the major work of Pearson's early period, 1844 through 1856.

Holy Trinity was much admired; Pugin, Barry, and Scott all praised it enthusiastically. Scott even labeled it "the best modern specimen of a fourteenth century English church."[2] Unfortunately, the church was demolished in the early 1950s. It was an elaborate, aisled, cruciform church with a central tower and spire. In it, many details that were to characterize Pearson's mature work appeared for the first time.

Holy Trinity was plainly a work of Pearson's formative period. The interior lacked the finesse of the exterior, and its space, details, and proportions had little of the refinement or the vigor of his mature work. However, Pearson's experiments during this first decade of practice led him to an understanding of architectural space and form that is rare at any age. He learned how to design churches that were visually solid and satisfying without depending upon ornament or unessential buttressing; he also learned how to apply classical proportional systems, particularly the golden section, to Gothic design.

In 1857, with the design for the Church of St. Leonard, Scorborough, North Yorkshire, Pearson entered a new phase of his career. This middle period of Pearson's work is a mature High Victorian phase that lasted until 1870. During this period Pearson produced designs for a number of new churches in the High Victorian style.

Pearson's High Victorian manner is quite different from that of most of his contemporaries. He had no "rogue" tendencies at all; he was much more interested in producing harmonious visual combinations than in being novel or surprising. Throughout his life his work is characterized by restraint. He used constructional polychromy subtly and sparingly, usually to differentiate structural parts rather than to add pattern. He used decoration lavishly, but he always contrasted it with plain areas; his decoration was more likely to be sculptural and architectural than planar applied work. He utilized High Victorian heavy massing of building components. He never allowed masses to collide but instead composed and integrated them into classically ordered compositions. Anthony Quiney, in his biography of the architect, observed that Pearson controlled the vigor of the period instead of abandoning himself to it.[3] The observation is apt; Pearson was always totally in control.

The Church of St. Leonard, Scorborough, Humberside

In 1854 Pearson was contacted by Baron Hotham of Dalton Hall about the design of a church for his estate. Nothing came of this meeting except that Pearson met James Hall, a local landowner and agent of Lord Hotham. Hall employed Pearson to design the Church of St. Leonard for him. The church was completed during the period from 1857 to 1859.

St. Leonard is small but extremely powerful in its forms and rich in its decoration. It is built of local yellow stone dressed with a hard, light gray stone that could be carved successfully. It has red stone decoration. The massing is very simple; the church is formed of two major elements—an extremely tall tower centered on the west end of the longitudinal axis of the church and a gabled horizontal mass that contains the nave and chancel. These two elements establish an occult equilibrium. The gabled horizontal block has no exterior indication of the division between nave and chapel; it is a simple block of five bays, twice as long as its vertical wall is high.

The east wall of the chancel is composed of an equilateral triangle over a square. The two geometric forms are connected by a recessed, arched, three-lancet window, placed so that the dividing line between square and triangle is also the spring line of

Exterior View of the Church of St. Leonard, Scorborough, Humberside, from the East
The east facade is composed of two forms, an equilateral triangle superimposed on a square, which are interlocked by the large east window.

both the large tracery arch and the three lancet arches. This line is marked on the yellow stone of the facade by a gray stone band of carved quatrefoils. Gray stone is also used for the frame and plate tracery of the window, the gable coping, and the carving that decorates the upper portions of the buttresses that frame the composition. The window itself is a layered composition. The plate tracery of gray stone seems to be thinly applied upon the yellow stone wall. Yellow stone shows behind the red shafts that carry the tracery arches above the three lancet windows.

One bay of the north side of the church receives a small gabled vestry/organ chamber wing. The westernmost bay on the south side receives a gabled entrance porch of precisely the same size. In each case the roof of the wing intersects both the main roof and the vertical side wall of the church, locking the parts together. The bay divisions of the church are marked by buttresses. Each bay, except the two where wings occur, has two lancet windows with a blind quatrefoil panel above them. The windows are framed in red stone, and a red stone band runs continuously behind the buttresses at the spring line of the arches and below the window sills.

The tower design is a masterwork of classical proportioning. Like the church itself, the tower is composed of two parts—a simple vertical base element and an elaborate belfry and spire. The vertical base unit is built of yellow stone and is relatively plain; even the corner buttresses are de-emphasized. It is composed of the double gray stone plinth on which the entire church sits, next a cubical unit, then a unit based on the golden section derived from the square below. As in the east chancel wall, an arched window with its spring line at the division be-

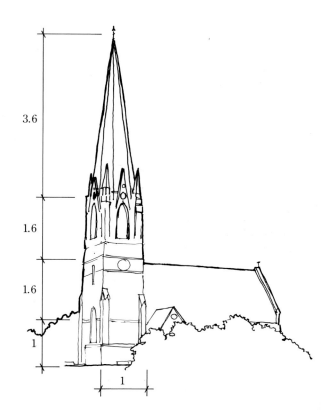

Exterior View Showing the Proportions of Tower and Spire at the Church of St. Leonard, Scorborough, from the South

tween the two stages serves to interconnect them. The belfry stage is the same height as the upper portion of the tower below and is as elaborate as the stage below it is plain. The belfry is made of the same gray stone used for decoration in the main body of the church. Hexagonal pinnacles at the corners camouflage the transition from square tower to octagonal spire. The belfry openings between the pinnacles are lucarnes with tall, slender canopies of the same height as the pinnacles. The octagonal

115

Interior View toward the Chancel at the Church of St. Leonard, Scorborough
The interior is a single large space covered with a handsome wood roof structure, plus a small, polychromed, stone-vaulted baptistry in the base of the tower.

Inside the church, the interior wall surfaces are pale gray stone. Bands of dark gray stone occur at wainscot height and below the window sills. Bands of red stone occur at the spring line of the window arches and below the cornice. Colored stone moldings are used to emphasize the arch of the opening from nave to baptistry. A polychromed tile floor—predominantly red and black laid in a diaper pattern—leads to the altar. Polished black marble shafts carry both the arches of the window openings and the roof trusses that occur at the bay divisions. (Every other roof truss has shafts.) The shafts are single except at the division between nave and chancel where they are doubled and in the triple-lancet chancel window where they are clustered. The shafts that mark the bay divisions are carried by carved brackets placed at the same height as the capitals of the window shafts. The exceptions are the double shafts (the only space dividers between nave and chancel), which are three times as tall as the shafts which mark bay divisions. Instead of being supported on upper wall brackets, the double shafts rise from the floor.

Cornice, column capitals, and brackets are deeply and richly carved, as are pulpit and font; and a band of carved quatrefoils similar to those that decorate the exterior is placed below the sill of the chancel window. (The carved brackets that carry the roof trusses are a Pearson trademark.) The carving is chaste, elegant, and refined—almost classical in feeling.

Pearson's carved decoration even at its most lavish is always controlled, and constructional polychromy invariably functions to articulate space and form. Pearson uses wall layering in a similar fashion. The double wall treatment given to all windows not

spire, including the cross it carries, is almost exactly as tall as the square tower below, including the belfry.

The visual result of these carefully considered relationships is amazingly satisfying. Its success is due in large measure to Pearson's unerring eye for proportion. It is also due to the utilization of constructional polychromy to emphasize structural and proportional relationships of the simple geometric units employed.

Interior View toward the West of the Church
of St. Leonard, Scorborough
The baptistry is located beyond the arch in
the west wall of the nave.

117

The natural wood framing of the roof structure is exposed. The roof is carried by a series of arched trusses (really arched, braced scissors rafters) that echo the shape of the arched altar wall. The bottom edges of the trusses are rhythmically notched in a typically bold High Victorian manner that gives them a dentilated look. The spaces between the truss members are filled with wooden tracery. The trusses are cross-braced by "Wells-like" double arches. The effect is extremely powerful, yet elegant. The wood roof structure here is as elaborate as some of Lamb's wood roofs, but it has none of Lamb's "rogue" characteristics.

The Church of St. Mary, Dalton Holme (South Dalton), Humberside

Soon after St. Leonard was started, Lord Hotham, undoubtedly feeling the need to keep up with his estate agent, reconsidered the idea of building a church of his own and engaged Pearson to begin work on the design of the Church of St. Mary, Dalton Holme. Pearson's first design (1857–58) was rejected, but his second design was found to be acceptable. Construction began in 1858 and continued until 1861. (Additions, including an awkward vestry on the north side, were made in the years from 1868 to 1872 for the fifth Baron Hotham.) The church that resulted is larger, more elaborate, and, at twenty-

Roof Structure at the Church of St. Leonard, Scorborough

only reinforces the spatial organization and enriches the altar wall focus, but it also diminishes the apparent weight of the heavy stone walls which might otherwise seem oppressive in such a small, narrow space.

St. Leonard's roof structure contributes significantly to the power of the church's interior space.

five thousand pounds, vastly more expensive than the Scorborough Church. Even so, the church is not large; the combined length of nave and chancel is only ninety-two feet.

The plan of St. Mary, Dalton Holme, is much more complex than the plan of St. Leonard. St. Mary's plan is cruciform in shape; it has transepts off of which chapels open to the east, parallel to the chancel. All plan elements are articulated in the exterior massing of the church. As at St. Leonard, the slender tower is placed on the west end of the longitudinal axis of the church; it contains a baptistry in the chamber in its base. The south porch is vaulted. The remainder of the church has wooden roofs similar to St. Leonard.

Although Pearson employed many of the same proportioning devices that he used at Scorborough, the exterior of this church is not characterized by the same graceful harmony of the parts that gives St. Leonard its special exterior appeal. St. Mary is a composition of seven major masses (not including the entrance porch and the vestry addition) instead of two. The church plan is not organized on a regular grid; consequently the heights and roof pitches of the various masses are variable. No polychromy is used to articulate exterior masses. No clear, logical organizing system seems to exist. Only the tower and spire have the same graceful energy as those at St. Leonard.

St. Mary's spire is extremely tall and slender, rising to a height of two hundred feet. Here the

Exterior View of the Church of St. Mary, Dalton Holme, from the Northeast
The composition of the church is unusually complicated for Pearson; it is formed of seven major masses.

Exterior Detail of the Sacristy Entrance at the Church of St. Mary, Dalton Holme

open, elaborately carved belfry stage clearly belongs to the tower mass rather than to the steeple, but the octagonal spire is linked to it by the pinnacles and lucarnes that rise from the walls and corners of the square form below. The design of St. Mary is much more English than is St. Leonard's. St. Leonard's spire was based on those at Chartres and Caen; St. Mary's spire is more like the spires at St. Wulfran's at Grantham and at Salisbury Cathedral. *The Ecclesiologist* was pleased with St. Mary's Middle Pointed style. This is not the Middle Pointed style of Pearson's early churches; here the style is used to a very different effect because of the elegant proportions of the interior spaces and the church's elaborately carved decoration.

With the interior of St. Mary, Dalton Holme, Pearson takes a giant step toward the elegant, complex interiors of his later, mature work. In it Pearson abandons polychromy (except in the beautiful pavement of encaustic tiles) but enriches the carved decoration. The great height of the space is emphasized by the tall, slender proportion of all openings and by the vertical emphasis of the shafts that run from cornice to window sill on each side of each window opening. (Pearson's correspondence indicates he was after an effect of great height. In a letter he wrote to Lord Hotham about the effect of the transepts upon the proportion of the space, he said, "These additions opening into the nave by side archways have a very material influence upon both the effect of width and height by adding to the former and taking away from the latter and which it is necessary to make due allowance for."[4])

The nave is composed of three bays that are organized in a Renaissance manner. Pearson uses a Gothic reinterpretation of the interlocking triumphal arch motif used by Alberti at San Andrea and by countless subsequent Renaissance, Mannerist, Baroque, and Neoclassical architects. Window openings occur between portions of solid wall decorated with blind arches at smaller scale and defined by the shafts described above. Window reveals are perpendicular to the wall instead of splayed as they are at Scorborough. Consequently, the contrast in solid and void, dark and light is much greater here than at Scorborough. The rhythm is one of solid, heavy, narrow wall surfaces alternating with deeply recessed, brightly lighted, open spaces.

What is most interesting at St. Mary is the increased spatial complexity that is revealed as the chancel is approached. Space opens up at the crossing, and light flows in from the large transept windows. Although emphasis is clearly upon the richly decorated chancel, partial views into the flanking chapels distract the eye. In contrast to the darker nave and the mysterious chapels, the chancel is flooded with light from enormous windows that completely fill its upper wall on three sides. In contrast to the other spaces of the church where weight and thickness of wall are deliberately emphasized, the chancel enclosure is almost dematerialized. The effect is truly splendid; it suggests the complex spatial manipulation of Pearson's later churches like St. Augustine, Kilburn Park. Only in its strength and vigor is it truly High Victorian.

Interior View toward the Chancel at the Church of St. Mary, Dalton Holme
The vertical emphasis of the decoration and the tall, narrow proportion of the spaces (the nave is twenty-three feet wide and fifty feet high) create a sublime interior.

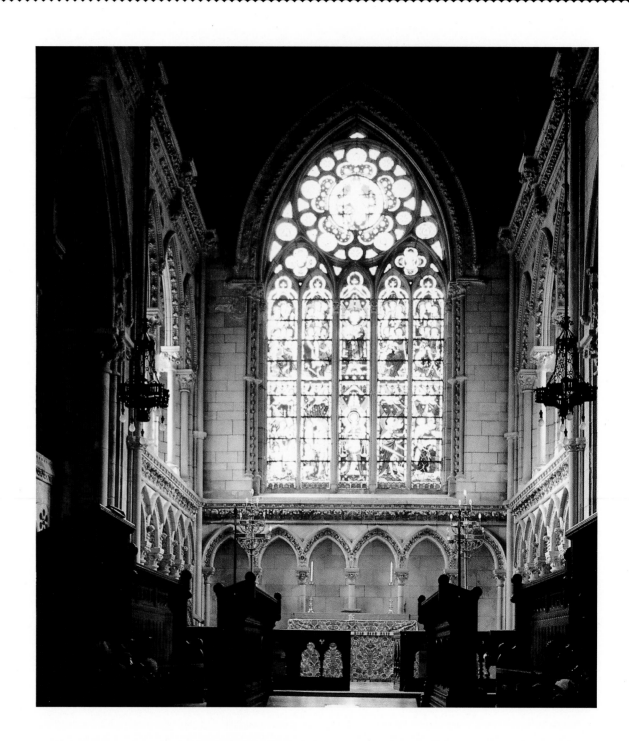

Interior View of the Chancel at the Churc'
of St. Mary, Dalton Holme
The weight of the lower chancel wall is
diminished by a layer of detached arcading
placed some distance in front of the solid
wall.

Other churches of the late 1850s

Pearson designed three other High Victorian churches during the last years of the decade—St. Peter, Daylesford, Worcestershire/Gloucestershire; St. Mary, Catherston Leweston, Dorset; and St. James, Titsey, Surrey.

St. Mary, Catherston Leweston, is a tiny two-cell (nave and chancel) church built of flint with Bath stone dressings. It has no spire but rather a bellcote over the west entrance door. The inside, however, is decorated with the same richness of carved detail found at Dalton Holme.

In St. James, Titsey, Pearson returned to constructional polychromy. In it he used polished marble shafts and bands (and even inlaid patterns) of red and green stone, much as at Scorborough. The Surrey volume of *Buildings of England* calls it "crisp and hard in the Butterfield sense."[5] This is an exaggeration. The addition of color is done subtly and in a manner that assists in the articulation of structure and space; it has nothing of Butterfield's pattern for pattern's sake.

The most interesting of these three churches is the church of St. Peter, Daylesford, an estate church built for Harmon Grisewood of Daylesford House.

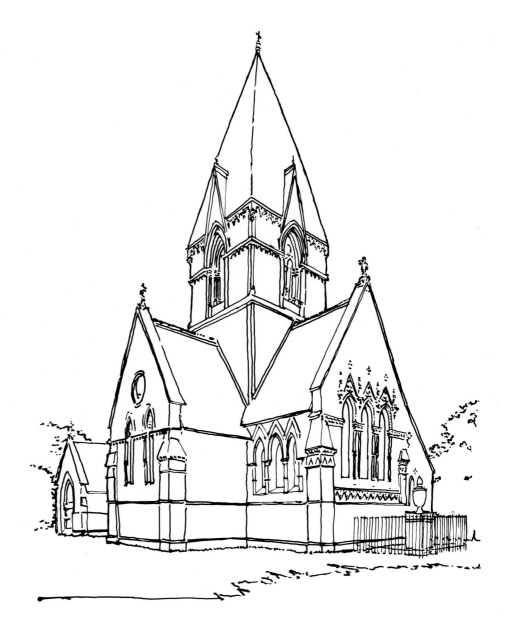

Exterior View of the Church of St. Peter, Daylesford, Worcestershire/Gloucestershire, from the Southeast
The composition is very powerful; nave, transepts, and chancel are locked together in a bold, compact, pyramidal mass by the strong tower form that rises from the crossing.

St. Peter is much more like the church at Scorborough than the church at Dalton Home in spite of the fact that it is a Latin Cross church like St. Mary, Dalton Holme. For its design, Pearson reverted to early French Gothic style—a style that accommodates simpler and bolder masses and details than does the English Decorated style. The character of the interior, in spite of the complication added by the transept spaces and the vaulted sanctuary, is much like that at Scorborough.

But it is the exterior massing that gives St. Peter, Daylesford, its very special character. The Daylesford exterior has the power and surprise of the works of rogue architects like Teulon; it substitutes mass and skill in composition for height and elegance. Window openings are few and small; the solid is much more important than the void. Window plate tracery is only slightly recessed from the exterior wall plane. Buttresses are short and squat. The south entrance porch seems to completely fill the space formed by nave and transept. Most powerful of all is the tower, which rises above the roofs by only a single cubical stage. It is capped by a simple pyramid 1.6 times as high as the cube beneath it. (This dimension was obviously established by the golden rectangle.) Canopies above deeply recessed belfry openings rise from the tower walls to create lucarnes that interconnect the pyramid and the cube.

The whole is built of golden local stone, subtly decorated with brown bands and red column shafts. The use of constructional polychromy and carved bands of a repeating quatrefoil pattern is reminiscent of St. Leonard. St. Peter has a gutsy quality that is very unlike the calm equilibrium of St. Leonard, however. Here angular broken lines, overscaled and crowded masses, and bold contrasts of light and dark contribute to a muscularity of form unusual to Pearson if not to other, less restrained, architects of the High Victorian period.

The Church of St. Peter, Vauxhall, London

The first church Pearson designed upon his return from an 1859 trip to France was St. Peter, Vauxhall. The trip must have been a seminal experience for Pearson, because its date represents a turning point in his style. Pearson's earlier churches had all had English plans, and their forms and details had been an interesting stylistic mixture of English decorated and French Early Gothic styles. In contrast, St. Peter's plan and form are Romanesque, and Italian Romanesque at that.

Pearson's client was the Reverend Robert Gregory. Gregory desired to establish a social center, including a large new church and schools for children and apprentices, to combat poverty in the south London area of Lambeth, of which Vauxhall is a part. Pearson received the commission for the design of the church in 1860 and rapidly produced a scheme. Pearson's first design was deemed to be too expensive, however, so he reworked the design, stripping it of most of its carved decoration, in order to bring its cost in line with available funds. The church, in its revised form and without its campanile, was constructed from 1863 to 1864.

Although the exterior impact of the church was

greatly diminished by the deletion of the tower and spire, the interior was relatively unaffected by the elimination of carved ornament. The powerful effect of the interior is created by its plan and proportion and the use of vaulting throughout; these elements of the first design were retained in the revised scheme.

The church has much in common with Street's Church of St. James the Less, designed in 1859. Both reflect Italian influence, both are constructed of polychromatic brick, both have interior arcades supported by stumpy circular columns with elaborately, boldly carved capitals, and both use interior painted decoration. Street's church has a detached campanile; Pearson's campanile would have been attached very gingerly, with its base joined to the west end of the north aisle wall. Except on the entrance facade, Street's church used a plethora of exterior buttresses for strength and vigor; Pearson eliminated most buttresses in favor of simpler, calmer geometric volumes.

St. Peter, Vauxhall, is an extremely powerful, muscular church. Its west facade is a masterful, pyramidal composition that begins at its base with a triple-arcaded narthex which seems to be fitted in and between three overscaled, almost crude, brick buttresses. These buttresses divide the middle zone of the facade into two equal elements. Between these buttresses, in the center of the facade, are arched recesses filled with French-type Decorated windows. The windows are composed of two lancets with a large oculus above, all in absolutely flat,

The Church of St. Peter, Vauxhall, London
This is the west elevation as originally designed. The tower was not built.

Exterior View of the West Facade at the
Church of St. Peter, Vauxhall
This facade is Pearson's most successful
essay in muscular Gothic design.

126

uncarved plate tracery. (Only the rose window in the gable above the central buttress has carved tracery.) The 3:2:1 composition—three arches in the base, two windows in the middle, one rose window at the top—is very strong and effective although, at least in the form here, it is certainly unorthodox.

A baptistry with a very steeply pitched roof on the right side of the entrance arcade creates a strongly asymmetrical composition that would have been balanced by the campanile intended for the left side. Pearson compensated for the absence of the campanile by adding a small bell tower with a pyramidal cap to the top, right side of the facade gable, subtly shifting the axis of the composition to the right and resolving its occult balance.

The yellow-brown brick of the facade is decorated with cream-colored stone bands and window tracery and red and black brick diapers. Roofs are slate. Side and apse walls are sheer, unbuttressed brick planes. (The thrust of the main vault is carried by the clerestory wall, the aisle vaults, and flying buttresses hidden in the aisle roofs.)

The polychromy is much more restrained than in Street's church of St. James the Less, but the geometry of the various compositional elements is much stronger and simpler. The elevation of the apse is illustrative; even the shapes, proportions, and placement of the windows in the exterior wall surface emphasize the tall, slender, largely undecorated volume of the chancel, which seems to have two stories rather than three, as it has inside.

The interior of St. Peter, Vauxhall, is as powerful and bold as the exterior. Like the church at Scorborough, St. Peter combines nave and chancel into a single space with only a minimal indication of separa-

Exterior View Showing the Tall, Simple Volume of the Apse at the Church of St. Peter, Vauxhall, from the East

tion—a chancel arch that is actually an exaggerated transverse vault rib carried down as shafts on the side walls. The church is brick-vaulted throughout. (This is astonishing since vaulting is expensive and St. Peter is a relatively large church, built for the modest sum of eight thousand pounds—less than a third of the cost of the much smaller Dalton Holme estate church.) The nave and chancel vault is fifty feet high. Most bays are quadripartite vaults with

127

stone transverse and diagonal ribs. Exceptions are the quinquepartite fifth nave bay (the fifth or ridge rib engages the center facade buttress) and the apse vault and the sexpartite first chancel bay. The vaulting here represents Pearson's new commitment to vaulted construction—a commitment that resulted in a series of subsequent vaulted church designs.

The visual strength of the brick walls and vaults and the proportions of the spaces give St. Peter a power and spaciousness that is exceptional. Pearson originally intended for the interior to be decorated lavishly with carved ornament as at Dalton Holme. The absence of this ornament calls attention to the strength of construction and the elegant proportion of the space, and the interior is actually more powerful without it. The proportions throughout the

Interior View toward the Chancel at the Church of St. Peter, Vauxhall
The vaulting emphasizes the vertical proportion of the space and camouflages the simple blocky design of most architectural elements.

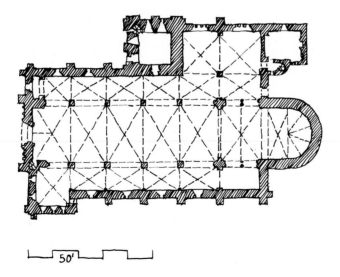

50'

Plan of the Church of St. Peter, Vauxhall
Each nave and aisle bay is a golden rectangle, and the entire church is vaulted.

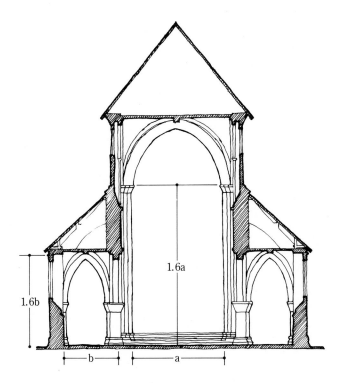

Cross-Section through the Nave at the Church of St. Peter, Vauxhall
As in the plan, the section is composed of golden rectangles at related scales; a = 1.6b.

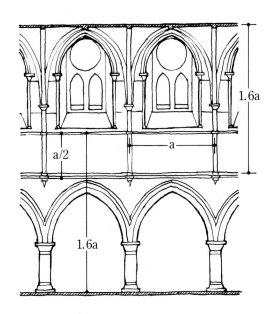

Nave Arcade and Clerestory at the Church of St. Peter, Vauxhall
Pearson's reliance upon the golden section as a proportioning system is apparent in the design of all parts.

church are based upon the golden section, a ratio of 1:1.6. The height to the springline of the main vaulting ribs is 1.6 times the width across the nave and chancel. The height to the apex of the aisle vaults is 1.6 times the aisle bay width. The golden section is also applied to the layout of the nave and chancel walls, controlling the size and configuration of each bay.

The nave space is simple and severe. Clerestory windows that are a variant of the facade window design light it brightly in comparison to the dark aisles that flank it on either side. The brick arches and blind triforium are decorated with the thinnest possible stone bands used as lines to emphasize design geometries. The thickness of the clerestory wall is emphasized by the deeply chamfered window surrounds. A minimum of constructional polychromy—bands in the walls and stars in the ceiling vaults—gives life and vitality to the otherwise undecorated brick wall surfaces. The column capitals are square and massive.

129

Interior Detail of Apse Wall and Vault at the
Church of St. Peter, Vauxhall
Pearson's simple planar geometry evolves
into a complicated intersection of wall and
ceiling planes in the apse.

In contrast to the nave, the chancel is much more
richly decorated. A very solid freestanding altar and
reredos—almost like a Byzantine building of red,
black, and gold—stand on a three-stepped platform
in the apse. The unperforated curved wall around it,
to the height of the nave arcade, is divided into
three painted bands. The lowest band is a green
wainscot, the middle band is a red and black stenciled diaper pattern with rosettes, and the upper
band is a series of cream grisaille sgraffito scenes
with alternating dark red and blue grounds. Yellow
geometric stenciled friezes separate the three
bands. The wall is double at the triforium level. The
inner wall is an arcade of heavy stone arches and
columns, two openings per bay. The outer wall has
a lancet window corresponding to each arch in the
inner wall. The bays of the clerestory zone are
treated as a series of space wedges (in contrast to
the planar quality of the triforium level) focusing on
single-lancet windows. The apse vault is carried on
an arch supported by colonnettes in the inner face of
each wedge. The vault ribs are carried down the

wall as shafts to brackets immediately below the triforium level. These shafts create an interlocking wall and ceiling geometry.

The effect of the chancel/apse space is enigmatic. It seems as strong and powerful as the nave, but, at the same time, lighter and more delicate. Emphasis is on void instead of on solid, and the composition is made up of much smaller elements. The Claydon and Bell stained glass in the sanctuary adds to the contrast. (The windows of the nave clerestory are glazed with white translucent glass.)

The complexity that is an important element in the spatial interest at Dalton Holme is de-emphasized at Vauxhall. The church has a single transept—a two-bay vaulted space that opens to the north through the last bay of the nave arcade and a similar arch in the chancel—but it is insignificant in effect. The rhythms of the great nave and chancel are so strong that the secondary spaces play no real part in the interior effect.

St. Peter, Vauxhall, in its proportioning, planning, and vaulting, was a High Victorian prototype for Pearson's Late Victorian churches of the 1870s and 1880s. In these churches Pearson would substitute elegance and refinement for St. Peter's boldness and muscularity, but the basic elements that would characterize his late work were fully developed in this High Victorian masterpiece. More important in Pearson's development was the discovery made at St. Peter that a church without much ornament or unessential buttressing could be made to satisfy the most demanding High Victorian critics by combining classical proportioning principles with Gothic design.

Christ Church, Appleton-le-Moors, North Yorkshire

St. Peter, Vauxhall, was followed in 1863 through 1866 by the design and construction of the small parish church at Appleton-le-Moors, Christ Church. Christ Church is a much smaller and simpler variant of St. Peter. Because Christ Church is a small rural parish church it is stone, not brick. It is built of local stone with bands and shafts of Rosedale firestone and red Mansfield stone, and it has a timber roof with tie-beams, crown post, and raking struts. One simple unbroken roof structure covers nave, chancel, and aisles; it is resolved in a conical form over the semi-circular apse.

As at Vauxhall, a small narthex is incorporated between the buttresses of the west facade. Here, however, the composition is much simpler. Instead of the tall pyramidal 3:2:1 composition of St. Peter, Christ Church's facade is a series of elements either on its center line (these include the square, shed-roofed narthex volume, the single entrance portal, and the large rose window) or bracketing it on either side (the buttresses and lancet windows). All is contained within a composition of right triangle and rectangle, locked together by the buttresses that embrace the narthex. Because the triangle sits on a rectangle rather than a square, as at Scorborough, the mass is much lower and broader than any of Pearson's earlier High Victorian churches. A projecting molding positioned at the springline of the west portal arch wraps the main body of the church en-

tirely, replacing the projecting plinth found in all his other churches.

A tower with pyramidal spire, very similar to that at Daylesford, is located at the east end of the south aisle. Its proportion is more slender than at Daylesford, however, and its position allows it to function as a separate vertical element counterbalancing the low, horizontal mass of the main body of the church. The tower has sheer, unbuttressed sides with virtually no fenestration. It is composed of a plinth, a cube, a stage whose sides are golden rectangles, and another cube—the belfry. Paired lancet grills are capped with triangular canopies that extend up into the simple pyramidal spire as dormers. The spire is the height of the tower minus the belfry.

The nave and apsidal sanctuary occupy a single unbroken space; only a pair of bracketed shafts marks the transition from one to the other. Pearson was much more interested in unifying the spaces than in dividing them. One continuous wooden roof structure covers both major spaces; the nave arcades continue into the choir (the north choir arch opens to the chapel; the south choir arch contains the organ); and the upper nave wall has a wide polychrome band capped by a deeply projecting, richly sculpted cornice that continues around the sanctuary. The polychrome band uses yellow, black, and white stone in geometric patterns; the shafts that carry the inner fenestration arches are also yellow

Exterior View of Christ Church, Appleton-le-Moors, North Yorkshire, from the Southwest
Christ Church has a much lower, more compact mass than do most of Pearson's churches; nonetheless, its proportions are determined by reliance on a classical proportioning system.

Interior View toward the Chancel of Christ Church, Appleton-le-Moors

Although Christ Church is not vaulted, the effect of the nave shape and decoration is much the same as at St. Peter, Vauxhall.

133

Interior Detail of the Secondary Arcade between the Chapel
and the Choir at Christ Church, Appleton-le-Moors

and black. Window shafts are almost ridiculously
slender; they must be tied to the outer wall with
braces at their tops and midpoints. (Pearson was
deliberately exaggerating the difference between
the decorative arcade and the structural wall.)

As at St. Peter before it, and at St. Mary, Freeland, which was to follow, the apse decoration features a red and white sgraffito frieze and reredos.
Sgraffito is also used to decorate the pulpit and the
small vaulted chapel located at the east end of the
north aisle. Bold, richly sculpted white marble sill
and cornice define the zone of the sgraffito frieze;
the cornice also functions as the sill for the arcade
above. A secondary arcade is inserted into the arch
between the chapel and choir; its two arches, and
the open rondel above them, are decorated with
notched, zig-zag moldings that are typical of the period but are unusual for Pearson. All arches, except
these special ones, have very simple square intrados. All are carried by short, stumpy round columns
with elaborately carved, square, white marble capitals. The nave columns are surrounded by banded
yellow shafts, placed at the corners of the capitals;
these shafts visually transform the circular columns
into basically square pier clusters.

Christ Church is a dark, heavy church. It has no
clerestory; its aisle windows are lancets in irregular groups. But its spaces are so handsomely proportioned, integrated and detailed that its effect is
powerful rather than oppressive.

Quiney says that Christ Church is "emphatically
expressive."[6] The phrase is descriptive of the bold,
muscular approach that characterizes the church's
design. Eastlake says that it "is modeled on the earliest and severest type of French Gothic, with an ad-
mixture of details almost Byzantine in character."[7]

Lloyd says that Christ Church is "more frenziedly rich than any other of Pearson's creations."[8]

The Church of St. Mary, Freeland, Oxfordshire

Pearson's last truly High Victorian church is another small variation of his great church at Vauxhall; this is the Church of St. Mary, Freeland, built for the Raikes and Taunton families, old friends and faithful clients of Pearson.

The exterior of St. Mary's church is reminiscent of Bodley's design for Selsley. It has a single pitched roof that covers both nave and sanctuary and is resolved at its east end in a conical form over the semicircular apse below. (The division between nave and sanctuary is expressed externally by buttresses and a restrained projection through the roof of the wall above the chancel arch.) Entry is through a porch on the south side. Like the towers of Bodley's churches at Selsley and Scarborough and Butterfield's at Stoke Newington, Freeland has a tower with a camel-back roof. Its nave windows are much like those at Vauxhall, except smaller. As at Appleton-le-Moors, a projecting molding wraps entirely around the main

Exterior View of the Church of St. Mary, Freeland, Oxfordshire, from the Southeast
This church, likes its predecessors, reveals Pearson's preference for simple, undecorated three-dimensional forms.

Interior View toward the Chancel at the Church of St. Mary, Freeland
The dramatic separation of nave and chancel at St. Mary is not typical of Pearson's approach to spatial design.

body of the church. The exterior impression it gives is of simple geometrical masses, carefully proportioned and artfully composed.

St. Mary's plan is extremely simple; it has a nave and a chancel. No secondary spaces beckon us to explore. It has a vaulted sanctuary that seems, at first glance, to be a miniature of that at Vauxhall. Present are the deep wedges of space holding lancet windows, a band of red and pink sgraffito decoration, and the polychromed, groined, quadripartite and quinquepartite vaults. Absent, however, is the triforium arcade (no triforium exists here) and the great sense of soaring space that is Vauxhall's chief glory. St. Mary, Freeland, is an intimate church. Unlike Vauxhall, or even Appleton-le-Moors, Freeland strongly separates nave and sanctuary. The vaulted sanctuary is seen, like a richly decorated set-piece, through a large chancel arch. The nave, as at Appleton-le-Moors, is severely plain, but no rich polychromy decorates its walls. The roof of the nave is a keel-shaped carpentry construction.

St. Mary, Freeland, is the least successful of Pearson's High Victorian churches. Its exterior decoration is so restrained that its planar surfaces do not seem to have adequate strength and weight. The interior lacks Pearson's typical spatial complexity and does not seem large enough to justify the dramatic separation between nave and sanctuary or the elaborate vaulting of the chancel and apse. Inside, it seems to be too small for the weight of its parts.

*The Church of
St. Augustine, Kilburn Park,
Paddington, London*

No discussion of Pearson's High Victorian churches can close without mention of his finest work, St. Augustine, Kilburn Park, because it is, in many ways, the culmination of the experimentation of the previous decade-and-a-half. Most architectural historians classify St. Augustine, in spite of its 1870 design date, as a Late Victorian church. (The same stylistic attribution is also given to the other two Pearson churches of the late 1860s—St. John, Sutton Veny, Wiltshire, and Holy Trinity, Wentworth, West Riding, South Yorkshire.) In my view, this Late Victorian attribution is simplistic. It is true that these churches do reflect a turn toward elegance and sensitivity and are not as brutally expressionistic as Pearson's earlier churches, yet they retain all the vigor and strength of his High Victorian work. Moreover, at St. Augustine at least, decoration remains richly polychromatic.

These churches are like Bodley's St. Augustine, Pendlebury; they are transitional in style between

Exterior View of the Church of St. Augustine, Kilburn Park, Paddington, London, from the West
The facade of St. Augustine is an assimilation of design features from Vauxhall, Dalton Holme, and Appleton-le-Moors, except it is modified by a new geometric crispness that diminishes the impression of weight and mass that characterized the earlier churches.

the High and Late Victorian periods, containing, remarkably, the best characteristics of both. This is especially true of the Church of St. Augustine, Kilburn Park, located in a fashionable north side suburb of London. St. Augustine is Pearson's masterpiece. It is bold, vigorous, and richly decorated in the High Victorian manner, yet it possesses a space as complex, majestic, elegant, and sublime as any Late Victorian church.

In St. Augustine, Kilburn Park, Pearson applies the best characteristics of his earlier churches. The height and proportions of the tower and spire, and their relationship to the body of the church, are similar to the design at Dalton Holme and the projected design for Vauxhall, but with the detail simplified and the basic form geometry emphasized.

The facade is a variant of the facades at Vauxhall and Appleton-le-Moors. At these churches Pearson used large, boldly projecting buttresses to subdivide the facade and organize its various elements. At Kilburn Park tall square towers with turrets perform the same function. Between them the shed-roofed narthex/baptistry projects and the arched-shaped wall that contains the major fenestration elements recedes. Only a vestigial west facade wall remains—an arch, supporting the gable, flies from tower to tower above the recessed rose window below. The geometry here is every bit as bold and unusual as the geometry of the Vauxhall facade. Here, however, a crispness of parts and edges, and a simplification of forms, replaces the brutal muscularity of Vauxhall. Also, as at Vauxhall, the main body of the church is extremely tall and unbuttressed. Pearson liked sheer walls of brick. Kilburn Park's brick walls are largely monochromatic; the strongly polychromatic diapering of Vauxhall is gone, and the stone dressing is very restrained. The power of the exterior of this church comes not from unorthodox elements, elaborate decoration, or constructional polychromy, but from the projection and recession of its major form components. At least in its entry facade, its principal wall plane is undefined.

The great glory of St. Augustine, Kilburn Park, is its interior, however. Pearson used a totally new plan for the church. It is a Latin-cross plan with

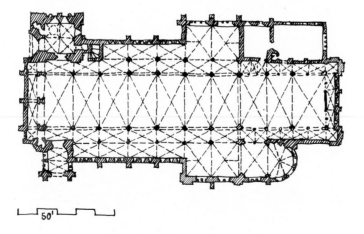

Plan of the Church of St. Augustine, Kilburn Park
This plan, Pearson's most complex, features an aisle/gallery construction that moves freely through space creating wonderful views into interconnected spatial units.

Interior View toward the Chancel at the Church of St. Augustine, Kilburn Park
The space of the sanctuary is screened, rather than separated, from the nave by a chancel screen which is a visual continuation of the aisle gallery.

double aisles, all vaulted. The inner aisles carry galleries. The divisions between the bays of the galleries are wall piers similar to those Bodley used at Pendlebury; these help absorb the thrust of the major vaults by functioning as interior buttresses. The galleries continue through the transepts (here the wall piers change to the most slender piers imaginable), establishing the nave and chancel as one great continuously vaulted space. The galleries bridge this space, establishing a rood screen at the entrance to the choir. Light floods in from the transepts to illumine the rood screen. From the nave it is possible to see through the gallery arcades into the spaces of the transepts, suggesting a spatial complexity belied by the simplicity of the major space. The effect is wonderful; the space is as baroque in its richness and complexity as any in English architectural history.

The interior of St. Augustine is richly decorated. Brick surfaces are either painted or laid in stripes of yellow and red brick. Vaulting ribs, shafts, arches, and most of the sanctuary surfaces are made of elegantly carved white stone. Gone completely is the heaviness of Pearson's earlier work. Slender vertical elements dominate.

Although the same classical proportioning system is used here that Pearson had employed in the design of his earlier churches (nave bays are a × 2a × 4a; wall bays are a × 3.6a), St. Augustine has a spaciousness that exceeds even that at Vauxhall. Moreover, like Burges' Cork Cathedral, St. Augustine seems much taller and longer than it really is. (The nave is twenty-five feet wide and fifty-eight feet high.) This expansiveness owes much to sensitive proportioning but more to the interaction of the spaces and the slender elegance of the parts.

Interior View from One Aisle Gallery through the Nave and into the Transept on the Other Side at the Church of St. Augustine, Kilburn Park
This view illustrates the extraordinarily rich spatial interrelationships that make this church a favorite of many architects today.

St. Augustine, Kilburn Park, was very well received by the architectural press of the day. The *Church Builder* hailed it "as a work of genius." The *Architect* said it had "about the noblest interior in London." The *Building News* labeled it "unsurpassed."[9]

St. Augustine is the logical culmination of the experiments in spatial interpenetration and classical proportioning that characterized Pearson's early work. In it, Pearson established himself as a master of spatial design. There is no question, however, that elegance and restraint, and slender, attenuated forms, have replaced the bold, muscular forms of the churches discussed above. Pearson has entered a new, Late Victorian, phase.

Handsome, carefully proportioned space is the hallmark of Pearson's churches throughout his career. He always made decoration subsidiary to proportion and spatial arrangement; this is not a new development at Kilburn Park. Similarly, he always eschewed irrational, idiosyncratic detail; his churches are invariably characterized by design restraint. In St. Augustine, Kilburn Park, Pearson's genius is clearly revealed in a church that combines the boldness of the High Victorian era with the sensitivity of the Late Victorian era. This church represents the artistic zenith of his career; with it he established himself as the preeminent church architect in England in the 1870s.

NOTES

1. David Lloyd, "John Loughborough Pearson: Noble Seriousness," *Seven Victorian Architects,* ed. Jane Fawcett (University Park, PA: Penn State University Press, 1977), 66.

2. *Building News* 73 (1897), 866.

3. Anthony Quiney, *John Loughborough Pearson* (New Haven & London: Yale University Press, 1979), 78.

4. East Riding County Records Office, DDHO (48), 236.

5. Ian Nairn and Nikolaus Pevsner, *Surrey,* 2nd ed., Buildings of England Series (Harmondsworth: Penguin, 1971), 409.

6. Quiney, 78.

7. Charles L. Eastlake, *A History of the Gothic Revival* (New York: Humanities Press, 1872; Leicester: Leicester UP, 1970), 304–05.

8. Lloyd, 67.

9. Quiney, 114.

WILLIAM BURGES

No architect responded more creatively or forcefully to the new High Victorian muscular Gothic style than did William Burges, yet his impact upon the development of architecture is negligible. Burges' work is certainly strong and massive in the best muscular tradition, but it is not characterized by rational design, constructional polychromy, or honest expression of function. Burges believed that Gothic architecture was an architecture of figures and subjects achieving its impact through the synthesis of figural sculpture, painting, and stained glass into the building fabric. He felt strongly that the poetry of a building lay in its decoration and that decoration should appeal to the mind as well as the eye; that is, that it should have meaning and tell a story. He was the first of the Victorian "art-architects," architects who were very much in the Renaissance tradition.

Burges was as much an artist, a furniture designer, and a decorator as he was an architect. Working closely with the artists and craftsmen who executed the various parts of his buildings, he controlled every detail of the work. Consequently, his buildings were so special, so individual, that they defied imitation and exist outside the mainstream of architectural development.

Billy Burges lived from 1827 until 1881. He was the son of a prosperous civil engineer who designed and built some of the principal harbors and lighthouses of nineteenth-century England. He received his architectural training in the offices of Edward Blore, a well-known "country-house" architect, and M. D. Wyatt, who was interested in all aspects of decoration and who wrote an interesting essay on medieval mosaic pavements. Burges continued his education by traveling on the continent where he spent eighteen months doing measured drawings of medieval buildings. (A portion of these drawings was published posthumously by his brother-in-law; they reveal an ability to draw with exceptional precision.) Burges produced precise mechanical drawings of the buildings he studied rather than beautiful pencil sketches or engraved renderings. In fact, he distrusted the effect of beautiful rendering techniques on the design process. It is said that he once remarked about G. E. Street, "What a pity that he cannot build his crosshatching."[1]

Burges had a great capacity to analyze and record accurately what he observed. He was, moreover, a great bibliophile and a fine scholar and writer. At least forty of his papers were published in the architectural journals of the day. He also found time for many interests outside of architecture. He loved animals and birds and studied them carefully. He was interested in all the arts and wanted art to permeate life. His only book, *Art Applied to Industry,* published in 1865, was devoted to improving the public taste. He was a bon vivant with an active social life; he belonged to at least twenty-eight social and intellectual clubs; and he rarely missed a theater opening. His sense of humor was legendary and is revealed repeatedly in his decorative schemes. Unlike Butterfield and Street, he had no great religious conviction. Nor was he a philosopher like Pugin, Ruskin, and Morris. There is no indication in either his writings or his work that he shared his age's earnestness about artistic integrity and truth.

As a personal, intuitive, creative artist, Burges was interested almost exclusively in appearances and effects. Three Burges characteristics can be seen over and over in his work. First, he was a hopeless romantic who sought to escape the reality of life in industrial Britain through medieval fantasy. Second, he could never resist architectural play-acting and visual humor. Third, he liked things to be larger than life, huge in scale. He was the great nineteenth-century master of scale manipulation; he could imbue small things—buildings, spaces, objects—with size, strength, and power far in excess of reality. Yet he managed to balance fantasy with common sense and sound architectural judgment. Although his work was extremely experimental, it was disciplined by a thorough grasp of construction practice. He had an archaeologist's knowledge of Gothic architecture, yet he felt free to borrow widely from history, combining and reinterpreting traditional elements in fresh new ways. He could function equally well in both the Gothic and classical styles; like Wren and Hawksmoor before him, he varied his style to suit the situation.

Burges' work is invariably bold, sculptural, and highly personal and distinctive; it is easily recognizable. He was unique in his age in his ability to handle plain walls and simple geometric shapes with consummate assurance. He was the inspired decorator of his era. Because private means allowed him to restrict his practice (he produced only twenty-two or twenty-three buildings in three productive decades), and because he was fortunate in having clients with the money, taste, and patience to allow him to give his personal attention to every design detail, Burges put his own stamp on every part of each building he designed.

In his book, Burges postulated a set of rules to govern the design of "modern Gothic" architecture. First, and most important, he preached "regularity." He felt that an unbridled enthusiasm for the pictur-

143

esque had produced buildings that looked as if they had been "shaken around in a hat."[2] He believed that a strong organizational system should govern plan and form arrangement.

Burges' other rules dealt mostly with design detail or the use of materials. He loved color and made an eloquent plea for the return of color to the modern city; he believed, however, that color should be used sparingly and carefully in order to avoid the "piebald" appearance of much contemporary work which featured multi-colored brick and tile patterns.[3] In fact, he felt that tiles should be used only for floors, that the use of marble should be limited to large slabs and column shafts, and that wall surfaces should be free of veneer. He despised small scale and fretful detail that obscured major architectural elements. He believed that nothing should be done to compromise understanding of the nature and strength of building forms and materials. He made the aesthetic of the sublime rather than the aesthetic of the picturesque preeminently important in his work.

Burges established his reputation as an architect through his participation in several important design competitions. In association with Henry Clutton, he won the 1855 competition for the design of the new cathedrals to be built in the French city of Lille. Although the Burges-Clutton design was not built (nationalism reared its ugly head and the commission was given to a team of three Frenchmen), Burges received much favorable attention through the publication of the winning design.

Burges repeated this success by winning, in the following year, the competition for the design of the Crimea Memorial Church to be constructed in Istanbul. Again Burges' design was set aside and another

design built. (It was felt that the stone vault that Burges proposed made his scheme prohibitively expensive.) This disappointment had an important impact on Burges' later work because it led him to abandon stone vaults entirely and substitute in their place the wooden internal roofs that are one of his chief design achievements. This competition also affected his work in a second important way; his visits to Istanbul and his study of its indigenous architecture resulted in the fascination with Islamic forms and geometries that is revealed in much of his subsequent work.

Waltham Abbey, Essex

In 1859 Burges received the commission to design an east, sanctuary, wall to transform the remnant of the medieval nave of Waltham Abbey into a complete parish church. (The abbey's choir and transepts had been pulled down at the time of dissolution, but no permanent east end to the truncated building had been constructed.) Burges deliberately designed his new sanctuary wall to be different from the old building; it was designed in the Early French style rather than the Early English style of the nave. Burges felt that as cathedral buildings had historically involved the combination of work in different styles built in different periods, he was free to depart from the original style in his new work.

Burges' work at Waltham Abbey is sympathetic in scale and mass to the heavy early English style of the existing building, but it is much richer and more complex as befitting its place as the visual focus of the church. It introduces the idea of spatial complexity through the device of layering an arcade in front of the enclosing wall. It includes a sculpted, strongly horizontal reredos panel above the altar that is reminiscent of a classical sarcophagus frieze, thereby alluding to an architectural era even earlier than the style of the original church.

The glory of the Burges work at Waltham Abbey is the stained glass. It incorporates the most jewel-like colored glass imaginable in the Burne-Jones/Powell "Tree of Jesse" and "Creation" windows.

The three design devices—arcade, reredos, and rose window—organize the wall into three carefully

Interior View toward the East Chancel Wall at Waltham Abbey, Essex

Interior Detail of the Altar Wall at Waltham Abbey, Essex

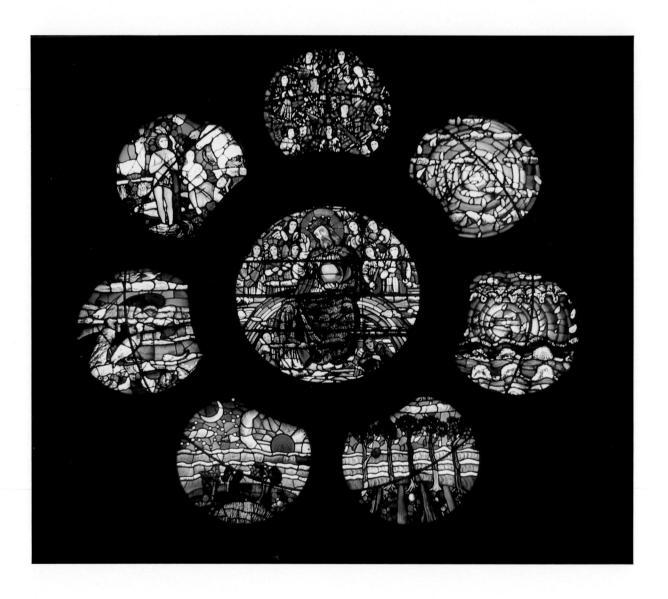

Detail of Burne-Jones' "Creation" Rose
Window in the Burges East Wall of the
Waltham Abbey Chancel, 1860–61

proportioned units that seem uniquely right even
though they do not line up with the organizational
scheme of the adjacent walls. In particular, the screen
wall's short columns with overscaled capitals relate
sympathetically to the heavy circular piers of the
nave. This project is also interesting in that it reveals Burges' ability to coordinate and direct the
efforts of a talented design team—Nicholls (sculptor), Burne-Jones (glass designer), and Poynter
(ceiling painter)—to a single aesthetic effect.

All Saints Church, Fleet, Hampshire

In 1860 through 1862, Burges was involved with the design and construction of the Church of All Saints, Fleet. Burges' client was Charles Edward Lefroy, Secretary to the Speaker of the House of Commons, who intended the church to be a memorial to his late wife, Janet Walker, daughter of Alfred Burges' engineering partner. Lefroy died before the church was completed; Walker paid for the completion of the church as a joint memorial to his daughter and son-in-law.

The church is small and its plan is simple—an apsidal basilica. It is constructed of red brick over a concrete core. The nave is covered with a steep (sixty degree) roof that is extended, at a gentler slope, over the wide aisles. The church has no clerestory. An arcaded porch with a lean-to roof runs completely across the west facade; above it a large wheel window is the single major decorative feature of the facade. All details are simple and bold—typically Burgesian.

The interior is much more elaborate. Mordaunt Crook calls it an "excursion in polychrome abstraction." He describes the interior in the following passage from his seminal work on Burges, *William Burges and the High Victorian Dream*:

> Taking Ruskin half-literally, Burges produced an overall scheme of coloured geometrical patterns which accentuated the interior structure without being in the least constructional. Mouldings are limited to the shape of the plainest brick. The brick-pointed piers are

Exterior View of All Saints Church, Fleet, Hampshire, from the West
With All Saints, Burges' mature, simplified, Early French inspired style emerged.

clean and bare. Coloured brick bands, painted white and blue on red; stenciled geometrical motifs scattered on capital and cornice; a vaulted ceiling boarded and painted, dappled with applique signs—North Italian and Sicilian sources have been diluted without distortion.[4]

At All Saints, Burges perfected his simple, bold, Early French-inspired forms and details. He must have been disappointed with the brick and the painted polychrome decoration, however, because almost all his later work was done in stone, and painted geometrical decoration disappears altogether.

Apparently, Waltham Abbey; All Saints, Fleet; and the competitions for the churches at Lille and Istanbul were ample preparation for the design of Burges' first true masterpiece, St. Fin Barre's Cathedral, Cork.

The Cathedral Church of St. Fin Barre, Cork, Ireland

In 1862 a competition was launched for the design of the Church of Ireland cathedral, St. Fin Barre's, to be built in Cork. Undaunted by his earlier unsuccessful competition experiences, Burges tried again.

The competition stipulated that the cost of the proposed structure should be limited to fifteen thousand pounds. After having been disappointed in the Lille and Istanbul competitions, Burges felt justified in departing from the constraints of the program. Instead of designing a modest provincial parish church,

buildable for the stipulated amount, he submitted plans for a grand edifice appropriate for a cathedral church. He freely admitted that construction of his design would cost twice the projected amount, and he appended a statement to this effect to his competition entry. Burges' hope was that the pride and imagination of the selection committee would be stimulated by his design. Apparently his hope was justified, since his design was chosen as the winner.

The venture might still have ended in disaster if Burges had not had the wholehearted support of the Bishop of Cork, John Gregg. Bishop Gregg was an extraordinary fund-raiser; he was also a man of unusual vision who wanted a great cathedral church for his city. By playing upon civic pride and personal rivalries, particularly in stimulating competition between owners of the whiskey and beer industries in Cork, he was able to raise the one hundred thousand pounds actually required to build and decorate the church.[5] Bishop Gregg's accomplishment is even more remarkable considering the size of the Anglican population to be served. R. B. McDowell, in his book *The Church of Ireland, 1869–1969,* indicated that only five percent of the population of the city were Anglican. Cork today is a city of approximately 125,000 people; although County Cork has lost population in the last century, the city itself was considerably smaller at the time the cathedral was built than it is today.

The competition stipulated seating for seven hundred people. It is doubtful, however, whether either Burges or Gregg took this number very seriously. To accommodate that number in St. Fin Barre's Church, half would have to be seated in pews in the aisles with no view of the service. It is more reasonable to assume that Burges designed a church to accommodate three hundred and seventy-five people routinely, with the possibility of adding additional seating for special occasions.

The church that resulted from the efforts of Architect Burges and Bishop Gregg is one of the true masterpieces of the muscular Gothic style. In its form and plan it is as bold, vigorous, and powerful as any other High Victorian church. Its monumental quality is particularly interesting considering the cathedral's small physical size.

Burges' design for the exterior demonstrates amazing virtuosity in the manipulation of scale, material, and mass to monumental effect. From a distance St. Fin Barre's gives the appearance of a great French cathedral transported to Ireland. It dominates its city as its French counterparts do, yet it is less than half their typical length or height. Mordaunt Crook described it as exuding weight, power, and majesty. He said, "It crouches, heavily muscled, like some tumescent beast, waiting to spring."[6]

Burges borrowed freely from French prototypes, but he always modified the element borrowed so that it would relate properly to the much smaller size of St. Fin Barre's. Everywhere the emphasis is upon the geometry of the wall rather than the sculpture of the mass; and the number of elements is, of course, reduced. The limited budget and small size of the church necessitated this change of emphasis, yet little architectural impact is lost in the transition. Burges was able to accomplish this architectural

Exterior View of St. Fin Barre Cathedral, Cork, Ireland, from the West
Burges combined the shallow triple arches of Chartres with the triangular pediments of Laon.

miracle by careful proportioning of all parts, by utilization of an ordering grid that affected the design of all facade elements, by skillful optical manipulation of the ordering geometry, by the choice of an exterior wall material that reflects light and reveals form whatever atmospheric conditions prevail, and by the marriage of architectural form and sculpture in a uniquely successful way.

Burges used three spires to offset the stumpy horizontality of the church's main mass. The crossing spire, in particular, is a vertical element designed to be in equilibrium with the horizontal line of the main body of the church and to anchor the church to its site while carrying the eye heavenward. The twin spires of the west front frame the crossing spire and bracket the central bay of the facade with its major entrance portal, rose window, and pediment. The three spires and the ambiguity of exterior scale contribute more than anything else to the successful silhouette of the building and to its impression of monumentality.

Careful examination of the entrance facade reveals Burges' ordering system. The basic module of the facade, and the center of the composition, is the square panel filled with the rose window surrounded by the sculptures of the symbols of the four evangelists in the corner spandrels. This square is the basis for the design of each of the four vertical stages of the facade, excluding the spires. Burges builds his composition upon a triple porch which is three modules wide and one and one-half modules

Exterior View of St. Fin Barre Cathedral, Cork, from the Northeast
The three spires are hybrid simplifications of Chartres' southwest spire and the spire at Senlis.

Exterior View of St. Fin Barre Cathedral,
Cork, from the Southwest

Exterior Detail of the West Facade at St. Fin Barre Cathedral, Cork
Nicholl's four evangelists fill the spandrels and bracket the rose.

high. To increase the importance of the central doorway, its recess is allowed to occupy the entire central module and its enframing pediment is permitted to project above the module and the pediments of the flanking doorways. The recesses of the side portals plus their surrounding wall surfaces are each one module wide.

To emphasize the projection of the triple portal from the main body of the church and to form a horizontal baseline for the composition of the upper facade, Burges inserts an open balustrade between the pediments of the portals. This balustrade becomes the visual baseline upon which the second tier of squares seems to sit; it also allows the sec-

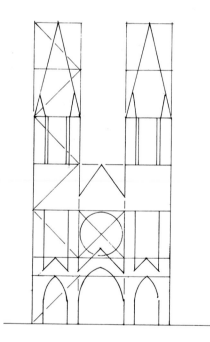

Diagram of the Facade Geometry at St. Fin Barre Cathedral, Cork

ond tier to be seen in its entirety from the ground in spite of the projection of the porch—an important consideration inasmuch as the square containing the rose window is the only perfect expression of the facade module.

The third tier of the facade retains a square module in each of the towers but inserts a triangular pediment between them as an expression of the roof ridge and pitch. This third tier of geometric modules is separated from the tier below it by a sloping horizontal cornice line that continues around the building to become the eave line of the building's major roofs.

The fourth tier of the facade towers repeats the module once again but gives it a very open character in contrast to the closed stage below; here the spires change from square to octagonal in form, with most of their wall surface opened to grills.

The same sort of ordering system is obvious on the sides of the building. Buttresses function as grid lines; the clerestory wall is expressed as a series of square modules; the aisle wall is a series of rectangular modules the same width as the modules in the clerestory above but half again as tall.

Burges was particularly prescient in his choice of stone for the exterior masonry—Cork limestone—for it weathers to a beautiful uniform white which changes color as the sun appears or disappears and the time of day changes. In bright sunlight it sparkles like crystal, and it changes from brilliant white to gold as the sun sets. On dark days and in the moonlight it takes on a luminous silvery gray glow. The stone is hard; it resists deterioration from weather and urban pollution; it reflects light;

Exterior View of St. Fin Barre Cathedral, Cork, from the South, Showing the Geometry of the Side Walls

153

Exterior Detail of the Sculpture on the
South Tower of St. Fin Barre Cathedral,
Cork
Burges' sense of humor is most often
revealed in Sculpture.

and it encourages and retains crisp, hard edges that
help define wall modules and sculptural decoration.
The figures in the western portals, however, were
carved in London by Burges' sculptor associate,
Thomas Nicholls, of Ballinasloe limestone that has
not weathered nearly so well as the local stone.

Because the size of the building dictated walls thinner than the monumental constructions of thirteenth-
century France and because of Burges' ordered
geometrical approach to design, the building's mass
is less sculptural and more planar in form than is the
norm in medieval cathedrals. Instead of sculpting
the total mass, Burges decorates his planar forms
with sculpture—1,260 pieces of sculpture in all according to R. Caulfield, secretary of the building
committee who documented the progress of the ca-

thedral's construction.[7] Almost all pieces were first
sketched by Burges, then modeled in plaster in
London by Nicholls, and finally carved in place by
R. McLeod, a local stone-mason, and his assistants.
Exceptions are the saints and virgins that decorate
the portals mentioned above and the four evange-
listic beasts that surround the rose window. The
latter were inspired by Assyrian reliefs in the British
Museum, according to an article in the *Building
News* of 1883.[8]

Nicholls' models for these four sculptures were
transformed into the actual stone of the wall by
C. W. Harrison of Dublin, a sculptor of note. The
resulting integration of sculpture and architecture is
awesome. The integrity of the square wall module is
undamaged, even accentuated, by the taut composi-

tion that completely fills the slightly recessed plane. Moreover, the four spandrel sculptures, with their gleaming gold mosaic grounds, reconcile the circular form of the window to the rectilinear grid of the facade. Other sculpture, though less dramatic, serves to enliven planar architectural forms while adding meaning and even humor to the ensemble. The encounter of the monk and griffin on the southwest corner tower, for example, is delightfully witty.

The plan reflects Burges desire for order and regularity. It is a Latin cross plan with an apsidal sanctuary surrounded by an ambulatory. It is an ordered simplification of the plan of Noyon Cathedral, minus half the nave and the outer ambulatory, and with the transepts shortened; the basic bay size is even approximately the same. The plan is modular in much the same way that fifteenth-century Florentine Renaissance basilicas are modular. The basic

plan module is a square, approximately twenty-eight feet to a side, contained within the four great piers that mark the crossing. The transepts each repeat this basic module. The nave is composed of five rectangular half-modules. (Burges originally intended only four half-modules so that the nave would have a more perfect geometrical relationship to the choir and sanctuary but was impressed into lengthening it by his client.) Both aisles are composed of square quarter modules. The ambulatory continues the aisle width; the spatial units, however, change from square to trapezoidal as they encircle the sanctuary.

Pure geometric modularity is adjusted at the sanctuary to counter the diminution of depth resulting from foreshortening and from the change of shape from square to half-round. The first two bays of the sanctuary are rectangles that are approximately seven and one-half feet by twenty-eight feet rather than fourteen feet by twenty-eight feet. The sanctuary is completed by a semicircular bay with a radius of fourteen feet. The semicircle is divided,

Plan of St. Fin Barre Cathedral, Cork
Burges' plan is a simplification of the plan of Noyon Cathedral.

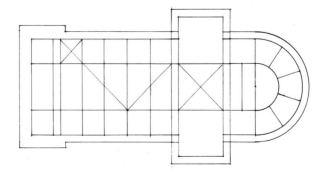

Plan Diagram of St. Fin Barre Cathedral, Cork
The basic module is the twenty-eight square at the crossing.

155

however, into five arcs with chords of approximately seven and one-half feet each. Because the strong regular rhythm of the nave columns with their engaged shafts continues into the sanctuary after its interruption by the crossing/choir, the eye of the viewer is deceived into assuming that the modular dimensions of the nave and sanctuary are the same and that the sanctuary is, consequently, considerably larger than it really is.

Optical adjustment of this type does not diminish the strongly regular order of the space but rather reinforces it. Without this adjustment, the sanctuary would have seemed extremely shallow; with it the sanctuary is spatially strong enough and, at two and one-half modules in height, vertical enough to be the logical climax of the powerful longitudinal plan dynamic. The result is a space that is superbly organized, ordered, and proportioned.

The emphasis on the sanctuary is reinforced by a change of colors and materials as well. The interior of the nave and choir seems monochromatic. The great piers that define the crossing, and contain the choir, are built of a warm light gray-brown Stourton stone. The columns, arches, and shafts of the nave are constructed of a local stone of similar color. The wall surfaces between these architectural elements are slightly darker, grayer stone. Color changes emphasize geometry, modularity, and verticality, but in a soft, understated way. The strong horizontal movement is arrested by a great flood of light that enters the space from the lantern at the crossing and prepares the viewer, much like an angelic trumpet fanfare might, for the glories of the sanctuary.

Colors and materials are anything but monochromatic in the sanctuary. The three-storied shafts and the columns of the first story arcade are polished

Interior View toward the Chancel at St. Fin Barre Cathedral, Cork
The impression of great size is due in part to the extreme verticality of the space that suggests the spaces of the great French cathedrals.

Interior View of the Chancel Wall and Ceiling
at St. Fin Barre Cathedral, Cork

St. Fin Barre Cathedral, Cork
The Chancel window is by Weeks and Saunders, under Burges' direction. Christ appears as King and Priest.

red Cork marble. The columns of the second and third story arcades are polished Irish green marble. The column capitals are painted green and gold. The wall surfaces and arch soffits are inlaid with patterns in red, green, and gold, with touches of blue and white. The great tre-foiled roof is predominantly blue and gold; it is painted to portray Christ in Glory surrounded by angels carrying either churches, one of which is St. Fin Barre's Cathedral, or candlesticks. The angelic host continues down onto the wall of the arch spandrels of the upper tier. The sanctuary pavement is a multi-colored marble mosaic executed by Italian craftsmen but designed by Burges. It illustrates Matthew 13:47, in which the Kingdom of Heaven is likened to "a net cast into the sea that gathered up of every kind." It includes all sorts of human and animal forms. The colored pavement continues down the sanctuary steps into the choir where the pattern changes to a more traditional geometric one. The choir is separated from the sanctuary by a low brass screen and from the nave by a low white marble wall inlaid with colored marbles and gold mosaics.

Colored light streams in brightly from the clerestory windows in the third tier of arches; these windows contain single figures posed against white glass grounds. Burges' design for the central of these windows, above the high altar, is a powerful figure, almost Assyrian in appearance. It portrays Christ reigning from the cross as King and Priest and is a pendant figure to the Christ Enthroned on the ceiling. More color but less light is admitted by the windows of the first level ambulatory. The sanctuary itself was intended to be filled with light; the ambulatory that surrounds it, and can be seen through the first level arcade, is intended to be dark in contrast. Consequently, its windows include virtually no white or transparent glass; their designs are made of brightly colored glass that gleams like jewels in the dark space beyond the sanctuary.

Both Mordaunt Crook, in his description of Cork Cathedral in *William Burges and the High Victorian Dream,* and the local guidebook to St. Fin Barre indicate that Burges originally intended to extend the polychromy of the sanctuary to the nave as well. If this is true, it is fortunate that either financial constraints made it impossible or that Burges changed his mind. At present we have a sanctuary that is a dramatic conclusion in its color, richness, verticality, and manipulation of light to the powerful longitudinal movement of the nave. If the nave had received similar polychromatic treatment, the balance between the longitudinal nave space and the vertical sanctuary space would have been diminished, as would the symbolic portrayal of pilgrimage to God through a dull world to His radiant presence on the altar in the sanctuary. (It is interesting to note that Burges, in his churches at Skelton and Studley Royal in North Yorkshire, where money was no object, again contrasted brilliantly decorated, reliquary-like sanctuaries with monochromatic naves.)

Burges was extremely conscious of the power of spatial movement from narthex to sanctuary. He equated spatial movement to the passage of time and used the iconography of the stained glass to illustrate this idea. Consequently, the great west rose window in the entrance facade is filled with stained glass depicting the creation of the world as described in Genesis; the windows in the aisles portray scenes from the Old Testament which foreshadow New Testament events; the clerestory windows include signs of the Zodiac; and the sanctuary and ambulatory windows portray events in the life, death, and resurrection of Christ. The entire iconographic program culminates in the figure of Christ Enthroned on the sanctuary ceiling—the visual focus toward which the column shafts and roof ribs seem to point.

The early French Gothic style that Burges chose to use for St. Fin Barre's Cathedral—the style of the cathedrals of Sens, Senlis, Noyon, and Laon—is a heavy style much like the Early English style of the thirteenth century. It is a transitional style that retains much of the massive masonry wall that characterizes French Romanesque architecture but uses pointed arches and geometric traceried windows and a taller, more slender, more graceful proportion of space and architectural elements. The viewer is very conscious of the weight of the masonry construction at St. Fin Barre; massive masonry walls carried by heavy circular columns at the first level rise three stories on either side of a narrow nave and sanctuary. Burges is very skillful, however, in minimizing the apparent weight of the construction by opening up the wall in arcades at all three stories, by layering the wall so that the inner surface appears to be much thinner than it actually is (this is particularly noticeable in the windows of the aisles and clerestory), by manipulating the light so that the inner space is seen as bright against darker spaces beyond except at the clerestory level, and by substituting a painted wooden ceiling for the stone vaults that are found in most early French churches. (Only the aisles, ambulatory, and lantern are vaulted at St. Fin Barre.) The result is emphasis upon light rather than mass—light that floods into the church through the lantern and clerestory windows, pulling the worshipper forward toward the altar and directing his gaze upward to heavenly realms above.

Burges was faced with the problem of how to imbue a relatively small church building with the power, grandeur, and monumentality associated with a cathedral. He solved this architectural problem through selection of an appropriately monumental architectural style, modular design in three dimensions, optical spatial manipulation, emphasis upon light and spatial interpenetration, imaginative design detail and decoration, and equilibrium between vertical and horizontal movement. Burges produced an ordered architectural form and space that testify to his understanding of the architect's palette.

The Churches of Christ the Consoler, Skelton-on-Ure, and St. Mary, Studley Royal, North Yorkshire

Burges' most celebrated ecclesiastical works are the two churches near Ripon in North Yorkshire done for the mother-in-law and wife of George Frederick Robinson, First Marquess of Ripon, a wealthy landowner and politician, prominent in the political and social life of the day. (Burges was exceptionally fortunate in having clients of virtually unlimited wealth who were willing to give their architect carte blanche to design whatever he thought appropriate. From 1868 until his death in 1881, Burges spent a considerable portion of his time upon the design and deco-

ration of two castles—Cardiff Castle and Castel Coch—for the Third Marquess of Bute, the richest man in the world at that time.)

Lord Ripon shared Burges' and Bute's fascination for things medieval, so it is not surprising that he desired churches in the Gothic style. (Incidentally, Ripon's estate at Studley Royal contains the grandest medieval ruin in England, Fountains Abbey, incorporated as a feature of the garden lay-out.)

The two churches were built as memorials to Lord Ripon's brother-in-law, Frederick Granthan Vyner, who was killed by Greek bandits in 1870. Burges had been a friend of Lord Vyner, Frederick's father, at Oxford, and Ripon and Bute were close friends, so it is not surprising that Burges was chosen to design these churches. Lady Vyner is responsible for the construction of the Church of Christ the Consoler at Skelton, on the Vyner estate, Newby Hall. Her daughter, Lady Ripon, built the church of St. Mary, Studley Royal, on her estate nearby.

The churches were commissioned in 1870 and begun in 1871. The church at Skelton was consecrated in 1876. The church at Studley Royal took two years longer to build and was twice as expensive as that at Skelton (fifty thousand pounds versus twenty-five thousand pounds) although it is about the same size. The naves of both churches are about sixty-four feet long, by nineteen feet wide, by forty-two feet high. Both churches involved the same artist team— Burges, the architect in charge, directing Nicholls the sculptor, Weekes the glass designer, and Lonsdale the painter.

Of the two churches, Christ the Consoler is the more picturesque. Here Burges chose to place the tower in the east end of the north aisle where it connects and balances the horizontal nave and chancel

Exterior View of the Church of Christ the Consoler, Skelton-on-Ure, North Yorkshire, from the South

blocks. The chancel is much lower than the nave; its roof eave occurs approximately at the level of the intersection of aisle roof with nave clerestory wall. The result is a balanced composition with its center of gravity at the visual center of the composition. Each compositional unit is boldly and precisely edged; the silhouette is crisp and linear. The design of the spire reveals Burges' mastery of form manipulation. The transition from square tower to octagonal spire is not managed with broaches but with crisply cut, steeply sloped pyramids that look more like obelisks than pinnacles.

At Skelton, the surfaces of the forms are richly sculpted; they are boldly cut away to reveal figurative and architectural sculptures that emphasize the thickness and plasticity of the mass. These surfaces are the opposite of Butterfield's planar compositions; they are perfect examples of architecture designed as sculpture. Tracery does not seem to be inserted into the walls. (Each window's outermost tracery molding is flush with the surrounding wall face, and the stone of the tracery is the same as the stone of the wall.) Buttresses are strong, blocky, and simple in silhouette and decorated with carved heraldic emblems.

Shadow is carefully manipulated to emphasize mass. For example, the upper half of the great wheel window of the west facade is flush with the wall face above so that shadow will fall into the recess created by the window, but its lower half projects past the face of the wall below so that its shadow will visually reinforce the circular shape of the window. Burges accomplishes this seemingly impossible feat by engaging the circle on either side with buttresses and sculpted figures, allowing him to make the thickness of the wall different above and below the window.

Exterior View of the Church of Christ the Consoler, Showing Burges' Use of Overscaled Detail, from the Southwest

The gable recesses that hold the figures of the Good Shepherd with sheep (the south entrance porch) and Christ the Consoler (the east facade) are plainly carved out of the walls. The figures themselves, although richly three-dimensional, engage the wall; they are never completely separated from it. Consequently, the figurative sculpture seems to have an intrinsic relationship to the architecture; it is not extraneous sculpture introduced to fill architectural niches. The entire architectural ensemble is *sculptural;* it is not architecture *decorated* with sculpture.

The interior of Christ the Consoler seems larger than it really is. It is characterized by the same sort of scale manipulation Burges had employed so successfully at Cork. The various parts—piers, arches, chancel wall, organ, pulpit, etc.—are so richly sculptural and monumental that they have a power and presence considerably greater than their size would indicate. Most notable is the sculptural treatment of the chancel wall that completely fills the space between arch and roof.

What is truly amazing is that the combination of these massive elements does not seem to be overbearing or cramped. Burges lightens the composition by making all parts light in color, by flooding the interior with natural light, and by introducing a second, very delicate and light-weight architectural system. The deeply recessed windows of the chancel are filled with a second layer of delicate tracery placed in the plane of the inner wall surface; slender black Irish marble shafts support the arches of aisle and clerestory windows and the cross-braces of the wood wagon roof of the nave; clusters of equally slender multi-colored marble shafts carry the stone ribs of the chancel vaults.

Exterior Detail at the Church of Christ the Consoler, Skelton-on-Ure
Nicholl's Christ the Good Shepherd is on the gable of the south entrance porch.

163

Interior View toward the Chancel at the
Church of Christ the Consoler, Skelton-
on-Ure
Exaggerated scale and heavy proportion give
importance to the small interior.

164

The introduction, at Skelton, of elements that are light-weight into a very heavy architectural armature is eminently successful and uniquely Burgesian. The secret of the success of this interior is not, however, due exclusively to the contrast of delicate elements with heavy ones or to the beauty of the sculptural forms. If Burges had chosen to use the rich, varied color palette characteristic of the High Victorian era, the interior of Christ the Consoler would have been oppressive indeed. Burges' heavy architectural forms and rich sculptural elements work in this restricted space *only* because of the light (almost white), monochromatic color scheme and the flood of light introduced into the space which reveals the exquisite sculptural detail. With the exception of the stained glass and the tile floors, color is used only to emphasize the importance of critical ecclesiastical features—altar, pulpit, font, organ chamber, and sanctuary.

It would be misleading to infer that color plays no part in the effectiveness of the interior of Christ the Consoler, however. Burges' use of color, while restrained, is singularly effective. The use of red, green, and black marble for the chancel shafts, the gold and multi-colored mosaics that decorate the altar reredos and chancel rail, the pavement of red and yellow tile, and the jewel-like hues of the stained glass add richness and vitality to the largely monochromatic interior. In particular, the stained glass, both in this church and in St. Mary, Studley Royal, is among the very best produced during the Victorian era. Its interesting, creative patterns are executed in very bright colored glass, but the backgrounds are white. The colored glass throws bits of colored light on the white architectural surfaces; the white glass admits lots of natural light.

The Church of Christ the Consoler, Skelton-on-Ure
The interior detail of the chancel wall shows the layering of a light interior screen wall over a heavy exterior wall.

165

Like the Church of Christ the Consoler, St. Mary, Studley Royal, has a four-bay aisled and clerestoried nave and a lower unaisled chancel divided into choir and sanctuary. The plan is derived from Pugin's Church of St. Giles at Cheadle. The tower and spire, as at St. Giles, is located in the center of the west facade. The silhouette of the church is much more formal and traditional than at Skelton, undoubtedly because the church is sited at the head of the avenue that led through the park at Studley Royal to the house and the abbey ruins.

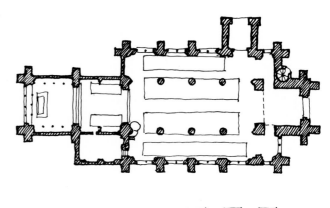

Plan of the Church of St. Mary, Studley Royal, North Yorkshire
Burges' plan is based upon Pugin's plan for St. Giles, Cheadle.

Exterior View of the Church of St. Mary, Studley Royal, from the West
St. Mary's spire replaced an eighteenth-century obelisk; its form was carefully developed to perform the same symbolic function.

The style of St. Mary is more elaborate and much less English than Christ the Consoler. It is an interesting blend of French, Italian, and English Gothic architecture. The crocketed gables over the chancel windows are French, as are the rose window in the west facade, the lean-to porch, and the treatment of the junction of tower and spire. The geometrical window tracery and most interior details are English and borrow from the cathedral churches at Salisbury, Ripon, and Lincoln. The wooden nave roof is based upon San Zeno in Verona, and the sanctuary vault is inspired in part by the sacristy of the cathedral in Padua and in part by Islamic vaulting. It is a mark of Burges' true genius as a designer that these divergent elements merge to become a totally satisfying unity.

The exterior of St. Mary, particularly of the chancel, is so heavily encrusted with canopies and crockets that the bold balance between architecture and sculpture, between mass and detail, which characterizes the exterior of Christ the Consoler, is lost. Although the figurative sculpture is equally fine and the church includes some bold Burgesian details—notably the complex composition of paired cinquefoil-headed lancets at various scales that make the east facade so unusual and the play of three different arch forms (cusped, pointed, and segmental) in different planes in the west portal—the exterior of the church at Studley Royal is not as satisfying as the church at Skelton. It does, however, perform its nodal function admirably. It seems to be much larger than it really is because of the careful proportioning of the parts and the pyramidal build-up of aisles, chancel, and nave to support the dominant vertical form of the spire.

Exterior View of the Church of St. Mary, Studley Royal, from the Southeast
This drawing shows the rich, unconventional encrustation of the east facade with sculpture.

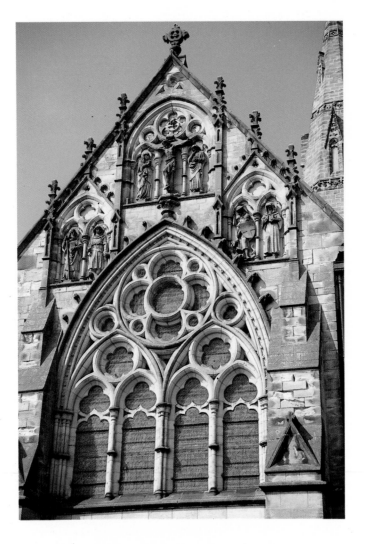

Exterior Detail of the East Facade at the Church of St. Mary, Studley Royal

The glory of St. Mary is its interior. Although it is similar to Christ the Consoler in many ways—its parts are richly sculptural; it plays a delicate architectural system against a massive heavy architectural envelope; it uses similar materials and a similar color scheme; its figurative sculpture and stained glass are similar in design approach and quality—the differences in the two churches are also important.

The interior of St. Mary is not only much more richly decorated but is much taller, more vertical in character, than is Christ the Consoler; consequently, the architectural elements are much less stumpy, blocky, and massive and are much more attenuated. The church does not have Skelton's extreme muscularity of form either inside or out. The height of the arcade is increased and the importance of the clerestory is diminished, although the cusped-arch form of the clerestory window recesses is one of the church's bolder, more masculine design details. The three-lobed wood nave roof, similar to the one at St. Fin Barre, echoes the cusped form of the clerestory windows and, at the same time, emphasizes vertical thrust. The opening into the chancel is also higher than at Skelton—an important difference inasmuch as the elaborately painted choir and sanctuary ceilings are made more visible and, hence, more effective. In proportion and in design detail, St. Mary seems to be more traditional, more true to historic precedent, than does Christ the Consoler.

Burges' most successful allusion at Studley Royal is not, however, his borrowings from the Gothic past but rather his concept of the sanctuary as a golden reliquary safely contained within, and detached from, the stone walls of the enclosing church. The density of color and light increases as one moves toward the chancel, which is designed as a precious, jeweled

Interior View toward the Chancel at the
Church of St. Mary, Studley Royal

Interior Detail of the Sanctuary Ceiling at the Church of St. Mary, Studley Royal

tabernacle—the destination at the end of the worshipper's path marked by a faceted golden dome over the altar, a development of the chancel roof at St. Fin Barre. The outer building shell is heavy and monochromatic; it stands for the world inhabited by fallen man. In contrast, the chancel is light and polychromed; it represents God's heavenly abode. Like a Byzantine sanctuary, it gleams with rich colors and materials—alabaster walls, mosaic floors, gilded and painted ceiling—all flooded with colored light from the windows which portray scenes from the Revelation of Saint John. No detail is without symbolic significance. The floor mosaics depict the shrines of the Holy City and the chancel steps symbolize, in their colors, man's original purity (white), his fall (black), and his ultimate purification through the blood of Christ's sacrifice (red). The beasts of the world carved on the pew ends join the heavenly chorus of angelic figures overhead and the saints and martyrs in the Te Deum parade in singing God's praise. The chancel is a theatrical glimpse of the glories of a heavenly eternity in the presence of God. What a reassuring message this is for the devoted family of the slain young man. It is also a fascinating essay in architectural symbolic language, if we are perceptive enough to read it.

Interior View toward the West Entrance Showing the Organ
on the Right at the Church of St. Mary, Studley Royal

NOTES

1. J. Mordaunt Crook, *William Burges and the High Victorian Dream* (Chicago: University of Chicago Press, 1981), 66.

2. William Burges, *Art Applied to Industry* (London: n.p., 1865), 113–18.

3. Crook, 123–25.

4. Crook, 194.

5. Maurice Carey, *St. Fin Barre's Cathedral,* Irish Heritage Series: 48 (Norwich: Eason, 1984), 7.

6. Crook, 199.

7. R. Caulfield, *Handbook of the Cathedral Church of St. Fin Barre* (Cork: n.p., 1881), 51.

8. *Building News* XLIV (1883), 868.

Butterfield locator:

1. All Saints, Margaret Street, London
2. St. Matthias, Stoke Newington, London
3. St. James, Baldersby, Yorkshire
4. St. Alban, Holborn, London
5. Holy Cross, Ashton New Road, Clayton, Manchester
6. St. Augustine, Penarth, Glamorgan
7. All Saints, Babbacombe, Torquay, Devon
8. St. Augustine, Queen's Gate, South Kensington, London
9. Rugby School Chapel, Warwickshire
10. Keble College Chapel, Oxford, Oxfordshire

Street locator:

1. St. Peter, Bournemouth, Hampshire
2. All Saints, Boyne Hill, Maidenhead, Berkshire
3. St. John, Howsham, Yorkshire
4. St. James the Less, Vauxhall Bridge Road, Westminster, London
5. St. Philip and St. James, Oxford, Oxfordshire
6. All Saints, Denstone, Staffordshire
7. St. Saviour, Eastbourne, East Sussex
8. St. Mary Magdalen, Woodchester Square, Paddington, London
9. Bristol Cathedral, Bristol

Pearson locator:

1. St. Leonard, Scarborough, Yorkshire
2. St. Mary, Dalton Holme, Yorkshire
3. St. Peter, Daylesford, Worcestershire/ Gloucestershire
4. St. Mary, Catherston Leweston, Dorset
5. St. James, Titsey, Surrey
6. St. Peter, Vauxhall, London
7. Christ Church, Appleton-le-Moors, Yorkshire
8. St. Mary, Freeland, Oxfordshire
9. St. Augustine, Kilburn Park, Paddington, London

Burges locator:

1. Waltham Abbey, Essex
2. All Saints, Fleet, Hampshire
3. St. Fin Barre's Cathedral, Cork, Ireland
4. Christ the Consoler, Skelton-on-Ure, Yorkshire
5. St. Mary, Studley Royal, Yorkshire

PART II

The Followers

HENRY WOODYER
WILLIAM WHITE
GEORGE FREDERICK BODLEY

HENRY WOODYER

 **enry** Woodyer (1819–96) was one of the first and most successful followers of William Butterfield. In fact, he received his architectural training in the Butterfield office during the 1840s. Apparently he learned much from his experience there; his work, like Butterfield's, is always original and carefully studied throughout, and the forms and spaces of his buildings are invariably satisfying.

Woodyer was the son of a successful Guildford physician, and his first architectural commissions were received from clients in the region. His practice quickly expanded to other regions, particularly in the County of Surrey. When his practice was successfully established, he purchased a small estate at Graffham, near Cranleigh, on the Sussex border, where he lived for the rest of his life, except for summers which he spent cruising the Mediterranean on his yacht, the Queen Mab.

Although Woodyer shared Butterfield's dislike of publicity and professionalism, never allowing his designs to be published and never joining a professional society, in other ways he was very different from his mentor. He was something of a Bohemian, greatly enjoying the good life. His pupil and colleague, Harry Redfern, described him as follows in a paper read to the Ecclesiological Society:

> What a distinguished looking man Henry Woodyer was! Tall, rather spare; always attired in an easy-fitting blue serge suit, loose shirt collar and crimson silk tie. His soft black hat—rather wide in the brim—bore a small steel brooch in front. During inclement weather a long dark Inverness cloak was worn. . . . A most picturesque figure, often smoking an extremely fragrant cigar. I envied him.[1]

Woodyer worked consistently in the Middle Pointed or Decorated English Gothic style. Even when most other English architects of the Gothic Revival embraced French Gothic architecture in the second decade of the High Victorian period, Woodyer remained true to the Decorated style. Yet he rarely copied Decorated prototypes directly. Eastlake commended Woodyer as being able to catch the spirit of Old English work without imitating it. In describing Woodyer's church and orphanage at Bovey Tracey, Eastlake said, "It is the design of an architect who has profited by antiquarian study—not that of an antiquary who has tried his hand at architecture."[2]

Although Woodyer tried various approaches to design in the 1850s—Tenbury Wells is almost a "rogue" design, whereas Highnam is an orthodox design that carefully follows Tractarian percepts—his work was always scholarly, beautifully proportioned, and elegantly decorated. He developed a number of stylistic characteristics that help identify his work. These include the tendency to concentrate decoration on critical features rather than distribute it generally and to design interiors that are spatially simple. He liked naturalistic sculptural ornament, acutely chamfered window mullions, and cusped tracery that is "thorny" in silhouette. All his buildings have idiosyncratic features or details, yet nowhere do these seem extravagant or out-of-place. Woodyer always managed to make every design decision within the larger context of his design concept for the job at hand.

Holy Innocents Church, Highnam, Gloucestershire

Holy Innocents was Woodyer's first major work after leaving Butterfield's office, and many regard it as his masterpiece. It is a Decorated church, built in 1849 through 1851. It is contemporary with Butterfield's great church, All Saints, Margaret Street, but it is very unlike it, although both were extremely well received by the Ecclesiological Society. Henry-Russell Hitchcock called it a "most important Anglican example of painted internal polychromy, rivaling Pugin's St. Giles, Cheadle," and Goodhardt-Rendel called it the "fulfillment of the Pugin ideal."[3] These comments are certainly apt ones, because the church is much more like Pugin's masterpiece than anything of Butterfield's.

Both Holy Innocents and St. Giles are dominated by extremely tall west towers and spires (two hundred feet tall at Holy Innocents) set on the longitudinal axis of the church, and both have extremely rich painted decoration on their interior surfaces. (Unlike St. Giles, however, Holy Innocents has no portal in the west, tower facade.) Both share the Decorated style and both have monochromatic stone exteriors. Both have extremely tall, narrow naves with slightly lower chancels. Both have five-bay naves with north and south aisles. Both have rood screens to divide the nave from the chancel.

But just as the similarities between the two churches are significant, so are the differences. The gray stone of the exterior wall at Holy Innocents is left with a much rougher texture than the beige ashlar of St. Giles. The silhouette of the tower at Holy

177

The West Facades of Holy Innocents Church, Highnam, and St. Giles, Cheadle
The exterior appearances of the two churches are very much alike. Their towers and spires are of similar height and design and are located on the centers of the churches' longitudinal axes.

Interior View of a Clerestory Bay Showing the Unusual Clerestory and Dormer Windows at Holy Innocents Church, Highnam, Gloucestershire

Innocents is much simpler than at St. Giles. Holy Innocents' broached spire has one instead of two pinnacles, and the crockets that give the spire at St. Giles such a spiky appearance are de-emphasized. The result of these exterior differences is that Holy Innocents has a much stronger, more muscular character than St. Giles.

Interior differences are also significant. Holy Innocents is much more brightly lighted than St. Giles. The interior of the Pugin church is lighted exclusively by the aisle windows and the great east window of the chancel; consequently, it is very dark.

Woodyer adds clerestory windows of two extremely interesting and unusual types. The clerestory wall has quatrefoil oculi set in very deep cusped, arched reveals that look like something from a Portuguese Rococo church. Centered above these windows are slender, bifurcated, arched, dormer windows. Because the nave bays are lifted to achieve double clerestory light, the proportion of the space is much taller and narrower than at St. Giles.

Woodyer improves over St. Giles in the design of the rood screen for Holy Innocents. Pugin's rood screen at St. Giles is so heavy that it effectively cuts off the chancel from the nave. Woodyer lightens and simplifies his so that separation is subtly suggested rather than enforced.

The particular glory of the Highnam church is its interior decoration. This decoration was designed in part by Woodyer and in part by his client, Thomas Gambier-Parry. Woodyer is responsible for the pattern decoration of stenciled walls and painted moldings; Gambier-Parry is responsible for the frescoes in the aisles—the expulsion from Paradise, the Annunciation, and the Entry into Jerusalem—and the Last Judgment on the chancel arch. Woodyer approached painted decoration very differently from Bodley. Bodley's decoration invariably minimizes weight and de-emphasizes structure; Woodyer uses decoration to emphasize mass and delineate structure.

The decoration of the moldings that comprise the chancel arch is typical; each molding is picked out in

Interior View toward the Chancel at Holy Innocents Church, Highnam
The chancel wall is decorated with particularly successful frescoes by Woodyer's client, Thomas Gambier-Parry.

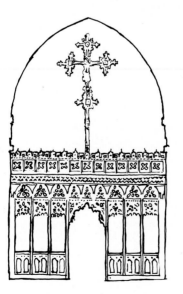

Choir Screen Designs at St. Giles, Cheadle, and Holy Innocents Church, Highnam
Woodyer's design features fewer, but larger and simpler, elements than does Pugin's.

Aisle Window Detail at Holy Innocents Church, Highnam

its own color and pattern, emphasizing that the arch is made-up of a collection of moldings. Similarly, decoration is used to emphasize the thickness of the wall where windows occur in the aisles; each recessed window is designed as a discrete space with its side walls recessed behind the arch molding on the inner face of the aisle wall. Painted continuous patterns emphasize these recessed planes. Gambier-Parry's aisle processions are made even more dynamic by

the drapery and wainscot patterns Woodyer paints below them. (The drapery of the middle tier is an unusual bit of trompe-l'oeil painting; most patterns are strictly two-dimensional geometric ones.)

In all decorative details, it is clear that Woodyer was in total control. In this he was like Bodley; but where Bodley's patterns are painterly, Woodyer's are strongly architectonic in character.

181

Exterior View of the Church of St. Michael and All Angels, Tenbury Wells, Worcestershire, from the Southeast

Steep roofs, tall clerestory, and full-height transepts contribute to the impression of great height.

The Church of St. Michael and All Angels (R.C.), Tenbury Wells, Worcestershire

The Church of St. Michael and All Angels and the college for the education of church musicians to which it is attached were built in 1856. Its patron and benefactor was the Reverend Sir Frederick Gore Ouseley, who paid for its construction.

The church and college make a very picturesque group. They are built on the north and south side, respectively, of a large raised court; they are connected at the back, or east side, by a low wood cloister. The church and college are comparable in mass; the church is taller but the college is longer. The college has three main stories plus a basement and a full attic story under the very steeply sloping roof; stairs are articulated in tower forms with their own roofs. The group would have been even more dramatic if the tower and spire intended for the crossing of the church had been built, although it is extremely handsome in its present form; it seems to be complete as it is.

The church has a four-bay aisled nave, full-height transepts, and a very deep five-sided chancel. Nave, transepts, and chancel are equally tall; they share a common roof ridge and eave lines. The entire church has a wood vaulted ceiling with all ribs expressed. The vertical dimension is dominant throughout. Major roofs have a steep, (sixty degree) pitch; west and transept facades are more than twice as tall as they are wide; a very tall clerestory rises above the low aisle roofs; and chancel windows are extremely slender two-lancet arched windows. Buttresses are used sparingly; the simple geometry of the major masses dominates the composition. The building material is beige field stone, laid in a tight ashlar pattern, dressed with cream stone. Window frames are minimal in width, installed flush with the surrounding wall. Exterior decoration is concentrated on the west and transept facades; blind arcades flank the entry portal in the west facade and span the transept facades in the zone established by the height of the adjacent aisle roofs.

The base of the west facade composition is strengthened by the projection of the north entry porch which was intended to correspond to an unbuilt cloister on the other side. (Woodyer intended to enclose the court with a west cloister similar to the one built on the east. The square headed windows would have continued along the cloister facade.)

The interior of St. Michael and All Angels is disappointing. Only the amazingly modern chancel tile floor (triangles and circles in a free Art-Deco-like design in bright colors), the colorful decoration of the organ pipes, and the magnificent Hardman stained glass suggest the color and vitality of the original church. All wall surfaces have been whitewashed. Moreover, few interior design details reflect the boldness of the exterior composition. The three notable exceptions are the handsome freestanding altar structure, the cusped-arch and canopy of the sedilia with its recess filled with tile sculpted in a geometric pattern, and the two-bay arcade between chancel and chapel (the large arch is divided into two very tall narrow pointed arches by the insertion of a column that carries a panel with a blind rondel). Woodyer's preference for all things steep and vertical remains apparent, however.

Interior View toward the Chancel at the
Church of St. Michael and All Angels, Tenbury Wells
Only a delicate iron screen divides the chancel from the nave. The exterior impression
of great height is confirmed by the tall,
narrow proportion of the interior space.

Christ Church, Reading

Christ Church, Reading, was built from 1861 to 1862 and was enlarged in 1874. It is a typical Woodyer church, powerful and strong in form and silhouette, Decorated in style, with all details carefully coordinated into a well-resolved unity. (Some of these details are idiosyncratic and surprising. This, too, is typical of Woodyer.)

The church is large, 140 feet by 62 feet, and the spire is 150 feet tall. It is built of blue Pennant stone laid in courses so narrow that it looks like brick. It is dressed with Bath stone, generously used. The cream color of the Bath stone makes a dramatic contrast against the very dark stone of the body of the church.

The church is prominently sited; its silhouette dominates the approach to town from the south. The generous churchyard is surrounded by a low wall of the same dark Pennant stone. The tall church rises from between handsome mature trees. The tower and spire dominate the ensemble.

The tower is unusually large. It is placed at the northwest corner of the church; the main entry to the building is through the portal on the north tower facade. The tower rises above the apex of the nave gable of the west facade before the transition to the simple, slender, octagonal spire occurs. The tower is dark stone for two-thirds of its height. The top third is belfry and is constructed of the light Bath stone. The tower is much larger than the base of the spire. The transition from square to octagonal is made by flying buttresses placed on the tower diagonals. This diagonal line is echoed in the diagonal

Exterior View toward the Tower and Spire at Christ Church, Reading, Berkshire

Exterior View of Chancel and Sacristy at Christ Church, Reading
Woodyer uses a gabled form to resolve the different longitudinal
forms of the nave, aisle, and chancel into a unified composition. (Note the use of diagonal buttresses that relate to both
directions.)

buttresses at the corners of the tower. The effect is
very powerful—heavy at the base, becoming lighter
and lighter as the tower rises. Moreover, the massive tower is effectively anchored to the ground by
the splay of the buttress bases. Woodyer showed
unusual perception in the tower design. Anything
less large and strong would have been unable to
stop and resolve the horizontal dynamic of the very
large, very steep aisle and nave roofs or give the
church a silhouette that balances horizontal and vertical masses.

At its east end, the horizontal dynamic of the
major roofs is stopped by the addition of a gabled
sacristy wing that resolves nave, aisle, and chancel
roofs into a particularly harmonious composition.
The corners of the sacristy wing and the square-
ended chancel block all receive diagonal buttresses
like those on the tower. Woodyer uses these to turn
all exterior ninety-degree corners; they add visual
strength and design continuity to the complex three-
dimensional composition.

The exterior design contains a number of Woodyer's interesting design eccentricities. The narrow
band of wall that is the nave clerestory is constructed
completely of the light colored stone; this band is
carved to make a paneled frieze of crocketed arches,
two to an aisle or nave bay. A small portion at the
center of each arch is devoted to a single stumpy,
lancet window. The exterior door to the sacristy engages the sacristy north wall and the diagonal buttress adjacent to it, and it penetrates the row of
lancet windows above. It is suprising that this composition works to integrate these features, but it
does. Fenestration of the west facade—two bifurcated lancet windows, widely spaced, with a triangular window centered in the space above them—

Interior View toward the Chancel Showing the "Veil" That Fills the Arch at Christ Church, Reading

Exterior Detail of the Clerestory Fenestration at Christ Church, Reading
A continuous tracery frieze gives importance to the small lancet windows.

is organized within a decorative cusped-arch molding of Bath stone.

The interior of Christ Church is disappointing, primarily because Woodyer's painted decoration no longer exists; all plaster walls have been painted a uniform cream. Comparison of Christ Church with Holy Innocents reveals what an intrinsic part of the overall design Woodyer's painted patterns were. Some interior details are worth discussion, however.

Certainly the most arresting feature of the interior is the design of the chancel arch. Its upper portion is filled with a "net" of stone tracery. (This net represents the veil of the temple that was lifted by the Passion of Christ.) Through this arch can be seen an elegantly proportioned chancel in which the altar, reredos, and east wall are integrated into a wonderfully unified composition. The altar and reredos are the width of the five-lancet, arched window that echoes the shape of the chancel arch. The canopy of the reredos is divided into the same five divisions as the window above and is visually linked to it by the pinnacles of the canopies that rise up in front of each lancet. (It is a pity that the background wall of Birnie Phillips' bas-relief of the Ascension, which is the feature of the reredos, is painted baby blue; the power of the architectural ensemble is seriously diminished by this color choice.)

Woodyer's pier capitals are as egocentric as his chancel arch. Eastlake found them "difficult to accept as agreeable."[4] They certainly are unusual, but they are designed to echo the canopy forms of the chancel reredos, and, as a device to tie the various parts of the design together, they are successful. The piers are composed of squat, round columns surrounded by eight darker colonnettes at equal intervals, establishing an octagonal form. They carry arches that are composed of clustered moldings. The capitals that marry these two forms are extremely heavy; they are designed as an octagon of eight tall, pointed canopies which are carried by the colonnettes and are decorated with Woodyer's typically naturalistic foliage sculpture. These capitals are not graceful, but they are powerful and interesting, and they are consistent with other details in this strongly individualistic design.

The Church of St. Peter, Hascombe, Surrey

Woodyer's skill as an architect is revealed most clearly in one of his smallest churches, St. Peter's, Hascombe. This church is a favorite of Nikolaus

Pevsner, as it must be of anyone who visits it, for it is a High Victorian gem. Pevsner writes, "St Peter, 1864, [is] worth a very special look to see how good and how free from period associations a Victorian country church could be when the architect took pains over it."[5]

The composition of the masses is simple but delightful because of the careful arrangement and proportioning of each part. There are five elements—a major one, the steeply gabled nave block to which the other forms are attached, and four secondary ones, an apsidal chancel with a roof that echoes the pitch of the nave roof at the lower level and becomes conical over the curve of the apse, a separately roofed lady chapel that is like a repeat of the nave mass at smaller scale, a belfry with a small steeple, and a gabled entry porch at the southwest corner. The relationship of these parts is so carefully considered that their composition is equally successful from every vantage point. (The composition of St. Peter's, Hascombe, is similar to Bodley's composition of Selsley, but it is more successful because all elements are visible from the entry side of the church.)

At least nominally, the style of the church is Decorated, but, in reality, all details are original. All windows are single lancet with Bath stone surrounds that are flush with the Bargate stone of the walls. The windows of the nave and chancel are so tall and slender that they are little more than slits in the wall. The windows of the lady chapel are more generous; they are organized in a frieze of arched panels (much like the clerestory windows of Christ Church); they rest upon a projecting stone sill that wraps this block and differentiates it from the main body of the building. This molding is also the base

Exterior View of the Church of St. Peter, Hascombe, Surrey, from the South

for the chapel's large east window. The east window of the chancel actually penetrates the stumpy buttress that stops the longitudinal axis of the church as its east end. (Pevsner calls this a "roguish detail"; I see it as one of the devices Woodyer used to make every detail an inseparable part of the larger whole.)

The church is as successful inside as out. Almost all decoration is concentrated in the chancel. (The exception is the wonderful painted wainscot pattern of net, stylized waves, and fishes. The fresco of Christ Enthroned on the chancel arch and the upper wall frescoes are 1890 additions. Woodyer intended a simply decorated nave to contrast with the sumptuously decorated chancel.)

Entry into the nave is beneath the floor of the belfry-loft. This lower ceiling in the first nave bay creates a narthex area for entry and font. The nave space is a simple gabled one with steeply sloping (sixty degree) beamed ceilings. Heavy timber beams divide the bays; smaller timbers almost flush with the white ceiling establish a fast rhythm between them. These rafters turn down on the upper nave wall and are laced with horizontal boards that establish a criss-cross pattern. All wood is very dark in contrast to the white plaster of the walls.

The tall slit windows of the exterior are transformed inside, almost magically, into generous windows that flood the nave with light. They are paired into deep, bifurcated recesses with widely splayed reveals that reflect light extremely successfully. The motif of cusped-arch that is the outstanding feature of the chancel ceiling is echoed here.

The most exciting part of St. Peter's is its chancel. It glows from the reflections off its gilded ceiling rafters and wall and ceiling surfaces as if it were

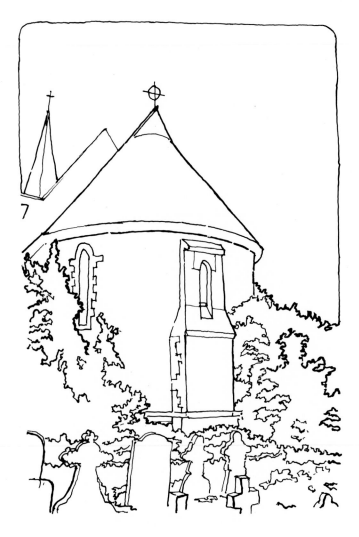

Exterior View of the Chancel at the Church of St. Peter, Hascombe
This drawing shows the insertion of an east chancel window into the buttress that stops the longitudinal axis of the church.

generating its own light. It is viewed from the nave
through an extremely delicate rood screen that reinforces the special nature of the space beyond. The
moldings of the chancel arch, and the colonnettes
that carry it, are accentuated in geometric patterns
of red, blue, green, and gold. The shape of the arch
is emphasized by painted bands on the face of the
wall which carry Biblical references to Christ as
Savior and Peter as the rock upon which the church
is built. The arch soffit is decorated with a tier of angels standing in painted canopies. The delicate gold-
touched filigree of the rood screen continues as a
wainscot around the apsidal sanctuary. The plaster
above the wainscot is stenciled to look like stone.
The window reveals and the spandrels between
them are decorated with angelic figures. The base
of the reredos is a marble arcade that repeats the
cusped-arch form. It supports a paneled wooden
section that surrounds the central window, extends
into its reveals, and rises to meet the ceiling ribs.
All of the reredos panels are filled with painted angels picked out in gold.

The timber ribs of the chancel take the cusped-
arch form. They are closely spaced and project
deeply from the ceiling plane. They rotate around the
apsidal end of the chancel to carry its half-conical
roof. All are gilded. Gilded starburst designs decorate the ceiling spaces between them. The effect is
dazzling and exotic—almost Islamic in character.
Only William Burges in his magnificently decorated
chancel ceilings equals the effect here.

Although the total body of Woodyer's work is un-
even, these churches reveal him to be at his best a
master of composition, sensitive to proportion and
form, original and imaginative in his re-interpretation

Interior Detail of the Decoration of the Chancel wall at the
Church of St. Peter, Hascombe
This view shows the beginning of the net and fishes pattern that
continues around the nave wainscot.

Interior View toward the Chancel at the
Church of St. Peter, Hascombe

Interior Detail Showing the Nave Window Design at the Church of St. Peter, Hascombe

NOTES

1. Harry Redfern, "Some Recollections of William Butterfield and Henry Woodyer," *The Architect and Building News* (14,4,44), 22.

2. Charles L. Eastlake, *A History of the Gothic Revival* (New York: Humanities Press, 1872; Leicester: Leicester University Press, 1970), 330.

3. David Verey, *Gloucestershire,* 2nd ed., Buildings of England Series (Harmondsworth: Penguin, 1976), 269.

4. Eastlake, 330.

5. Ian Nairn and Nikolaus Pevsner, *Surrey,* 2nd ed., Buildings of England Series (Harmondsworth: Penguin, 1971), 302.

of historical forms, and deeply appreciative of the contribution of applied decoration to spatial character. His works are not as bold as Butterfield's, as complex spatially as Pearson's, or as daring or unusual as Teulon's or White's, but they always seem to be "right," and they are eminently pleasing to the eye.

WILLIAM WHITE

illiam White (1825–1900) grew up in comfortable circumstances in Northamptonshire, where his father was curate of Blakesley and private chaplain to Sir Henry Dryden of Canon's Ashby. In 1840 White was apprenticed to the architect Squirhill of Leamington, from whom he learned a great deal about construction but little about design. He taught himself design by studying and sketching old buildings.

Around 1845 White moved to London, where he was employed in the office of Scott and Moffatt along with G. E. Street and G. F. Bodley. Although White was a year younger than Street, he seems, at least at first, to have been the leader in the development of an architectural philosophy largely shared by the two young men. (The attitudes expressed about form and color in White's early writings were echoed by Street in his own, slightly later, speeches and essays.)

White left the office of Scott and Moffatt to set up his own firm in Truro, Cornwall, in 1847. Street followed him to Cornwall in 1848. For two years, until Street moved to Wantage in 1850, the two architects were constant companions, and their work during this period was similar. Both designed a number of small parish churches, schools, and vicarages in Puginesque Gothic characterized by informal planning, the use of local stone or brick, and a picturesque quality that derived from utilitarian articulation of function. Everything was straightforward, honest, and, to use an expression of the day, "real."

White, like most of his peers, was a devout Christian and High Churchman, interested in Anglo-Catholic ritual and the attitudes of the Ecclesiological Society. He was never a fanatic about High

Church matters, however; he was too interested in other things. He was as fascinated with building technology as he was with design; many of his essays dealt with construction technology. He was an inventor, a mountaineer, and a physical fitness enthusiast; he wrote on all these subjects. One of his most charming essays is a piece entitled "The Tourist's Knapsack and its Contents"—a bit of advice for the serious vacationer. Paul Thompson, whose paper "The Writings of William White" is an excellent evaluation of the man as revealed by his writings, says that White loved controversy and was never reluctant to engage in debate even about such unlikely subjects as the authorship of Shakespeare's plays.[1] White loved his work—his obituary said, "to him everything connected with his art was a delight"[2]—and he loved life as well. Thompson concludes, "One comes from his writing with the impression of a man of conviction and enthusiasm, with genuine personal warmth and kindness."[3]

In an 1851 lecture, "On Some of the Principles of Design in Churches,"[4] White recommended that church buildings be characterized by strength, massiveness, and repose. He argued that breadth (horizontality) is more important than verticality because of the necessity for all worshippers to see the sanctuary. He liked what he called "picturesque utility"—a philosophy he shared with Lamb—whereby a picturesque silhouette could and should grow out of a functional plan; important plan components would be articulated with tall, major volumes and lesser components would be tucked into lower, smaller volumes.

In reality this philosophy led White away from the picturesque to an architecture of simple massiveness. Other attitudes reinforced White's preference for simple, massive compositions. He liked thick walls because "they lend comfort, both in appearance and reality." He felt that a building's roof planes were its most expressive features. He produced polyhedral forms which emphasized volume and silhouette. He used restraint in the application of buttresses; he simplified roof lines; he liked window tracery that was flush with the face of the exterior wall. In general, the massing in his buildings is more unified and blocky and less segmented than in Street's buildings, although White's fenestration is often much more irregular.

White had strong feelings about light and color. He believed that the quantity of light affects mood; he liked dark churches because moderated darkness fosters "reposeful attention."[5] Color, he believed, had an "unconscious influence" on the mind; he called it a "luxury upon which the eye can feast." In his article "A Plea for Polychromy" he said, "I am not pleading for the indiscriminate, inharmonious, strongly contrasted and fantastic colouring which earnest advocates for polychromy are sometimes supposed to delight in but for the deep, full, rich, harmonious luxuriance which has the power of exhilarating whilst it soothes."[6] White continued to employ constructional polychromy in the 1860s and 1870s even when it was no longer in vogue; however, his color is invariably subtle and pleasing, never jarring in pattern or contrast.

White had similar views about ornament. He believed, like Pugin, that ornament must be related to structure, but he believed, like Ruskin, that it was a luxury which should not be applied to the ordinary or utilitarian but should be saved for the extraordinary or special. Moreover, he believed ornament to be art which should be produced only by hand; he felt that machine-made ornament could only be crude and mechanical. Churches, as special, sacred places, deserved rich ornament; schools and parsonages as utilitarian structures did not.

White's buildings of the late 1840s and very early 1850s are varied in form, plan, and details and reveal no clear overriding philosophic stance. There are even instances of rogue-like experimentation. By 1853, however, White's beliefs about architecture had jelled, and he would be true to them throughout his lifetime. His mature approach to design is more nearly consistent with that of Butterfield than of Street. White, like Butterfield, would adhere to the English Middle Pointed, Decorated style throughout his career; he was never interested in the continental Gothic details that characterize the work of Street and Burges in the 1860s. He would also continue to employ constructional polychromy long after it had been abandoned by Street, Burges, and Scott. He also continued to lay his brick in patterns and to cut it to create spiky, notched profiles. He remained a true High Victorian architect long after the era had passed. He was more interested in the "real," the "truthful," than he was in style; in fact, in a letter of 1856 to *The Builder* he said, "Truthfulness has nothing to do with style, as such." [7]

Paul Thompson, in the essay cited above, gave three reasons why White should be regarded as an important architectural figure of his age. First, his best buildings are unequalled as perfect examples of High Victorian architecture. Second, White, in his writings, clarifies High Victorian architectural philosophy more clearly and completely than anyone else. Third, White's writing and buildings, at least in the 1850s, directly influenced the ideas and style of his contemporaries, especially Street. Yet White is

perhaps the least known of the major High Victorian architects. His style did not evolve with the times; he designed no important public buildings, and the unfavorable publicity he received from the lawsuit brought against him by the aristocratic client for whom he designed his one great country home, Humewood Castle, effectively blocked him from further important secular work. Perhaps now, as High Victorian architecture is again admired for its strength and vitality, White will regain his rightful position in the history of nineteenth-century English architecture.

All Saints Church, Talbot Road, Notting Hill, London

One of the first works of White's maturity, and his first important London commission, was the Church of All Saints, Notting Hill, built from 1852 to 1855. The church was to be part of a complex which included a college of priests that White's Cornwall client, the Reverend Samuel Edward Walker of St. Columb Major, intended to build as a memorial to his parents. Unfortunately Walker ran short of money in 1855 and work on the church was halted. It stood unglazed and undecorated until 1861, when work resumed under the direction of an engineer. None of the furnishings are White's designs, and the white walls of the nave, aisles, and transepts would certainly not be to the liking of an architect who found the color white to be somber and distressing, like black, fit only for funerals and nuns' garb.

The design is stately, but vigorous. Its dominant feature is its tall west tower, based on the famous tower in Ghent—one of the very few instances where White used a foreign detail. This tower is unique in the High Victorian oeuvre. It is slim. In its present form it consists of two equally tall, square stages, plus an octagonal stage that rises from between four corner pinnacles which are as tall as the octagonal stage itself. Several different colored stones are used in the construction of the belfry. White intended for the octagon to carry a tall octagonal spire which, together with the octagonal belfry, would have been as tall as the two square stages of the tower; but the spire was never built. White also intended for the tower to be buttressed on the west with two colossal flying buttresses between their bases. White planned an entrance porch with portals on the north and south sides. If completed in this manner this tower and spire would have been one of the most unusual and dramatic in the country. The boldness of its design was uniquely High Victorian.

All Saints has a Latin Cross plan. The clerestory windows are very large four-light windows; the clerestory walls are carried across the transepts as screens with unglazed windows. Aisle fenestration

Exterior View of All Saints Church, Talbot Road, Notting Hill, from the Southwest
This is a drawing by White; the spire was never built; neither were the two flying buttresses shown attached to the tower's west face.

Interior View of the Intersection of Nave, North Transept, and Chancel at All Saints Church, Notting Hill

The large arch on the left opens into the chancel. The low arch on the left opens into the north transept, which is placed adjacent to the last bay of the nave. The slightly higher arch on the right opens from the chancel into the Lady Chapel.

in the north and south aisles is different; the windows in the north aisle are very high to accommodate a cloister that was planned but not constructed. A very tall, broad chancel arch opens the chancel space to view. Aisle arcades are carried by clusters of marble columns. The aisles are broad and open to the transepts with tall, wide arches similar to, but slightly smaller than, the chancel arch. The church has a very open spacious quality; it also has interesting spatial interrelationships.

Originally, the interior of the church received a great deal of constructive coloration, most of which has been covered with plaster and white paint. The lower parts of the walls were lined with black, red, and buff tiles. The decoration increased in height and complexity from west to east, becoming full-height and most complex in the chancel. There was a handsome inlaid design of red and blue circles and triangles and flowers with green stems in the heads of the clerestory windows. Holiday executed the strongly pre-Raphaelite fresco of the Annunciation in the chancel.

Eastlake made the following comment about All Saints, Notting Hill: "[It is] a work exhibiting great cleverness in design allied with a certain inclination to peculiarities which are not always justified by their effect. Among these may be reckoned the treatment of the chancel roof and sedilia, and, externally, the gable turrets of the north transept. These, however, are but details. By a judicious attention to the proportions of the interior, Mr. White has managed to secure for it a great appearance of size."[8]

The Church of St. Michael and All Angels, Lyndhurst, Hampshire

In the late 1850s and the 1860s, White turned away from the massiveness and simplicity of his earlier works to churches with more lively plans and silhouettes which were more direct expressions of the relationship of interior to exterior. White's masterpiece, St. Michael and All Angels, is illustrative of this development.

The church was built in the years 1858 through 1870 for the Reverend J. Compton and the church commissioners. Its plan is very similar to the plan of All Saints, Notting Hill. It is a large church, 120 feet by 50 feet, with a spire 135 feet tall, but, like All Saints, it seems even larger because it is so spacious inside. Its spaciousness occurs because the wide arches of the aisle arcades are carried on very tall brick piers—the piers are encircled with banded clusters of eight Purbeck marble shafts—and because the aisles are very wide and their sloping roofs seem to be extensions of the nave roofs. (In reality there is a short clerestory wall between the aisle and nave roofs, but it is not tall enough to accommodate any sort of traditional clerestory fenestration. Consequently, White introduces huge dormer windows to admit clerestory light.) As at All Saints, the nave arcades continue through the transepts; aisles open to the transepts through half arches. Unlike All Saints, however, the nave opens to the chancel through an arch that is only slightly higher than the arcade arches. The chancel is divided from the nave

by an extremely delicate wood rood screen. The east end of the chancel is square; the east window is a complex design of alternating narrow and wide lancets supporting a large rose.

The exterior of St. Michael and All Angels is dominated by its massive, tall square tower with broached octagonal spire located at the northwest corner of the church, occupying the west bay of the north aisle. The tower is composed of three equal stages; each chamfers back from the stage below. The bottom stage is unperforated; there is a continuous small, blind arcade at the base of the second stage; the third stage is divided between large recessed clock faces and three-lancet belfry openings. The tower is buttressed at its edges on all sides; the buttresses on either side of the northwest corner are joined with a diagonal infill to make a single, massive corner buttress. The vertical sides of the tower extend up the sides of the spire to form large lucarnes.

The west facade includes a portal with a very low arch recessed in two stages carried on very short Purbeck marble shafts. The arch is made of carved Bath stone; its face occupies the same plane as the brick of the surrounding wall. A broad yellow, red, and black brick arch parallels the stone arch. Above the portal is an extremely large arched west window, similar in design to the east window but larger. It seems to be pushing the portal below it into the ground.

Exterior View of the Church of St. Michael and All Angels, Lyndhurst, Hampshire, from the Northwest
The complex pyramidal composition terminates in the massive tower attached to the west facade.

The north side is the church's most interesting aspect because it is composed of so many different yet harmonious forms—the tower, the tall volumes of the nave and the slightly lower chancel, the long shed roof of the nave aisle, the shorter shed roofs of the chancel aisle and vestry, the tall gabled projection of the transept, the lower but longer projection of the gabled porch, and the gables of the two large clerestory dormers—all built of red brick banded with yellow and black brick. (This listing suggests a complex chaotic composition. In fact that is not the case. Forms are related by materials and shape and derive from and are expressive of the functions of the plan arrangement. Moreover, individual forms are all massive and simple in outline. The result is a composition of extraordinary vitality and charm.)

The dormers are particularly interesting. They are triangular with their faces completely filled with plate tracery and glass. The triangular five-lancet window pattern has no historical precedent and, in fact, looks amazingly modern. White brick makes a spiky pattern of dentils around the window edges. The dormer roof structures seem very thin because no wall is expressed above the windows.

The north portal is much more elaborate than the west portal. Its corners are anchored with colossally heavy buttresses—heavier than any used elsewhere—and colored brick bands turn diagonally to meet the portal arch like voussoirs. The effect of the porch design is extremely massive and sculptural in contrast to the planar quality of other walls, which have tracery placed flush with their exterior surfaces. This design dramatically expresses White's preference for the massive.

Inside, White has made the decoration much richer than in his earlier churches, but he has sim-

View of the Exterior Detail of the South Aisle Showing the Dormer Clerestory Windows at the Church of St. Michael and All Angels, Lyndhurst

Exterior Detail of the West Facade Portal at the Church of
St. Michael and All Angels, Lyndhurst

plified the structural details. The nature of materials
seems to dictate both decoration design and structural profile. All brick walls in the nave, aisles, and
transepts are evenly striped in two colors of red,
plus yellow and black brick. Brick piers and arch
profiles are square. Arch decoration comes from the
notching of the brick and the expression of different
colored brick voussoirs. Arches and spandrels are
outlined with black brick bands. In contrast, timber
ceilings are left plain.

Windows in the heavy aisle walls are treated as
openings in an outer plane seen beyond and through
concentric arches in the inner wall plane. This layering does not occur in the clerestory windows, however, where walls are not masonry but are thin
tracery and glass. All details respond logically to
their situation.

The interior decoration is concentrated on particular features and in the chancel area. Polychrome
brick patterns become more elaborate above the
aisle windows and the chancel arch. The bases of
the roof beams are decorated, appropriately for the
Church of St. Michael and All Angels, with sculpted
life-size wooden musical angels of unusual elegance.
Arch intersections are decorated with carved stone
portrait heads. Pier capitals are carved with extremely naturalistic foliage; each capital is different
from every other.

All wall surfaces of the sanctuary are covered
with polychrome frescoes. (The fresco of the Wise
and Foolish Virgins on the lower east wall above the
altar is by Frederick Lord Leighton; the others are
by John H. Pollen.) White was more fortunate here
than Street was at St. James the Less; the frescoes
at St. Michael and All Angels—perhaps because
they are contained in an architectural volume that is

Interior Detail of the North Aisle Showing
the Polychrome Brickwork at the Church
of St. Michael and All Angels, Lyndhurst

Interior View toward the Northeast Corner
of the Nave and North Aisle at the Church
of St. Michael and All Angels, Lyndhurst

Eastlake said that St. Michael and All Angels "exhibits evidence of Mr. White's ingenuity and vigour in design side by side with those eccentricities of form either structural or decorative which distinguish nearly every building that he has erected."[9] These eccentricities, coupled with design consistency predicated by a thoughtfully defined philosophy, account for the special, anti-archaeological appeal of the church.

The Church of the Most Holy Saviour, Aberdeen Park, Highbury, London

Interior View toward the Chancel at the Church of St. Michael and All Angels, Lyndhurst

seen as a recess, a special feature defined on all sides by architectural elements—enhance rather than detract from the interior effect. Incidentally, the stone arch that divides chancel from sanctuary is so richly cusped that it achieves the same spiky effect which the notched brick arches of the nave have. (The church is also enhanced by an extremely fine set of stained glass windows of 1862–63 by Morris and Company; Edward Burne-Jones was their principal designer.)

The Church of the Most Holy Saviour, Aberdeen Park, is White's masterpiece of the 1860s. F. T. Mackreth of Canonbury contributed the site, and the funds for the building were given by Canon Morrice of Salisbury. Their intention was to establish a High Church for daily service in the Low Church parish of Islington. The bishop approved their proposal, White was commissioned, and the church was constructed from 1865 to 1866.

St. Saviour is a small church built almost entirely of brick. It appears to be a centrally planned church. It is organized around the twenty-three foot square crossing bay. The nave is short, only two and one half bays long. The chancel, in contrast, is very

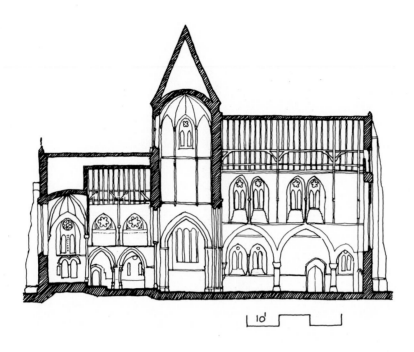

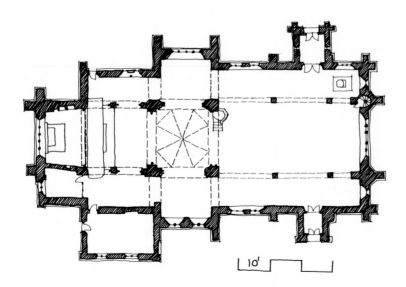

deep; it is composed of a square choir bay, almost as wide as the nave, and a sanctuary only slightly smaller. The total depth of the chancel is thirty-two feet; it appears almost as long as the fifty-four foot nave. Both nave and choir are flanked with narrow aisles, eight feet wide. The transepts project four feet past the aisles on either side. Choir and clergy vestries are attached at the northeast corner.

The exterior of St. Saviour is not particularly pleasing. Hitchcock described it as shapeless, and the adjective is appropriate. Forms are grouped around the vertical projection of the crossing which takes the form of a very low octagonal tower capped with a short octagonal spire. The nave is short but very tall; its ridge line intersects the crossing tower just below the eave of the spire. The long chancel is much lower than the nave; it is only slightly taller than the transepts. Heavy stepped buttresses used extravagantly give the whole composition an amorphous shape. How different this building is from the elegant composition of the precise forms of St. Michael and All Angels, Lyndhurst.

What makes St. Saviour fascinating is its bravura, almost organic, approach to brick construction. What

(above) Longitudinal Section of the Church of the Most Holy Saviour, Aberdeen Park, Looking South
The crossing tower mediates between the extremely tall nave and the much lower chancel.

Plan of the Church of the Most Holy Saviour, Aberdeen Park, Highbury, London
The importance of the crossing and the depth of the chancel cause St. Saviour to appear to be a centrally planned church.

makes it a masterpiece is the quality and character of its interior spaces and its constructional decoration. Like few other buildings in history, St. Saviour is an essay in the decorative possibilities of brick. It is small but it is rich in its design ingenuity and intricacies. Virtually everything is brick. Even the window tracery is more brick than stone. The exterior is red brick with black brick used for pattern work in the gables and on the upper nave walls. The interior is beige, brown, black, and mauve brick arranged in subtle decorative patterns. The nature of brick accounts for the unusual profiles of the overall silhouette and the various individual components; everywhere brick steps back or corbels out to create changes in building forms. The brick patterning is obviously influenced by Butterfield, but St. Saviour's organic forms are as different from Butterfield's crisp, planar volumes as they could possibly be.

Inside, the total commitment to brick leads to design idiosyncrasies that range from awkward to extremely handsome. The huge brick arches of the nave arcades and the walls that define the crossing are extraordinarily powerful. The edges of the arcade arches are made of molded brick with a curved corner; otherwise their surface conforms to the plane of the wall. Their spandrels are filled with multicolored brick laid in a basketwork pattern. Clerestory windows are paired two-light lancet windows; they are placed close to the exterior wall surface and high in the clerestory wall. Their deep sills step out in four stages. However, the treatment of the heads of the recesses is most peculiar. The windows are set close together so there is little splay in the pier that separates them, but the outer reveals are deeply chamfered. The result is a pair of asymmetrical arched recesses whose arch apexes do not

Exterior View of the Church of the Most Holy Saviour, Aberdeen Park, from the Southwest
St. Saviour's great height coupled with its central crossing tower gives it the most compact silhouette of any High Victorian Church.

Exterior Detail of the West Window at the Church of the Most Holy Saviour, Aberdeen Park
At St. Saviour, even the window tracery is constructed, at least in part, of brick.

conform to the shape of the windows they contain.

The arcades are carried on square brick piers. Their bases are brick; only their simple carved capitals are stone. The edges of the piers are made of curved, molded brick much like that used in the arches. The capitals feature bold geometric forms rather than naturalistic foliage. The piers are certainly non-traditional and are extremely handsome.

The focus of the space is, of course, the chancel which is seen through the crossing bay which is empty except for the pulpit. The wall that divides the nave from the crossing is actually treated as if it were the chancel wall. Above its arch a cross in a nimbus is built into the wall with colored brick. This cross functions as the chancel rood; consequently the crossing bay belongs more to the chancel than to the nave, creating an ecclesiastical area longer than the nave.

The arches in the walls of the crossing bay are taller and more elaborate than the arcade arches. The brick arch surfaces are painted with scriptural quotations. The intrados are elaborated with curved brick ribs (made of molded brick) that are carried on slender brick shafts (also made of molded brick). Molded brick shafts are also used in the aisle window arcades. The crossing bay is very tall, nearly sixty feet to the center of its wooden vault. The octagonal wooden vault has sixteen facets; it is lighted by lantern windows on three sides. The brick construction, faceted vault, and squinch supports give it a decidedly Moorish appearance.

The constructional patterns of the nave continue into the chancel. The brick of the chancel walls is over-painted with conventionalized floral decoration in gold, red, green, and blue. Brick moldings are also emphasized with paint. Gavin Stamp and Colin

Interior View toward the Crossing and
Chancel at the Church of the Most Holy
Saviour, Aberdeen Park
The interior is heavy and dark—a study
in brick construction.

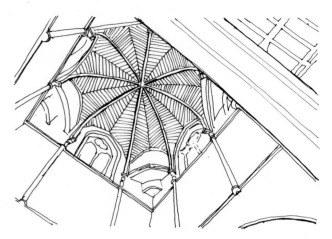

Interior Detail of the Crossing Vault at the Church of the Most Holy Saviour, Aberdeen Park
The vault is wood but is supported on brick squinches that transform the shape from square to octagonal.

Interior Detail of the Painted Decoration on the Brick Surfaces at the Church of the Most Holy Saviour, Aberdeen Park

Amery described this decoration as "a kind of see-through lace."[10] The focus of the chancel is the altar and the sanctuary window above a traditional five light fourteenth-century English window, except that only the tracery in the head is stone. The altar reredos and window are identical in width, so they create a single unified composition. White's reredos is a bold, non-traditional, three-compartment baldachin with Salviati mosaics in the compartments. Its heavy upper structure is carefully designed to appear to be the sill for the window. The sanctuary is given a quadripartite wooden vault similar to the vault in the crossing; the choir, like the nave, has an exposed, braced rafter roof system.

The Church of the Most Holy Saviour is unlike any other built during its age. It exemplifies the willingness of High Victorian architects to reinterpret traditional forms in their pursuit of a new style. It also exemplifies the boldness with which the best designers of the age used pattern, color, texture, and form. Finally, it reveals a growing sensitivity to the intrinsic nature of materials and their "natural" use in buildings. (No architect of the age was more perceptive than White in his understanding of the relationship between material and building form. White's great country house, Humewood Castle, is as perceptive to the nature of stone as St. Saviour is to the nature of brick.)

NOTES

1. Paul Thompson, "The Writings of William White," *Concerning Architecture*, ed. John Summerson (London: Allen Lane Penguin, 1968), 229.

2. Royal Institute of British Architects Journal VII (1900), 145.

3. Thompson, 229.

4. *Transactions of the Exeter Diocesan Architectural Society* IV (1851), 176–80.

5. William White, "On Windows," *The Ecclesiologist* XVII (1856), 319–32.

6. William White, "A Plea for Polychromy," *Building News* VII (1861), 50–55.

7. Stefan Muthesius, *The High Victorian Movement in Architecture 1850–1870* (London and Boston: Routledge & Kegan Paul, 1972), 162.

8. Charles L. Eastlake, *A History of the Gothic Revival* (New York: Humanities Press, 1872; Leicester: Leicester University Press, 1970), 291.

9. Eastlake, 292.

10. Gavin Stamp and Colin Amery, *Victorian Buildings of London 1837–1887* (London: Architectural Press, 1980), 84.

GEORGE FREDERICK BODLEY

**o** architect of the second half of the nineteenth century was more successful or more prolific than George Frederick Bodley (1827–1907), whose innumerable churches in the Gothic style represent the climax of the Gothic revival in England. Bodley received his architectural training as an apprentice (as did George Edmund Street and William White) in the office of Sir Gilbert Scott during the years of 1845–49. He was deeply impressed with Ruskin's writings and the work of his friend Butterfield, however, and early departed from Scott's Gothic style in favor of what Eastlake termed more "muscular" designs. The heaviness of Bodley's High Victorian work of the 1850s and early 1860s evolved by the end of the decade to church designs that featured simple spaces, magnificently decorated.[1] We are concerned with the first, High Victorian, phase of Bodley's work and will discuss in detail five churches designed during the 1860s.

Although Bodley was an architect of considerable ability, his greatest talent was as a decorator of churches. His talent in this area lay in his ability to see the interior as a whole and to be able to bring all decoration—patterns, fittings, glass—into a harmonious unity. In order to do this, he kept tight control over every design decision, often even designing altar vessels and vestments.

All Saints Church
Selsley, Gloucestershire

Bodley's mature High Victorian style emerged in 1862 with the design of the small French Gothic style church of All Saints, Selsley, Gloucestershire. Bodley claimed, to please his patron, that the design was based on an Austrian Tyrolean model, but this is highly unlikely considering the predominantly French character of the building. The church is magnificently sited on top of a crest overlooking the Vale and the factory tower at Ebley.

The building is composed of three masses, two major and one minor. The major masses are the vertical tower mass and the horizontal main body of the church containing the nave and chancel. The minor mass is the gabled mass containing the sacristy and organ loft. This minor form is vertical in its proportions but horizontal in the character of its roof. Its tall gabled form relates to the tower, but its ridge line parallels the ridge line of the nave and chancel block. Consequently, it mediates between and enriches the two major forms.

Analysis of the form makes it clear that Bodley wanted nothing to detract from his simple composition of powerful geometric objects. Fenestration is simple plate tracery set in the outer plane of the wall in order to minimize distraction from the basic building forms. The exterior is made of ashlar cut stone laid in a relatively smooth random pattern that emphasizes the strength of the masonry. Block subdivisions are marked either with small projecting moldings that help to tie the composition together

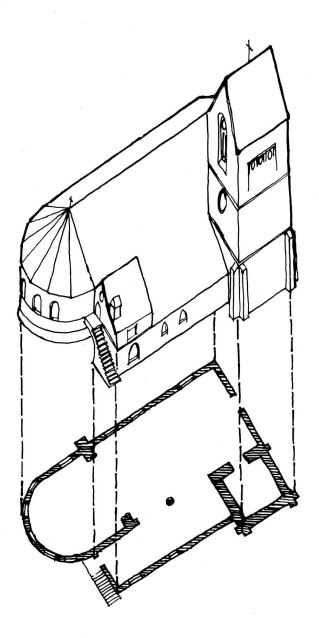

Plan and Isometric Showing the Three Masses—Nave, Chancel and Aisle, and Tower—and the Organ Loft of All Saints, Selsley, Gloucestershire

213

Exterior View of All Saints Church, Selsley, from the Southeast
Block subdivisions are marked either with small projecting
moldings that help to tie the composition together visually or
with simple buttresses.

visually or with simple buttresses. The walls thicken
to meet the ground. The total effect is muscular,
heavy, and strong. Moreover, there is a wonderful
design consistency in the way that Bodley featured
similar forms at different scales (similar triangular
gables of different sizes in parallel planes, particularly) as well as groups of three—three basic blocks,
three bays to the nave, three interior plan divisions,
three stages to the tower, three windows in the
west facade.

The effect of the exterior is simple yet picturesque. Its appeal depends upon the drama of the occult balance of the massive geometric units, especially the relationship of vertical to horizontal
masses, and the play of repeating design elements
at different scales.

Inside, a three-bay nave leads to the semi-circular
chancel; a massive chancel arch separates these two
plan units. The third plan unit is the single aisle on
the north side; it is two bays in length. (The tower
occupies what would otherwise be the first aisle
bay.) The south nave wall is a sheer vertical surface
broken only by a corbeled cornice at the top, a string
course at the spring line of the window arches, and
a series of sculpted memorial tablets that include
stations-of-the-cross in their tops like keystones.
The two bays of the aisle are divided from the nave
by arches of the same height as the arches of the
windows of the south wall, but because these arches
are much wider than the window arches (the entire
wall is opened up) the spring line is much lower.
The arch form is simply sculpted; the only decoration is half-round moldings at the arrizes. The visual
contrast of the three arches of different sizes but
similar shape is another example of Bodley's play
with similar elements in groups of three.

Interior View toward the Chancel at All Saints Church, Selsley
The interior is divided into three spatial units—nave, chancel, and north aisle

The arches are carried on Greek-cross-shaped column capitals. Stiff leaf carvings make the transition to a circular red granite column between the two arches and to the brackets that receive the arches at their other sides. Similar but elevated columns carry the arch of the chancel screen wall. The columns are stumpy but powerful. The spandrel above the column in the aisle wall is decorated with a large blind oculus made using the same half-round

molding that decorates the arch arrizes. All stone is the same light gray-beige stone of the exterior.

The ceiling in the nave and aisle is framed with exposed dark wood timbers with white plaster in the panels between them. At the apex of the nave ceiling, the rafters become scissors trusses which decorate and modulate the space. The roof timbers turn down on the upper face of the nave walls for a few feet, effectively tying the ceiling and wall planes together. The sanctuary ceiling is a dark wood polygonal vault.

The apsidal sanctuary has bands of carved molding above and below the lancet windows. These bands feature individually different leaf sculptures and are brightly colored, picking up the colors of the Morris glass in the windows. This church, unlike Bodley's later churches, has minimal constructional color or painted decoration. It depends for its effect upon the strength and vigor of its spaces and forms, and the effect is very strong, masculine, and simple. The splendid Morris glass compliments the architecture.

The Churches of St. Michael and All Angels, Brighton and St. Martin, Scarborough

The Bodley churches of St. Michael and All Angels at Brighton and St. Martin at Scarborough are contemporary with the church at Selsley and are similar to it in their design approach, although their materials are different and their stylistic details are thirteenth-century Decorated rather than French. The Brighton church is brick with stone dressings and is obviously influenced by the work of William Butterfield. The Scarborough church is dark stone. The composition of St. Michael's west front is very much like that at Selsley, and St. Martin's tower is a saddleback one very similar to that at All Saints. All three churches contain glass from the newly founded Morris company. All three share the bold masculine approach to massing that is characteristic of the High Victorian era; they draw their effect from scale, proportion, and simplicity of design. Incidentally, the design of all three was endorsed by the Ecclesiological Society.

St. Michael and All Angels, Brighton, was converted into the south aisle of a greatly enlarged church by William Burges in 1865. In the process it lost its north aisle and its west portal. Burges followed the Bodley design in the design of the addition. The original building and the addition share a symbiotic relationship much like that of the nave and sacristy/organ loft wing at Selsley. Both parts of the enlarged church have a similar tall, slender, gabled form, with their ridge lines parallel. The materials of the addition are the same as in the earlier Bodley church; however, the stone string courses of the two buildings are discontinuous. A contemporary designer would certainly have made the linkage of the two parts more secure by continuing the stone bands of the one around the other. Burges, however, preferred to allow the spacing of string courses to be determined by the scale of his addition; as a result, the new actually bear a closer resemblance in

Exterior View of the Church of St. Michael and All Angels, Brighton, from the Southwest
Bodley's church, the smaller element on the right, was converted into the south aisle of a much larger church by Burges' addition of 1865.

216

scale and proportion to the original than would otherwise have been the case. Bodley probably would have approved this design decision. There is a parallel in this to the discontinuity of stencil patterns and molding on interior partitions, not part of the structural shell, in a number of Bodley decorated interiors. (See the Tue Brook discussion below.)

The Church of St. Martin-on-the-Hill, Scarborough, is notable for its interior decoration. Although Bodley's chief accomplishment is in the area of decorative design—he had an unfailing color sense and a talent for pattern-making that rivaled William Morris' own ability—decoration of this church was not done exclusively by Bodley but was a collaborative venture between Bodley and the principals of the new Morris firm. Morris and Philip Webb painted the keel-shaped chancel ceiling (and probably the ceiling of the north chapel as well) as a series of rectangular panels outlined in gold with small gold rosettes on the grounds. The pulpit panels were designed by Morris, Daniel Gabriel Rossetti, and Ford Madox Brown. Bodley painted the wall above the chancel arch and the altar wall and designed the reredos and rood screen, although these were done nearly thirty years later. (Bodley liked to control every detail of his churches and often provided designs for fittings years after the original buildings were completed.) Unfortunately, the tempera paints used in the church's decoration have not lasted well; the church's once bright colors have peeled and faded, so no true appreciation of the character of the original space is possible. To truly appreciate Bodley's great strength as a decorator—his ability to see the interior as a whole and to sensitively and carefully relate everything from floor to ceiling to his single vision—we must look at another of his

Exterior View of the Church of St. Martin, Scarborough, from the Northeast
The saddleback tower, located in the westernmost bay of the north aisle, is similar in form and placement to the tower at Selsley. Unlike All Saints, however, St. Martin is a large town church; therefore it is larger in scale and more sophisticated in design detail.

churches, St. John the Baptist, Tue Brook, Liverpool, which has recently been carefully restored.

Interior View toward the Chancel at the Church of St. Martin, Scarborough
The interior decoration was a collaborative venture between Bodley and the members of the Morris circle.

The Church of St. John the Baptist, Tue Brook, Liverpool

The church of St. John the Baptist, Tue Brook, built in 1868, was Bodley's first work in his mature style, and it remains one of the few existing examples where the sumptuous unity of his decorative style can be seen and studied. Unfortunately, Bodley's wall paintings have not lasted well; at Scarborough and most of his churches they remain as pale, washed-out ghosts of their original appearance. At Tue Brook, however, a comprehensive, sensitive restoration has been completed, and the church today, with the exception of its great chancel window which remains badly deteriorated, is as bright and fresh as it was a century ago.

The exterior of the church gives no hint of the glorious decoration to be found inside. Though large and pleasing in its form, there is nothing especially distinguished about its exterior. It is an architecturally simple High Victorian church with a west steeple and spire, a long nave with lower side aisles and clerestory above, and a lower chancel, all built in a restrained Decorated style. The interior plan and resulting space is architecturally as simple and straight-forward as the exterior form. The nave clerestory wall is carried by low octagonal piers. The open character of this supporting structure minimizes the spatial separation between nave and aisles. The nave seating reinforces the tendency toward spatial unification in that it extends into the aisles and allows them to become part of the larger congregational space. The treatment of the clerestory is unusual in that the windows are over the spandrels rather than over the arch apexes. What truly astonishes the modern visitor of St. John the Baptist, Tue Brook, however, is the amazing variety of surface patterns which cover virtually all of the church's interior surfaces. Even more astonishing is the unity of decorative effect achieved in spite of the variety of devices utilized.

The weight of the structure is de-emphasized in the interior of the church, mainly through the utilization of painted, decorative devices. The stone of which the church is constructed is expressed in the interior only in the piers, arches, and lower wall surfaces. It is of two colors, gray-beige and pinkish-tan, and is laid in alternating courses of various heights; the stone almost looks as if it were another painted pattern. The stone coursing changes to smooth plaster above the arches of the nave arcade and at the sill line of the windows in the aisles. The stone seems very thin; it has a two-dimensional rather than a three-dimensional character. Only in the moldings of the arches themselves is the stone sculpted into three-dimensional forms. The planar quality of the stone is particularly apparent at the windows. Window reveals are stone surfaces, yet the stone does not turn the corner as moldings on the face of the adjacent wall. Instead, the patterns painted on the plaster wall surfaces continue to the arrize of the intersection of the wall plane and the plane of the window reveal perpendicular to it. In consequence, neither stone nor plaster has any apparent thickness; two-dimensional patterns dominate every surface; even the stone wainscot appears to have its pattern painted on.

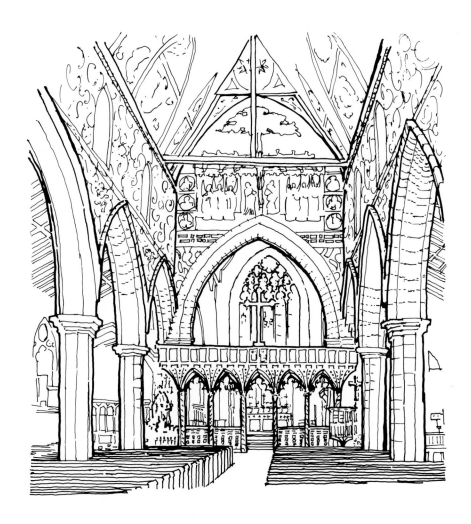

Interior View toward the Chancel at the Church of St. John the Baptist, Tuebrook, Liverpool
The nave is actually very high, but its apparent height is diminished by the very wide side aisles that are designed to appear to be part of the nave space.

Interior Detail of the Stencil Decoration of
All Surfaces at the Church of St. John the
Baptist, Tuebrook
The stenciling serves to diminish the weight
of the stone.

Various stenciled "wallpaper-like" patterns are used to decorate plaster wall surfaces. The side walls of the aisles receive one pattern from the sill line of the windows (the top of the stone wainscot) to the spring line of the window arches and a second pattern from the spring line of the arches to the top of the wall. The lower pattern is particularly Morris-like in character and is composed of cream-colored vines, leaves, and flowers moving diagonally across a putty-colored ground that approximates the color of the stone wainscot below. The upper wall pattern reverses the field/ground relationship of the lower pattern and plays alternating flower and letter medallions in straight vertical and horizontal rows against a cream background. Elegant stenciled borders separate different wall patterns and mark intersections of walls and ceilings. The lower wall pattern has a strong diagonal movement; the upper pattern is static. Both patterns use bits of dark teal blue as accent; this color is also used as the background color for the sloping aisle ceilings below which cream-colored rafter and purlin bottoms project slightly. The dark ceiling panels and the projecting beams and purlins are decorated with stenciled medallions.

In the nave, the spandrels between the arches of the arcade receive a scrolled, foliate pattern designed to fill the roughly triangular spaces formed by the sides of adjacent arches and the molding carried by the arch apexes. The clerestory wall above this molding features a regular pattern of alternating large and small flower patterns. The background color of both patterns is cream, as is the nave ceiling background and the truss-like crossties that mark the bays of the nave. All are stenciled. The crossties receive biblical quotations; the ceiling pan-

els are decorated with medallions that alternate the initials of Christ with star motifs. Accent colors include teal blue and an Indian lake red that picks up the color family of the pink stone.

The focus of the nave space is on its east screen through which the chancel is seen. The screen and the stenciled patterns are Bodley's designs; the crucifixion fresco on the chancel wall is by C. E. Kempe. The great east window of the chancel (a badly deteriorated Morris window) visually fills the space between chancel arch and rood screen. The elaborate figurative treatment of the chancel wall, the richly decorated screen, and the colored glass of the east window focus attention upon the chancel in an extremely successful manner. The crucified Christ of Kempe's fresco echoes the altar crucifix and relates well to the arch that supports it. The delicacy of Bodley's screen suggests spatial separation without obscuring the view.

Pattern complexity and color richness increase in the chancel. Gilt, red, and navy replace the restrained colors of the nave and aisles. The carpet that leads to the altar, the railing of the screen, the drapery of the altar, and the walls of the chancel on either side of the reredos use these colors in patterns borrowed from Safavid Persia. The coved arcade of the screen carries a paneled rail decorated with figures and fruit-and-leaf patterns that are similar to those used in many Morris windows. The baptism of Christ in the center of the screen is a motif used at larger scale in the center panel of the gilded reredos. Both crucifixions are flanked by lovely pre-Rafaelite angels. The lotus pattern of the altar drapery seems to be the logical termination of the carpet pattern. The cove of the reredos is suggestive of the form of the screen. The decoration of

Interior Detail of the Nave Roof and Clerestory at the Church of St. John the Baptist, Tuebrook

the organ case, and the arrangement of pipes within it, is consistent with the rest of the rich pattern decoration of the chancel. The upper walls of the chancel that are visible from the nave are decorated in a complex foliate stenciled pattern that is paisley-like in feeling and is consistent in color to other surfaces. The rear side of the chancel arch is decorated in the simplest of the church's stenciled patterns— John's initial alternating with a pine cone medallion. The chancel ceiling is paneled much like the nave ceiling but features gold star medallions against a teal background—a stylized variation of the Gothic and early Renaissance "starry sky" pattern.

The decorative patterns of St. John the Baptist, Tue Brook, do more than decorate the space; they establish its very character. Without them the space would seem heavy and ponderous because the rhythm of its structural components is slow and the amount of wall as opposed to window is great. In contrast, the decorative patterns are small scaled and their rhythms are lively and fast. In consequence, the space is lightened and humanized in scale. The color scheme and consistent overall character of the decoration give the space visual unity. The concentration of pattern complexity and color richness in the chancel area establishes its preeminence in the hierarchy of the building's spaces and attracts the attention of worshippers.

Unfortunately, most of the glass in St. John the Baptist, Tue Brook, is either clear glass leaded in quarry patterns or badly deteriorated stained glass;

this church is not an appropriate one in which to study the relationship of stained glass patterns to overall pattern decoration, generally an important element in the decorative scheme of Bodley churches.

Interior Detail of the Rood Screen with the Chancel beyond at the Church of St. John the Baptist, Tuebrook

The Church of St. Augustine, Pendlebury, Lancashire

The church of St. Augustine, Pendlebury, designed in 1869 and built from 1870 to 1874, is the finest example of Bodley's High Victorian style. Although it moves toward the perpendicular elegance of Bodley's Late Victorian period, it retains the strength, vitality, and creativity of his earlier work. Gone is the picturesque massing and the bold, chunky detail; although the mass of the church is powerful, it is a single form, not a composition of forms. Constructional polychromy and rich surface decoration are retained. It is an original creative work rather than a derivative one even though its decorative details are borrowed from earlier styles. Pevsner calls it one of the most moving of Victorian churches.[2] David Verey says it is Bodley's greatest achievement.[3]

St. Augustine is a large, impressive church that was financed by the banker E. S. Heywood, whose contribution toward its construction is variously put at something between thirty-three and fifty thousand pounds. Even so, it was not finished. The freestanding tower designed to stand near the southwest corner of the building was never built. (It is a pity that it was not, because the tower was an integral part of the entrance sequence planned by Bodley. The sequence as intended would have been as follows: entry at the gate in the gatehouse lodge, progression west along a walk on axis with the longitudinal axis of the church to a freestanding cross, left on the path toward the school, then right toward the tower, into the tower followed by a ninety degree right-hand turn through an open breezeway into the narthex of the church, and finally another right-hand turn into the church proper.)

The church is one great rectangle of nine bays with chamfered northeast and southeast corners. One bay constitutes the narthex. The rood screen is placed at the center of a bay dividing the main space into a four-and-a-half bay nave and a three-and-a-half bay sanctuary. (The screen is low and delicate and does not interfere with the unified character of the total space in any major way.) The church is a hall church; it does not have true aisles. The great piers that carry the roof project into the interior space, creating a series of great niches. The lower portion of each pier is perforated with an arch, and these arches are what create the semblance of aisles. (Movement along these narrow aisle spaces is very interesting visually because of the perspective effect of looking through a series of diminishing arched forms.) In this church the vertical is everything, inside and out.

The exterior wall is layered to emphasize its height. The piers, expressed on the outside as buttresses, project above the eave line of the wall and carry arched spandrels at their tops that bridge from pier to pier. Below these arches the wall is recessed and is treated like a great brick curtain. This

Exterior View of the Church of St. Augustine, Pendlebury, Lancashire, from the East, Showing Bodley's Unbuilt Tower in Dashed Line

recessed curtain wall is banded with stone. The banding helps to establish the independent curtain-like character of this second wall system; banding is continuous from panel to panel *behind* the piers. The bands to do not appear in the piers that have their own independent system of stone dressings that expresses changes in pier shape and emphasizes arch spring lines. The curtain is divided slightly below its mid-point into a solid lower wall and an upper wall almost entirely opened up to great arched windows. The tracery in the chancel windows is flowing; in the nave windows it is perpendicular.

The perpendicular aesthetic controls; it is apparent everywhere. This is particularly true in the elaborate decoration of the east and west facades. Both feature a decorated gabled center panel between tall, slender buttresses. The west wall unit features a single arched portal of white stone which divides it into three parts. The door panel is extended into the zone above, where it establishes the width of the great west window. This window is a five-lancet arched window whose divisions extend down through the brick to the banding course below. This upper wall stage is predominantly brick except for the window frame and tracery. Stone banding is restricted to the horizontal zone established between the window sill and the window arch spring line; stone courses in this zone stretch from the buttresses to the window. The center portion of the wall breaks up between the buttresses to create an almost weightless triangle/parapet to receive the gable of the roof. The roof slope is sixty degrees.

The east facade is both a simpler and a more elaborate composition. The largely undecorated lower stage receives a small, slender buttress at its center. This buttress has no structural function; its

Exterior Detail of the Window in the Gable of the East Facade at the Church of St. Augustine, Pendlebury
This window is divided into three parts with straight, vertical mullions that continue through the flowing upper tracery, past the window, into the decoration of the wall itself.

Exterior Detail of the Nave Clerestory Fenestration at the Church of St. Augustine, Pendlebury
Buttresses seem to be applied to the mass; wall banding continues from panel to panel behind them.

Exterior Detail of the West Facade of the Church of St. Augustine, Pendlebury
The east facade uses more stone than brick, but the west facade, except for the gable, is evenly divided between stripes of red-brown brick and white stone.

purpose is to mark the center line of the composition and reference the axis of altar and church inside. The upper wall is almost completely filled by a great seven-lancet arched window. The rhythm of window division is 2:3:2. The stone banding of the wall around the window makes a criss-cross horizontal/vertical pattern of blank paneling; this is stopped by the buttresses at either side. The buttresses continue up past the wall as pinnacles to the height of the apex of the gable. The composition of this facade shows Bodley at his most masterful.

The roof is a single uninterrupted gable that seems to disappear down behind the high side walls. In fact, the buttresses are the full thickness of the aisle and can be seen to continue past the outer wall to intersect with the roof plane at a point that marks the inside dimension of the aisle. In the interior, these piers form not only the aisles but also a series of full height wall niches that contain the great arched windows that flood the interior with light.

The materials and decorative scheme of the interior do not reflect the exterior at all. No brick is apparent, and only the extreme inner edge of the wall piers and the window arches are faced with stone. These pier fronts are molded to appear to be singularly tall, slender piers carrying upper wall spandrels that duplicate the arches of the outer layer of the exterior wall. The tall, slender stone pier fronts deemphasize the weight of the structure but reinforce the vertical emphasis that seems to govern most design decisions. All other wall surfaces are plastered and painted or paneled. The aisles and chancel have a paneled wainscot that extends to the spring line of the aisle arches. Above the wainscot the plaster walls are covered with stenciled pattern decoration. (The

Interior Detail of the Aisle Construction at the Church of St. Augustine, Pendlebury
Exterior buttresses continue inside to form the nave. Aisles penetrate the piers through arched doorways; giant clerestory windows fill the upper niches.

Interior Detail of the Stenciled Decoration of
the Chancel Wall and Ceiling at the Church
of St. Augustine, Pendlebury
Only in the chancel does Bodley's rich
painted decoration survive. Here, as at
many High Victorian churches, white paint
obscures most of the patterned decoration.

stenciling in the chancel remains; unfortunately in
the nave and aisles it has been painted out.)

Bodley's intention was for the worshipper to be
led to the chancel by the march of the tall stone
piers and the arches they carried. He intended for
the majesty and simplicity of architectural space—
the interior is 159 feet long and 80 feet high—to
dominate. He also intended for the interior to appear as a single space; there is no architectural division between chancel and nave—no chancel arch, no
change of ceiling. The entire sweep of space carries
the eye directly to the altar. It is no accident that

the easternmost aisle bays angle in toward the altar
wall; this is simply another device to concentrate attention there. For the same reason, the altar is elevated eight steps above the level of the nave floor.

The altar reredos accepts the seven-partite division of the window above and its basically rectilinear
geometry. It is a three-tiered golden sculpture that
is sympathetic in form and detail to the geometry of
the building and is important enough in scale, color,
and material to be the focal point of the entire space.
The wooden linenfold paneling on either side of it
and the stenciled wall above it are sufficiently rich to

harmonize with the altar, reredos, and window but sufficiently simple so as not to overwhelm these more important liturgical elements.

Bodley apparently worked closely with Burlison and Grylls on the great east window that fills the wall above the altar reredos. The lancets are orga-nized as tiers of vertical rectangular panels that contain large figures of saints and angels which fill their frames fully. There are three tiers of figures except in the three center lancets where there are four tiers. The centermost lancet, top, has a crucifix that is the focal point of the window. All other figures relate to it. The window is predominantly white, gold, and brown with touches of blue. The difficult shapes of the upper tracery are filled with angelic figures in the Burne-Jones manner.

Bodley's attention to detail can be seen in the starry sky that decorates the chancel ceiling and in all fittings, including the organ case, sedilia, door hinges, and furniture. Particularly effective are the stations of the cross done in the manner of the reredos—painted figures in gilded tabernacles—that decorate the upper east faces of the aisle niches. The whole is (or was) elaborately decorated; yet the result is amazingly serene, simple, restrained, and powerful.

Interior Detail of the High Altar at the Church of St. Augustine, Pendlebury
The lines of the reredos echo and harmonize with the design of the great window above.

Holy Angels Church, Hoar Cross, Staffordshire

St. Augustine is Bodley's last major work in the High Victorian idiom. The change in his style is demonstrated by a church that is contemporary with it but totally different in style—the Church of Holy Angels, Hoar Cross, Staffordshire, built in 1872–79. Pevsner says in the Staffordshire volume of

Interior View toward the Chancel at Holy
Angels Church, Hoar Cross, Staffordshire
With the design of Holy Angels, Bodley
moved from the muscular High Victorian
style to the elegant, attenuated Gothic of
the Late Victorian period.

230

the *Buildings of England* series that "Pendlebury is austere, Hoar Cross is luxuriant; Pendlebury is blunt, Hoar Cross is exceedingly refined; Pendlebury highly original, Hoar Cross essentially derivative. At Pendlebury Bodley meant to create something new, at Hoar Cross he intended to show what perfection was obtainable within the rubrics of English late medieval decoration and architecture."[4]

Holy Angels seems to be a perfect fourteenth-century church. The only clue to its nineteenth-century origin is the perfection of its fabric. It is magnificent in its elegance and beauty, but it has little in common with Bodley's earlier work. Bodley, perhaps due to the influence of Garner, his new partner, entered a new period that is essentially derivative and elegant rather than creative and bold. Holy Angels is a work of Late Victorian architecture; Bodley had left the High Victorian period behind.

NOTES

1. Nikolaus Pevsner, *Lancashire*, Buildings of England Series (Harmondsworth: Penguin, 1969), 303.

2. Pevsner, 303.

3. David Verey, "George Frederick Bodley: Climax of the Gothic Revival," *Seven Victorian Architects*, ed. Jane Fawcett (University Park, PA: Penn State University Press, 1977), 91.

4. Nikolaus Pevsner, *Staffordshire*, Buildings of England Series (Harmondsworth; Baltimore: Penguin, 1974), 148.

White, Woodyer, and Bodley locator:

1. All Saints, Talbot Road, Notting Hill, London
2. St. Michael and All Angels, Lyndhurst, Hampshire
3. St. Saviour, Aberdeen Park, Highbury, London
4. Holy Innocents, Highnam, Gloucestershire
5. St. Michael and All Angels, Tenbury Wells, Worcestershire
6. Christ Church, Reading, Berkshire
7. St. Peter, Hascombe, Surrey
8. All Saints, Selsley, Gloucestershire
9. St. Michael and All Angels, Brighton
10. St. Martin, Scarborough, Yorkshire
11. St. John the Baptist, Tuebrook, Liverpool
12. St. Augustine, Pendlebury, Lancashire
13. Holy Angels, Hoar Cross, Staffordshire

PART III

The Non-Conformists

PHILIP WEBB
EDWARD BUCKTON LAMB
SAMUEL SAUNDERS TEULON

PHILIP WEBB

The Church of St. Martin, Brampton

Philip Webb (1831–1915) is generally regarded as an Arts and Crafts architect; his early tastes, however, were distinctly High Victorian. He got the bulk of his architectural training as an apprentice in the Oxford office of G. E. Street. He greatly admired Street's work, as well as the work of William Butterfield, which was similar. Webb's sketch books are filled with studies of Street's and Butterfield's High Victorian buildings and details. In particular, he admired the straightforward use of materials, the simplified details, and the free functional planning that characterized their secular work, especially parsonages. He made these characteristics his own; they can be found in his entire body of work.

Philip Webb was the son of a country doctor. He grew up in comfortable circumstances in the university city of Oxford. From an early age he was fascinated by architecture, and he loved the fine old buildings of his city. In one of his letters he said, "I was born and bred in Oxford, and had no other teacher in art than the impressive objects of the old buildings there, the effect of which on my natural bent has never left me. . . . All my life, since leaving the then more beautiful place than now it is, has been coloured and even trained by its fashioning."[1]

In 1856, when Webb was chief clerk in the Street office, William Morris joined the firm. Two years later, Webb left Street's office to start his own practice. His first commission was a house for Morris—the famous Red House. Webb's association with

Morris lasted for more than two decades. Webb was a founding partner in the firm of Morris, Marshall, Faulkner and Company, which was established in 1861. Webb's architectural commissions were an important element in the firm's success. In addition, Webb participated actively in the design of stained glass and furniture. His involvement was a key factor in the particularly architectonic character of the glass produced during the firm's early years.

Webb and Morris were inseparable friends almost from the very beginning, although their personalities were very different; Morris was brash, ebullient, outgoing, often rowdy, while Webb was gentle, modest, patient, and deeply reserved. They shared many common attitudes about art and architecture, however, and together they forged a philosophy that would be the basis for the Arts and Crafts movement. They built on the writings of Pugin and Ruskin, accepting Pugin's fidelity to place and Ruskin's desire for surprise, variation, and picturesque composition. (Peter Davey, in *Arts and Crafts Architecture,* uses the term "changefulness" to describe this aspect of Ruskin's philosophy.[2] It is a good term to describe similar characteristics in Webb's work.) Webb and Morris shared an abiding passion for traditional building techniques and traditionally-used local materials. Webb often said that he desired to achieve the commonplace—to be able to design new buildings that would appear as if they were an organic part of their context and not new buildings at all.

These attitudes led Webb to design buildings that, while incorporating historical detail, took unusual, new forms. Although his early buildings were firmly rooted in the Gothic style, their forms and spaces had no Gothic prototypes and were often surprising and unusual. Consequently, they were not universally admired. Norman Shaw summed up the view of Webb held by many of his contemporaries when he referred to him as "a very able man indeed, but with a strong liking for the ugly."[3]

Webb is known almost exclusively as an architect of houses. He designed only one church—St. Martin's, Brampton, Cumbria. St. Martin's is a serious Gothic design and is as bold and vigorous as any High Victorian church. The composition and many of the details are extremely original, but it is in the spatial arrangement that Webb's true genius is best revealed.

Webb was selected as the architect of the church through the influence of Mr. Charles Howard, M.P., the brother of the eighth earl of Carlisle, and his son, George, later to be the ninth earl. (The Howards were faithful clients of Webb. They contributed more than half of the seven thousand pounds required for construction on the condition that they could select the architect. In fact, it was at their urging that the church was built at all; the parishioners were much more interested in using their money for a tram-way and a sewer system.) The church was designed in 1874 at the very end of the High Victorian period.

Webb designed a church that is fortress-like in many of its forms and details. His sketches indicate that he regarded the northeast view as particularly important. (The church sits immediately adjacent to an east-west road, slightly west of the town center.) He planned a powerful east-end composition consisting of a deeply recessed, gabled central (chancel) block bracketed by two-storied vestry and organ chamber blocks. The details of these blocks, as well as of the rest of the church, are very simple and very heavy. All stone is laid in an irregular ashlar pattern. The windows of this facade, except for the large chancel window, are small and square-headed with their frames flush with the wall. There is the suggestion of battlement in the design of the gable/parapet intersections.

The north facade is equally interesting. The composition builds from the powerful vertical vestry block, which is gabled and given an exaggerated chimney, through a triple set of tall, gabled aisle bays that repeat the intersecting gable/parapet motif of the east facade and establish a strong horizontal rhythm, to the sheer, almost unbuttressed, vertical mass of the tower. An arched portal with a shed roof mediates between the vertical mass of the tower and the horizontal body of the church and seems to marry the forms to each other. (Webb intended for the tower to receive an octagon and spire, but he designed the present tower when it became apparent that something more economical was called for. The scheme as built is more powerful than the original design; it is also more consistent with the fortress-church concept that controlled the design of the remainder of the church.)

The fortress image prevails everywhere. Tower walls are solid. Most windows are placed high in the walls. (Although the tower has a large west window in its base, its deep recess emphasizes the thickness of the wall, giving the impression of great weight and mass.) One great pitched roof covers nave and aisles. The gables of the north aisle windows are embattled, as are the north and south tower tops. (The tower has gables on its east and west facades; between these runs a pitched roof. From this major roof, smaller transept-like pitched-roofs run to north and south. At the intersection of the two tower roofs, like a crossing fleche, sits the small lead spire; its

Exterior View of the Church of St. Martin, Brampton, from the Northwest
St. Martin is fortress-like in appearance with embattled gables and a powerful, stumpy tower without a spire.

Exterior Detail of North Entry Porch Arch and Eave at the Church of St. Martin, Brampton

Exterior Detail of North Facade Aisle Gables at the Church of St. Martin, Brampton

delicacy emphasizes the strength of the tower. The merlins of the aisle-gable-embattlements become the horizontal parapet of the aisle block when it turns to meet the tower. The parapet of the entrance porch is also embattled but with merlins that establish a much faster rhythm than those on the aisle gables. These details are original but not capricious; they are totally consistent with Webb's fortress-church concept.)

St. Martin's is not a church building intended for a High-church, Tractarian congregation. Its plan is to-

tally unlike most other Victorian churches, except perhaps for those of Lamb. The plan of the church is almost square. It is a hall-church four bays long and three bays wide. There is no true chancel space, only a recess in the center bay of the east wall where the altar and the great five-lancet windows by Morris/Burne-Jones are located. The railings around the easternmost bays of the aisles separate the sanctuary from the congregation. These bays contain second-level vestry and organ chambers (these are the blocks discussed earlier); their different ceiling level makes them seem special and different, establishing a chancel of sorts.

The heavy, somber character of the exterior does not prevail in the interior, which is very light. Space rather than mass is dominant inside. Slender octagonal stone piers carry wide stone arches that divide nave from aisles and help to support the roof.

237

to a low side wall without breaking the single roof plane that covers the south half of the nave and the south aisle bays. There are dormers in each south aisle bay, as well as aisle windows in the aisle wall.

The north aisle is totally different. Each of the three north aisle bays has a wooden-tunnel vault perpendicular to the longitudinal axis of the nave. These vaults give the north wall the height necessary for the large arched windows in the gables of the north facade described earlier.

All interior masonry walls are plastered and painted white; all wooden ceilings are painted green. (Webb liked this color-scheme and often used it in his houses; it is more consistent with the Queen Anne than the Gothic style, however.) Only the piers, arches, altar recess, and window frames are gray stone.

The interior of St. Martin's is certainly unusual (Pevsner describes it as on the verge of gimmickry in his *Buildings of England* volume on Cumbria),[4] but its effect is extremely pleasant. Obviously, Webb appreciated the muscularity and vigor of High Victorian churches. The exterior of St. Martin's is certainly consistent with this style. Inside, however, St. Martin's is not a traditional High Victorian Gothic church. Its character, its lightness, suggests the Old English and Queen Anne styles to come. The building is transitional; it represents the end of one era and the beginning of another.

The stained glass windows, especially the great three-tiered east window, are glorious—certainly the most significant feature of the interior of the church. The entire set of windows was done by Morris and Company with Edward Burne-Jones as designer. Webb, who had been a partner in the earlier firm of Morris, Marshall, Faulker and Com-

Interior Section/Elevation Looking toward the Chancel at the Church of St. Martin, Brampton, Showing Its Unique Treatment of Aisle and Nave Spaces

The nave roof is flat and has wooden fan coving above the piers. (I find this to be a disturbing detail; I want these fans to be part of a complete wooden fan vaulting system—they seem strangely truncated as they are.) The south aisle is covered with a lean-to roof; but what might be expected to be a simple space is complicated with a large cornice-cove that sweeps out to intersect with a vertical wooden surface that rises to the sloping roof. The purpose of this spatial manipulation is to modulate the tall space

pany, secured the commission for his friends. Although there is no record of Webb's involvement in the design of the St. Martin's windows, it is reasonable to assume that he organized, supervised, and coordinated the stained glass here. (This had been his role in the earlier company.) The strongly architectonic character of the windows is consistent with the production of the firm while Webb was involved; it is inconsistent with the character of the other windows Morris and Burne-Jones produced during the late 1870s and early 1880s. (During this period Morris became increasingly absorbed in politics, in textile design, and in poetic composition and gradually withdrew from involvement in the design of windows, leaving even color selection to Burne-Jones. It is not surprising, therefore, that elsewhere the work of the firm changed from the strongly architectonic character of the artist-decorator-architect collaboration that had characterized its earlier production to a painterly pictorial style approximating in glass the style of Burne-Jones' panel pictures.)

The first designs completed were for the west and center windows of the north aisle; these date from 1878. The designs for the great chancel east window and the other north aisle window followed in 1880 and 1881 respectively. The remainder of the windows were added over the next two decades, culminating with the circular window in the baptistry at the west end of the south aisle which was installed in 1898. The north aisle windows consist of paired lancets with a single tracery opening in the arched head. Burne-Jones divided the lancets in half and placed a figure of a patriarch, king, or prophet in each part, creating a two-tiered composition. The figures are in the Michelangelesque style that had characterized Burne-Jones' designs of the earlier

1870s. Burne-Jones had returned to Italy at the beginning of the decade to continue his study of Renaissance painting. As a result of this trip, his earlier infatuation with quatrocento painters was replaced with a new enthusiasm for the works of High Renaissance artists. This enthusiasm is plainly visible in the designs for the St. Martin's windows. The figure of fallen Adam consigned to labor at the top left in the westernmost north aisle window is based upon a Michelangelo "bound slave," for example. Burne-Jones was not exclusive in his eclecticism, however; the Adam in the tracery light above is borrowed from Giovanni Bellini's St. Sebastian in the San Giobbe altarpiece. This window includes, in addition to Adam, figures of Noah (upper right, shown holding the ark in his left hand with the dove bringing the branch over his shoulder), Enos (below Adam, shown with his hand grasping a hand that reaches from heaven), and Abraham (shown holding a long sword.)

The other two windows of the north aisle are very similar to this one. The center window of the three includes the figures of Moses, David, Solomon, and Elijah. Each can be identified by the detail of the design. Moses holds the tablets of the law, David is playing the harp, Solomon holds the temple, and Elijah is being fed by the Raven. The east window of this set portrays the figures of St. John the Evangelist and St. Luke in the upper tier (both based on cartoons done originally for windows in the Jesus College chapel, Cambridge. Burne-Jones used the same designs over and over in reversed positions and new colorations.) The bottom tier is devoted to figures of St. Peter and St. Paul. The three windows all feature figures in rich jewel-like colors posed against a background of clear quarries. The clear glass not only sets-off the figures dramatically, but it

(left) Burne-Jones' "St. Luke" Window, Jesus College Chapel, Oxford, Made by the Morris Company in 1873

(right) Burne-Jones' "SS. John, Luke, Peter, and Paul," North Aisle, East Window, St. Martin, Brampton, Made by the Morris Company in 1881, Using Reworked Cartoons from the Jesus College Commission

also lets in the necessary light to see and appreciate the interior space. The figures do not have the monumentality of their predecessors at Jesus College, however. At Jesus College the figures completely fill their frames and seem about to burst from them into our world. At St. Martin's, in contrast, they are static and serene, and much less powerful, due to the balance between figure and ground.

The windows of the south aisle, done between 1887 and 1898, reveal Burne-Jones' late style—a style that emphasizes pictorial composition rather than the two-dimensional architectural plane in which the windows lie. The Sacrifice and Victory panels are illustrative of this development. They are not nearly as successful as integral components of the architectural whole as are the earlier windows.

The great chancel east window is Burne-Jones' piece-de-resistance here. It is, with the "Last Judgement" window at Easthampstead and the "Rivers of Paradise" window at Allerton, one of the Morris firm's great masterworks of the late 1870s. These three windows represent the beginning of Burne-Jones' practice of treating adjacent lights in a large window as a single picture plane having a unified pictorial composition that is seen through, or behind, the window tracery. In each case, the entire composition is symmetrical although the composition of individual lights is asymmetrical. The figures all seem to occupy the plane of the glass, yet suggest depth at the same time. The windows retain Gothic tiered organization and a tapestry-like background pattern that precludes spatial recession and binds the figures together. The figures themselves are classically conceived and realistically posed, however; they owe nothing to Gothic precedent. They contain something of the contraposto and agi-

tation of the great Jesus College figures but little of their monumentality and strength. Moreover, Burne-Jones counterbalances the figures so exactly that the effect of the window as a whole is not one of movement but of timeless stillness.

The east window figures include, in the top tier, Christ the Good Shepherd shown carrying a lamb and flanked by musical angels. The second tier is filled with angels with scrolls. The bottom tier shows a pelican feeding its young, flanked by figures of St. Martin, the church's patron, and the Virgin Mary on the left and St. Dorothea and St. George on the right. In Christian art, the pelican is both a symbol of charity and an emblem of Jesus Christ. This association is based on the fallacious medieval belief that the pelican fed her young with her own blood. The medieval bestiary tells us that when the young birds grow they rebel against the male parent, provoking his anger so that he kills them; whereupon the mother returns to the nest, sits on the dead birds for three days, pouring her own blood over them, until they revive. Shed blood, resurrection in three days—the parallel is plain.

Burne-Jones was particularly proud of this window. He wrote in his account book in May 1880:

> To Brampton window—a colossal work of fifteen subjects—a masterpiece of style, a chef d'oeuvre of invention, a capo d'opera of conception—fifteen compartments—a Herculean labor—hastily estimated in a moment of generous friendship for 200 pounds, if the firm regards as binding a contract made from a noble impulse, and in a mercenary spirit declines to re-open the question, it must remain—but it will remain equally a monument of art and ingratitude—200 pounds! [5]

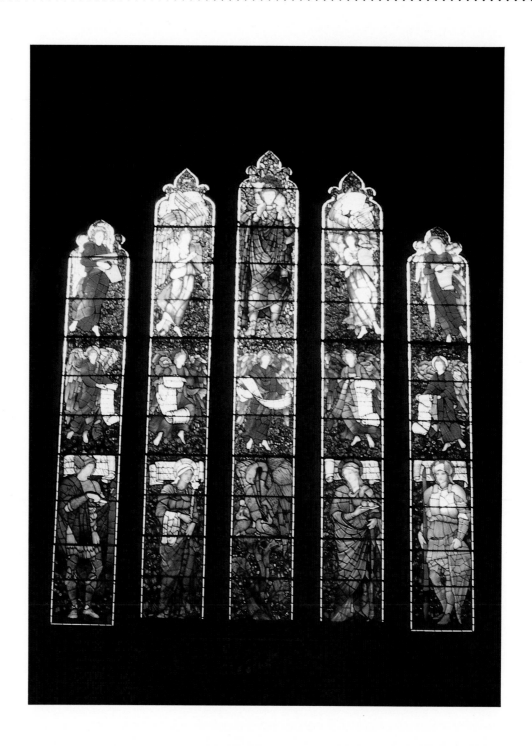

The East, Chancel, Window at the Church
of St. Martin, Brampton, Designed by
Burne-Jones in 1880

There is no record as to whether or not Burne-Jones was able to negotiate an adjustment to his fee. Nor do we know what the reaction of architect or client to the window was. To this writer, however, Burne-Jones' claims for his design are accurate, not presumptuous. The east window at St. Martin's, Brampton, is truly one of the masterpieces of Victorian art.

NOTES

1. W. R. Lethaby, *Philip Webb and His Work* (1935; London: Raven Oak Press, 1979), 7.

2. Peter Davey, *Arts and Crafts Architecture: The Search for Earthly Paradise* (London: Architectural Press, 1980), 30.

3. Lethaby, 75.

4. Nikolaus Pevsner, *Cumberland and Westmoreland*, Buildings of England Series (Harmondsworth: Penguin, 1967), 74–76.

5. A. Charles Sewter, *The Stained Glass of William Morris and his Circle—A Catalog* (New Haven and London: Yale University Press, 1975), 30.

EDWARD BUCKTON LAMB

B. Lamb (1806–1869) was described by H. S. Goodhardt-Rendel as the "arch-rogue" of the group of High Victorian architects he classified as rogue nonconformists.[1] Lamb is the originator of a High Victorian Gothic style that, while every bit as muscular and powerful as any other, is uniquely original.

Lamb was the son of a civil servant whose hobby was painting. When the young man demonstrated creative, artistic talent of his own, he was articled to the well-known restorer of Gothic churches, L. N. Cottingham. Lamb developed rapidly as both architect and artist. By the age of eighteen he had become a regular exhibitor at the Royal Academy.

In 1832, when Lamb was in his mid-twenties, he was employed by John Claudius Loudon to illustrate the *Encyclopedia of Cottage, Farm and Villa Architecture*. The house designs Lamb created for it are in the picturesque mode of Nash and Soane; however, they show a boldness, a muscularity, that picturesque Regency domestic architecture never possessed. Loudon admired the work of his young draftsman; Lamb's contributions to Loudon's *Architectural Magazine* were regularly accepted thereafter.

During his career, Lamb designed more than thirty churches and a number of country houses and vicarages. Although he is best known for his church designs, his most important commission was for the remodeling of Hughenden Manor (1863–66) for the prime minister, Benjamin Disraeli.

Lamb was an independent genius, an original creator, his own man. He was never a part of the mainstream Gothic revival as practiced by Butterfield, Street, and Pearson and as supported by the Ecclesiological movement. His work and his philosophy are not based upon Pugin's writing; Lamb had been a practicing Gothicist for over ten years when Pugin's writing first appeared. By this time Lamb had already developed his own Neo-Gothic style, and he persevered in it even when fashion took architecture in a different direction.

Today we are able to admire Lamb's consistent, highly personable style in spite of its crudities and its unusual planning. This was not the case in Lamb's lifetime; only in the recent past has Lamb's work received favorable consideration from architectural critics. (Summerson, in his splendid essay on Street and Lamb, "Two London Churches," suggests that today we find it agreeable to be shocked by Lamb's originality.)[2]

Lamb was either ignored or vilified by most Victorian critics. *The Ecclesiologist* despised his Christ Church, West Hartlepool, of 1854, and refused to comment on his subsequent work. *The Builder* and *Building News* were only slightly less hostile. Eastlake ignores Lamb entirely. Critics disliked Lamb's work because it was usually Perpendicular Gothic, a style labeled as debased by *The Ecclesiologist*, rather than the approved Decorated style, and because it ignored Tractarian demands for plans laid out to accommodate High Church ritual. Henry-Russell Hitchcock maintains that it was Lamb's scorn for ritualistic planning that really did him in with the Camdenians who were able to take the stylistic vagaries of architects like White and Teulon in stride.[3] Lamb did not design churches for High Church ritual; he was a Low Churchman sought out by other Low Churchmen to design their churches. He liked large amounts of usable space for congregational use near, not in, the chancel; he tried to plan his churches so

that all worshippers could be as near the pulpit as possible. Consequently, most of his churches seem to be centrally planned although in reality they are not; all have extended naves. However, the space in his churches expands near the chancel, and his great tent-like wooden roof constructions emphasize centrality.

Nevertheless, Lamb's churches, in many respects, are typical, rather than atypical, of High Victorian Gothic architecture. They are always picturesque and fanciful; they feature boldly sculpted forms that balance vertical and horizontal masses; they are heavy and muscular in effect; and they use strongly contrasting materials inside and out. Although Lamb rarely employs polychromy, he always features textural contrasts between smooth and rough stone and between stone and wood.

Hitchcock calls Lamb's Gothic "cranky" and cites the coarse detail and nervous silhouette of his forms as proof.[4] Lamb's crankiness comes, also, from contrasts in coarse and delicate detail and from an almost obsessive passion for broken lines and articulated structural elements. However, many of these characteristics and certain of his details, especially segmental-pointed arches and curious notchings and chamferings, are typical of the period.

Yet Lamb's architecture is truly unique. No one else shaped buildings to feature overlappings and penetrations in quite the same way. (He said, in his lecture on architectural composition published by the *Building News* in 1857, that the architect must use features, projections, solids, and voids to put his lights and shades, his forms, his effects, into the subject itself much like the painter uses trees, figures, sky, and clouds to compose a picture.)[5] He preferred complication to simplicity, and it shows.

He liked irregularity, but he achieved a kind of unity by repetition of the same sort of irregularity throughout a building. He was exceptionally bold in the contrast of very large and very small features. His picturesque effects seem uncontrived because they are inevitably achieved by the articulation of plan components. (Lamb preached that the articulation of major spaces resulted in a picturesque silhouette with little help from the architect; he practiced what he preached. Major spaces are given taller forms and richer decoration; minor spaces are given lower forms and less decoration.)

All of Lamb's work was based on a carefully considered architectural philosophy. In the lecture mentioned he said, "The main qualities necessary for the composition of a great work in fine art architecture are—unity, harmony of form, harmony of material, and harmony of construction. . . . Architecture may be considered the art of investing the useful with the garb of beauty, but only in such manner as will constitute perfect unity."[6]

Lamb was convinced that nineteenth-century Gothic should pick up where sixteenth-century Gothic left off. He believed that the Renaissance had been an interruption in the natural evolution of architecture; he said that if this interruption had not occurred, medieval architecture would have produced a style "possessing in its composition all the requirements of utility in its constructive elements, and of beauty in the harmonious combination of their parts."[7] He wanted to achieve this end in his century; it was for this reason that his forms were based most often on the last phase of Gothic, Perpendicular, rather than on an earlier period—he saw himself as picking up where the last Gothic architects left off.

Lamb followed a number of principles in his design. He tried to achieve a balance between conformity and variety in his work; he said that there should be nothing discordant (such as different roof pitches), or too much repetition of uniform elements. He believed forms should relate to each other without violent contrasts. He tried to emphasize the horizontal and the vertical and to de-emphasize the angular in order to avoid confusion in his designs. He believed that materials used should be limited in number and employed in large masses of simple construction. He also believed that buildings should rise organically from the earth; he liked powerful bases from which buildings rose in gradual stages. He said that the base, the string courses, and the cornice lines should bind the forms together into a unified composition. He felt that ornament should be integral to the structure; it should not be applied to it as decoration. He tried to achieve a balance of solids and voids sufficient for evident strength and durability, and he attempted to interlock all parts of his buildings visually so that no feature could be removed without damage to the whole. (He despised layering of blind arcades, screen walls, etc. for this reason.) The goal of all his rules was harmony of form and construction.

All Saints Church,
Thirkleby, North Yorkshire

Although All Saints, Thirkleby, 1848–50, is actually earlier than Butterfield's All Saints, Margaret Street, the church generally conceded to have inaugurated the High Victorian period, there is no question that it is High Victorian in style. It is hard to imagine a bolder composition of muscular sculptural forms than this. It is heavy and solid in the best High Victorian tradition. It even uses the Decorated style for its details, and its plan is orthodox—nave with clerestories and north and south aisles, lower chancel, and tower engaged to the aisle at the northwest corner of the composition. What is unusual is the manner in which the forms are handled.

The west facade is typical of Lamb's idiosyncratic design approach. The entrance porch is placed between the tower and the main body of the church; it effectively joins the two major forms in a carefully balanced composition. Its north roof slope is a visual continuation of the north slope of the nave roof. An octagonal stair tower, partly engaged in the corner of the larger tower and partly engaged in the porch, aids the porch in marrying the larger forms. The porch facade is asymmetrical; the roof on the left which overlaps the stair tower continues to a lower point than the roof on the right. The west facade of

Exterior View of All Saints Church, Thirkleby, North Yorkshire, from the West
The asymmetrical west facade composition is typical of Lamb's idiosyncratic design approach.

of the tower below. Overscaled diagonal buttresses are located at the tower corners; these recede in stages until they terminate two-thirds of the way up the tower's second, belfry, stage. The wall of the first stage corbels out, then chamfers in to form a base to support the belfry. The belfry is capped by a cornice that corbels out to support the spire, which, in turn, recedes sharply before it becomes steep and octagonal. The forms are different, but the transition from form to form is much like that between first stage and belfry in effect. Two pinnacles pierce the lower slope of the spire on each side. This is a tower of great weight, firmly anchored to the ground.

Pevsner, in his *Buildings of England* volume on North Yorkshire, says that All Saints "is a veritable riot of forms, perverse and mischievous, and one takes a perverse pleasure in it."[8] With the exception of the confused composition of the last end, which includes a chapel which looks like the base for a second incomplete tower, the building is eminently satisfying to the modern eye. It gains harmony and unity not from the repetition of identical forms but from a composition of similar forms which seem organically related by weight, shape, material, and relationship to the ground. Its idiosyncrasies—like the strange window forms, some segmental, some round, some bisected by buttresses—serve to add vitality and lightness to a composition that otherwise might seem leaden.

Inside, except for the incidental details, the church more nearly approaches the High Victorian norm than Lamb's other buildings do. Its great hammer-beam roofs are powerfully impressive, however. They foreshadow the emphasis placed on heavy, intricate wood roof structures in his later churches.

Exterior View of All Saints Church, Thirkleby, from the Southeast
Only the strange east end composition justifies the negative reaction that Lamb's work often receives.

the nave is also asymmetrical. It has a flying buttress on the right side of the great Decorated west window, and the south aisle climbs up in steps to meet the nave.

The tower is extremely powerful. It has three stages—two square stages plus a broached spire with concave sides equal in height to the solid mass

Christ Church, Church Square, West Hartlepool, County Durham

Christ Church, West Hartlepool, designed in 1849 and built in 1854, was Lamb's first important urban commission. It is considerably larger than the Thirkleby church and not nearly so pleasing visually. Although the emphasis upon the strength and weight of the stone construction and the desire for a picturesque silhouette are the same, the relationship between the masses, at least from the west entrance front, is much less satisfactory at West Hartlepool.

Christ Church is important, however, because it is here that Lamb first explored the syntheses he desired between longitudinal space and central focus and between stone wall and wood roof structure, features that would dominate his two great London churches, St. Martin, Gospel Oak, and St. Mary Magdalene, Addiscombe.

In its massiveness, design details, and play of sculptural forms, Christ Church's tower is a study for the tower of St. Martin, Gospel Oak. At Christ Church, the tower is located Wren-like in the center of the west facade. (How much more pleasing is the asymmetrical position of the tower at Thirkleby and Gospel Oak.) The primary entrance to the church is on the longitudinal axis through a portal in a small projecting porch in the base of the tower. The tower is very tall—too tall—in relation to the low forms of

Exterior View of Christ Church, Church Square, West Hartlepool, County Durham, from the Southwest
Here the tower is everything.

249

the church behind it. This height is exaggerated by the tower's forms. Lamb has chosen to substitute a very tall, square belfry, equal in height to the first two stages of the tower below, for the spire he had used at Thirkleby.

The tower is a study in the use of projection and recession. The entire church, including the tower, sits on a plinth that recedes in two chamfered stages. The tower repeats this plinth, making its base twice as tall as the base of the rest of the church. At the top of the first stage the tower corbels out slightly, then chamfers back dramatically to make a new base for tower stage two. Similar sculptural gymnastics create a base for the belfry stage. The belfry is capped by a cornice that corbels out, then sweeps back and up to make a concave parapet. (These are the same devices Lamb had experimented with at Thirkleby, repeated more often and more dramatically.) George Hersey, who ascribes gender to buildings in his book, *High Victorian Gothic*, says the tower has a phallic silhouette, "made almost naturalistic by the deep pent roof at the belfry stage."[9]

The forms of the larger tower are repeated in a much more slender form in the stair tower engaged to its southeast corner. The small broached spire of the smaller tower projects past the top of the main tower, like a finger pointing to God. Tower windows are all relatively small, and the portal is carved out of the mass and is cavelike in feeling. The weight and power of the stone masonry is everything. The slenderness and delicacy of the stair tower emphasize the strength and mass of the main tower. The flaw in the design is that the tower is too widely separated by the nave extension from the complex geometry of the east end of the church. Conse-

Exterior View of Christ Church, West Hartlepool, from the East
This shows the very long transept arms that were necessary for Lamb to develop the large central interior space he desired.

quently, the tower is unable to engage the critical mass of the composition and anchor it to its site.

Inside and out, the masonry has a wrought rockface surface. No polychromy is employed here. The details are vaguely Early English, although they are anti-archaeological in their originality.

The plan is interesting in its efforts to be both longitudinal and centralized. The east end of the church is laid out as a Greek Cross with one arm, the chancel, apsed octagonally. Between the arms of the crossing, in each of the four corners, is an aisle/chapel construction; each of these is given its own gabled roof with its ridge parallel to the ridge of the main body of the church. These four structures are treated as aisles which become part of the seating area of the church auditorium, creating a large central space before the chancel. The nave extends past its aisles further than do the transepts and chancel, adding a longitudinal dimension (and additional seating) to the plan. Transepts, aisles, and nave open to each other to make it possible for most worshippers not only to sit near the pulpit but also to have an unobstructed view.

Also interesting is the manner in which Lamb roofs the large central space. Heavy low-springing timber arches span all plan units. At the crossing similar timber arches—Pevsner calls them cyclopic[10]—are placed diagonally on crossing piers; these carry a tent-like open timber roof crowned by a small lantern that lets badly needed light into the dark, wide, low space. (This plan and this structural system will be repeated in Lamb's two London churches with only minor variations.)

The church follows Lamb's dictum that a good plan articulated in the building's forms can create a picturesque ensemble. The interior configuration of Christ Church is expressed in its exterior forms, and the church is dramatically picturesque in its silhouette. Hersey says that the building "telegraphs its functions with sculptural vim."[11]

The Church of St. Simon and St. Jude, Englefield Green, Surrey

In 1858, Lamb received the commission to design a parish church, a non-denominational chapel, and two mausolea for the Fitzroy Somerset family. The Church of St. Simon and St. Jude at Englefield Green is the result of this commission.

Hitchcock, in his *Surrey* volume of *The Buildings of England* series, says that St. Simon and St. Jude is not one of Lamb's most memorable buildings although he describes the constructional polychromy of the interior as "unforgetable."[12] This assessment is a serious devaluation of the church's bold High Victorian features and Lamb's unique design sensitivity.

The plan of the church and its relationship to the road is peculiar. Access is from the east, or chancel, end, which is seen by the passerby. Unfortunately, the south transept has received a modern extension; it has been extended to create a parish hall. Consequently, the original clarity of the parts—nave, tower chancel, south transept, and north

Exterior View of the Church of St. Simon
and St. Jude, Englefield Green, Surrey,
Showing the Major Entry through the South
Transept Tower

tower—has been obscured. Primary entry was intended to be through the north transept portal. How the High Church people must have despised this: it destroys the processional relationship of nave to chancel. (In fact, even today this door is locked and people enter "around back" through the south porch, a door located further to the rear of the nave.)

Lamb attempted to make the church's smallness a feature, striving for intimacy rather than formality. The church has no aisles and no true clerestory; the powerful wood trussed roof is supported on low exterior walls; the chancel roof is lower still. The nave

is broader than it is tall. Nave windows are two-light windows with segmental heads, and in the roof above each one is a two-light dormer window with small mullioned panes of glass. This nave fenestration looks more domestic than ecclesiastical. The exterior of the church is built of Kentish ragstone laid in a rough, irregular ashlar pattern that is extremely informal in appearance. There is very little dressed stone trim.

The major exterior design features of St. Simon and St. Jude are the great windows of the east and west facades and the tower. The west window is a five-lancet Decorated-style window that occupies more than a third of the wall. The east window is unique; it is similarly large and has an unusual cusped shape with blind tracery panels on either side of and below a three-lancet, Decorated, center window. Hitchcock calls it proto-typical Art Nouveau; it represents Lamb's personal adaptation of traditional forms.

The tower is much shorter and stockier than the tower at West Hartlepool, but it has a similar silhouette. It has three stages, a cubical base stage, a second stage a third again as tall, and a cap stage that is made up of a parapet with vertical center panels (the east one is triangular and is decorated with a clock) between corners that recede as if they were the corners of a pyramid. A short pyramidal roof is barely visible above the parapet. At the juncture betweeen the west tower wall and the nave, a tall slender octagonal stair tower is located; it extends past the cap of the main tower to form a picturesque turret. The silhouette of the church from the northeast is, consequently, the boldest, most interesting view.

The interior's constructional polychrome is far-and-away the most interesting feature of the work. This church is Lamb's great experiment with constructional polychromy; most of his buildings are singularly monochromatic. The nave walls feature alternate bands of brick laid in various ornamental patterns, dressed limestone, and Kentish rag. The brick is predominantly red with bits of blue, the limestone is cream, the Kentish rag is gray. Below the window sills and two-thirds of the way up the window, Lamb inserts a course of brick laid askew to form a row of notches. The two widest brick bands, one of which functions as cornice, are laid in

Exterior Detail of Nave Fenestration and Tower at the Church of St. Simon and St. Jude, Englefield Green
This shows the introduction of clerestory light through dormer windows.

253

a herringbone pattern. The window heads receive a segmental canopy of limestone that appears detached from the outer wall surface. The walls support a trussed rafter roof that is much simpler than Lamb's typical wood roof constructions. (This church does not expand the seating in front of the chancel; consequently there was no need for the kind of complicated roof construction given churches with more central planning.)

The chancel of St. Simon and St. Jude is seen through a particularly well-proportioned arch with a relatively low spring. Bracketed moldings decorate its soffit; a three-course brick and stone arch is concentric with the chamfered limestone arch. Through it is visible an elaborately decorated two-bay chancel. A graceful wood truss with a bottom chord formed to echo the shape of the chancel arch divides choir from sanctuary. The reredos, wainscot, and the blind tracery panels of the east window are inlaid with mastic and gold in both geometric and figurative designs. The upper east wall is gilded and frescoed with stars and angels that bracket the figure of the resurrected Christ in the stained glass. The effect is gorgeous, but Lamb must not have liked it, because the decorative treatment utilized in this chancel and the constructional polychromy of the interior walls disappeared from his oeuvre, not to be used again.

Interior Detail of Constructional Polychromy in the nave wall at the Church of St. Simon and St. Jude, Englefield Green

Interior View of Nave Looking West at the Church of St. Simon
and St. Jude, Englefield Green, Showing the Low, Wide, Simple
Character of the Space and Its Polychromy

Interior View of the Sanctuary at the Church
of St. Simon and St. Jude, Englefield Green
This is Lamb's most elaborately decorated
interior space.

The Church of
St. Martin, Vicar's Road,
Gospel Oak, London

Lamb's first opportunity to design a major London church came in 1862 when he was hired by John Derby Allcroft to design the Church of St. Martin, Gospel Oak. Allcroft was a self-made man who made a fortune manufacturing gloves. He was an evangelical churchman who paid to have St. Martin built in a London slum as an act of Christian charity. We don't know how he became acquainted with Lamb, but he certainly found the right architect for the kind of evangelical "low" church he had in mind. Construction began in 1862 and the church was completed in 1865.

St. Martin's exterior appearance has been spoiled by the addition of a chapel in the church's open northwest corner and by the destruction of its tower's pinnacles and turrets in World War II. Today the best way to appreciate the strength of Lamb's original scheme is to study his perspective of the church published in *The Builder* in 1866.[13]

The plan of St. Martin is almost identical to that of Christ Church except for the location of the tower. Here Lamb made the tower an almost freestanding element at the center of the composition, attached to a corner of the large central mass. The nave and north transept bracketed it on two sides. On the other two sides it stood free. From the northwest the tower appeared to stand on colossal masonry legs that seemed to "heave-up" (Summerson's expression)[14] the heavy masonry mass of the tower

Exterior View of the Church of St. Martin, Vicar's Road, Gospel Oak, London, as Originally Designed
Sketch from an illustration in the *Builder* in 1866.

257

into the air. (The addition of the chapel filled the open northwest corner of the original composition; now the tower seems to rise out of a disorganized composition instead of standing free of the other forms, as was originally intended.)

The relationship of the tower to the church was much the same as at Street's St. James the Less, but with a very different effect. The details of St. Martin's tower are essentially the same as those of the tower at West Hartlepool. It uses the same corbel-out/chamfer-back device to create bases for the upper stages; it eschews a spire in favor of a very tall tower; it exaggerates the weight and mass of the masonry in the way it is sculpted; and it has engaged at its southwest corner a tall slender stair tower with a turret rising above its roof. Because of its changed location, however, the relationship be-

tween the tower and the rest of the church was extremely successful before the chapel was added; at Christ Church this was not the case. This tower is the centerpiece that organized and anchored all other masses into a harmonious unity.

Lamb used another device to organize and discipline the church's coarse rock-face stone; all Kentish

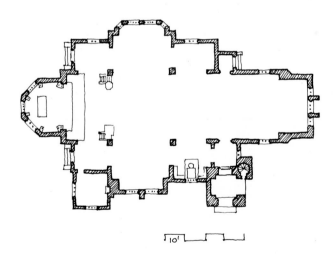

Plan of the Church of St. Martin, Gospel Oak
Lamb's hallmark is the great central space created by a dramatic expansion of transepts.

Exterior Detail of North Transept Window at the Church of St. Martin, Gospel Oak

Interior View toward the Chancel at the Church of St. Martin, Gospel Oak

Lamb's low, heavy, elaborate wood roof structures made possible the open congregational space that Low Church congregations desired.

Interior Detail of Nave and Transept Intersection at the Church of St. Martin, Gospel Oak

transept facade is typical of Lamb's idiosyncratic experimentation with Perpendicular details. The facade has a single buttress at its center between two three-panel perpendicular windows with segmental pointed-arch heads. The buttress continues up to bisect an oculus in the facade gable above. The buttress element is repeated inside in the form of a shaft. Another example of overlapping, repeating forms is the major entrance portal. In its review of the church, *The Builder* said, "The style . . . is that which was in general use at the time of Henry VII; but the building must be considered rather as a characteristic expression of that style, than as a reproduction, for it would be difficult to find an absolute precedent for any portion of the work."[16] Although few of his contemporaries used Perpendicular details, it is not surprising that Lamb did so. Lamb really saw himself as resuming the evolution of Gothic architecture that had been broken off at the time of the Renaissance.

In St. Martin, Lamb has abandoned the experimentation with constructional polychromy that was a feature of the church at Englefield Green. Only in the boldly diapered tile roof is color and pattern used as decoration independent of structure. Lamb has returned to the essence of his original design philosophy, which focused on the picturesque expression of a utilitarian plan. St. Martin's plan is extremely functional; virtually all the one thousand worshippers it can accommodate can see and hear the service. Moreover, the plan is translated directly into a very picturesque composition. Wherever you look there is a picturesque ensemble of gable ends, hipped roofs, eaves, and parapets. There is a great unity of forms; all speak the same language; all belong to the same family.

rag masonry planes are edged with crisply dressed Bath stone. About this device Hersey said, "[The] Bath stone skeleton interpenetrates and, especially in the tower, frames the mass. Often these elements, at least on the south side, form themselves into gratuitous gables and pinnacles, squeezing the panels of softer stone and pressing down vertical features such as turrets, tower, buttresses, etc. . . ."[15]

The exterior design details are Lamb's original reinterpretations of Perpendicular forms. Nothing is foreign; nothing is borrowed from any other architect. The treatment of the windows in the north

Lamb's concept of the picturesque derives from Nash and is unique at mid-century. In an 1846 article, Lamb wrote that the essential elements of the picturesque are "contrast, irregularity and inequality. . . . The convenient distribution of the apartments should be the foundation of the picturesque . . . in this principle alone can the picturesque be considered beautiful."[17]

The position of the entrance at the west end of the longitudinal axis at West Hartlepool de-emphasized the church's major central space. At St. Martin, however, the position of the entry leading to an aisle which divides the seats in the nave extension from those in the great square of the central space reinforces the strong feeling of openness and centrality that one perceives upon entering. The great open character of the central space is a surprise; it is not revealed outside. The exterior suggests a traditional Latin cross plan.

The size of the church is also surprising. The length from end of the nave to end of the chapel is about 140 feet; the great central space is approximately seventy feet square; and the space defined by the piers at the crossing is about thirty feet by thirty-four feet. The chancel, in contrast, is actually quite small—approximately twenty-five feet square. It is apparent from the plan that this is a "low" rather than a "high" church.

As at West Hartlepool, the roof is composed of mighty hammerbeams that turn at right angles into the transepts, creating a tent-like structure supported on long diagonal rafters carried by four central piers. The piers echo the corbel-out/chamfer-back theme of the tower. At their bases they are square in section; they evolve into octagons, then into squares again. The upper squares chamfer back

Interior Detail of Roof Framing at Transept/Nave Pier at the Church of St. Martin, Gospel Oak

horizontally to create smaller squares; brackets that support shafts corbel out from these sloping planes. The shafts support the butts of the hammerbeam arches. Pevsner said that the form of these piers defied description.

The interior is both extremely open and spacious and very heavy and hard. The stone walls are relatively low and are totally subservient to the power of the dark, intricate wood roof pressing down above. Little color has been added; the chancel roof has been painted blue and white and the floors are patterned with tile. Most color comes from the church's stained glass windows, all of which have pointed, segmental-arch heads, a Lamb trademark. Even the sanctuary is severe. Although it is given a dressed stone interior shell which is much finer than the coarse Hassock stone walls that exist everywhere else, the shafts and the arches they carry retain a heaviness that is appropriate considering the coarseness of all other details.

St. Martin is a powerful architectural statement, yet it was almost ignored by the architectural press of the day. Only *The Builder* reviews it, giving it grudging respect instead of praise. Twentieth-century critics find St. Martin much more appealing, however. The noted architectural critic H. S. Goodhardt-Rendel, commenting on the church in 1949, described it as "a completely original and, I think, almost perfect, solution of what a large auditorium for protestant services should be."[18]

The Church of St. Mary Magdalene, Addiscombe, Croydon, Greater London

In 1868, one year before his death, Lamb received the commission for a second great London church, St. Mary Magdalene, Addiscombe. The church was completed in 1870, minus its tower which was not added until 1928–30.

The church, in plan and form, is very similar to St. Martin, Gospel Oak. The tower is in a different location. (The church has a single road frontage on its east, or chancel, side; consequently, the tower is located adjacent to the south side of the chancel.) Only the base story is built to Lamb's design. St. Mary Magdalene's fenestration is Lamb's unique reinterpretation of the Decorated style instead of the Perpendicular style, as at Gospel Oak. (The windows are traditional in shape, but many are set in recesses with triangular heads.) The upper exterior wall of the apse seems to layer-out over the lower wall.

Inside, St. Mary Magdalene is more richly decorated than is St. Martin. The openings in the great hammerbeams and the panels of the wood chancel vault are filled with wood tracery; the chancel arch and stone inner chancel shell is elaborately carved; and shafts and colonnettes are dark polished marble. These elegant details do little to enrich the character of the interior space; if anything, they detract from its strength and power. (A modern altar has been placed under the lantern at the center of the crossing; a spindly stick canopy is suspended over

Exterior Detail of East Facade at the Church of St. Mary Magdalene, Addiscombe, Showing the Base of the Tower and the Polygonal Chancel

it. This feature is not at home here even though it is appropriate for the geometry and plan of the space. Its mean design simply emphasizes the strength and power of Lamb's bravura building.)

Pevsner's review of St. Mary Magdalene in his *Buildings of England* series is mixed. He describes the timberwork as "ingenious and unexpected," but he calls the interior effect "nightmarish." He goes on to say, however, that "The church certainly de-

serves study, chiefly as a reminder of how far some Victorian church architects were from a mechanical imitation of the medieval past. This ruthless individualism is the necessary counterpart of Pearson's noble correctness."[19]

Interior Detail at the Crossing at the Church
of St. Mary Magdalene, Addiscombe

Interior View of the Church of St. Mary
Magdalene, Addiscombe
The interior is very similar to that at St.
Martin, Gospel Oak.

NOTES

1. H. S. Goodhardt-Rendel, "Rogue Architects of the Victorian Era, *R.I.B.A. Journal* (April 1949): 251–52.

2. John Summerson, *Victorian Architecture: Four Studies in Evaluation* (New York: Columbia University Press, 1970), 75.

3. Henry-Russell Hitchcock, *Early Victorian Architecture in Britain*, 2 vols. (New Haven: Yale University Press, 1954), 1: 159–60.

4. Hitchcock, 32.

5. E. B. Lamb, "Architectural Composition," *Building News* (Feb. 20, 1857): 185–87.

6. Lamb, 185–87.

7. Lamb, 185–87.

8. Nikolaus Pevsner, Yorkshire: the North Riding, Buildings of England Series (Harmondsworth: Penguin, 1966), 365.

9. George L. Hersey, *High Victorian Gothic* (Baltimore, London: John Hopkins University Press, 1972), 132.

10. Nikolaus Pevsner, *County Durham*, 2nd ed. (Harmondsworth and New York: Penguin, 1983), 311–12.

11. Hersey, 132.

12. Ian Nairn and Nikolaus Pevsner, *Surrey*, 2nd ed., Buildings of England Series (Harmondsworth: Penguin, 1971), 213.

13. *The Builder* (Oct. 20, 1866), 778–81.

14. Summerson, 71.

15. Hersey, 134.

16. *The Builder* (Oct. 20, 1866), 778–81.

17. Summerson, 72.

18. Summerson, 74.

19. Nairn and Pevsner, 180.

SAMUEL SAUNDERS TEULON

S. Teulon (1812–73) was one of the most aggressively original of High Victorian architects. He was born the son of a French Huguenot cabinetmaker in Greenwich. Because he demonstrated talent in art and was interested in architecture, he was sent to the Royal Academy Schools. As a teenager he began his architectural apprenticeship in the office of George Legg but soon moved on to Bermondsey and the office of George Porter. Neither was an architect of distinction, and neither was particularly avant-garde. It is hard to say how they influenced the young Teulon other than to give him a thorough grounding in building construction.

Teulon established his own practice sometime between 1838 and 1848; accounts differ as to the exact date. His practice got off to a good start; he won the 1840 competition for the design of the Dyers' Almshouses. He quickly attained prominence as an architect of churches and country houses. He was a polished, sophisticated man who related easily to the aristocracy; most of his clients were aristocrats rather than newly rich industrialists. Among others, his clients included the Queen, the Archbishop of Canterbury, and the Dukes of Bedford, Marlborough, and Saint Albans.

Eastlake included Teulon among the architects he categorized as followers of G. G. Scott.[1] It is difficult to identify anything in Teulon's works to support this position, other than the fact that both he and Scott worked in the Neo-Gothic style. Teulon is actually the most strongly individualistic of High Victorian architects. Paul Thompson called Teulon's work the ugliest of the High Victorian period. In the 1980s, when bold forms and constructional patterns, colors, and textures are again appreciated, it is difficult to accept Teulon's work as ugly.

Goodhardt-Rendel included Teulon among the group he called "rogue-architects"—a metaphor he used as an architectural parallel to the term rogue-elephants—[architects who are] "driven or living apart from the herd, and of savage temper."[2] This group included, in addition to Teulon, E. B. Lamb, James Wild, Romieu and Gough, Joseph Peacock, Bassett Keeling, and sometimes Butterfield, White, and Woodyer. Their works were described as bizarre, grotesque, discordant, peculiar, naughty, and savage by late nineteenth- and early twentieth-century historians; these are not, however, adjectives that would have been used to describe his work during the High Victorian era. Even *The Ecclesiologist*, that most ruthless critic and arbiter of ecclesiastical taste, usually liked Teulon and had an occasional good word to say about Lamb. Muthesius says that the single common denominator in the work of the High Victorian rogues is complication rather than simplicity.[3] To the current generation, tired of the simplicity of Modern architecture, the complication apparent in the works of architects like Teulon is again interesting, even attractive.

Teulon's work was substantially different from the work of most of his contemporaries. It is an extreme response to Ruskin's pleas for polychromy and rich naturalistic sculpture. Although most of the forms and details of Teulon's churches can be traced to thirteenth-century Gothic prototypes, his buildings feature mannered reinterpretations of these prototypes. His work is massive and heavy; it features expressive personal experimentation with Gothic geometries and forms. Unusual massing and exaggerated proportions are also characteristic. He combined French and English details freely, fusing them to create a style that is uniquely High Victorian. (This is particularly true of Teulon's interiors.)

Like Pearson, Teulon was interested in complicated penetrations of space, but Teulon's buildings emphasize strength and boldness rather than elegance and classical proportion. Like many of his colleagues, Teulon liked to employ a great variety of decorative features in each of his buildings—arches, profiles, traceries, and concentrations of decorative sculpture. Sometimes he used extremely unorthodox building materials; his Church of St. Mark, Silvertown, Essex, for example, employs drainage bricks for its main walls. His constructional polychromy was often more strident than that of Butterfield at his most flamboyant. He led the way, along with White, in the use of gray and yellow brick patterns, polychromatic roof tiles, and notched and billet-molded brick.

The tracery in his windows might be exaggerated, fanciful and bold, or it might butt into the exterior wall as if the windows were cut-outs without frames. Sometimes his tracery would be composed of simple stone slabs with openings made with perpendicular cuts; sometimes it would be elaborately sculpted. Teulon could get away with an inordinate amount of idiosyncratic detail because his overall compositions of crisply defined, compact masses were so powerful, simple, and effective.

Teulon's early work is unremarkable Early Victorian design. In the early 1850s, however, with his designs for Tortworth Court, Cromhall, Gloucestershire, and Holy Trinity Church, Hastings, Teulon moved into his fully developed High Victorian mode.

The Church of
the Holy Trinity,
Robertson Street, Hastings

Exterior View of the Church of the Holy Trinity, Robertson Street, Hastings, from the Northwest
The duality of the facade with its twin gables was influenced by Carpenter's church at Munster Square, except that Holy Trinity has two gables instead of the more conventional three.

The Church of the Holy Trinity was built on an important, but cramped, triangular site in downtown Hastings in 1852 through 1859. It is a large church; its internal length is 132 feet, the nave is 35 feet wide, and the aisle is 25 feet wide. The church is built of local stone laid in a small-scale, rough, ashlar pattern—the kind of wall loved by High Victorians but which would have been plastered-over in medieval times. Exterior constructional polychromy is not featured here; smooth stone dressing is used sparingly, except on the exterior of the polygonal chancel where it is the dominant material. Inside and out, Tuelon intended to contrast a rough, almost crude, nave with an elegant chancel.

The church has a single (south) aisle. Nave and aisle are both covered with steeply pitched roofs; consequently, the west facade has two adjacent gables, of almost equal height, in the same plane. The duality of this bifurcated facade is relieved by an asymmetrical fenestration pattern. The left-hand portion (the nave facade) has a single, very large, six-lancet, Decorated-style, arched window placed fairly high in the wall. The adjacent aisle facade has an extraordinary arched portal with a hexagonal star-shaped window above it. The sill line of the large nave west window corresponds to the arch spring-line of the portal; this relationship is established by a single, small, projecting, stone molding.

The portal is an interesting and original design in its own right. It consists of two concentric arches—one very tall, one much shorter—with the space between (the tympanum) filled with a radiating tracery pattern of distorted triangles and lozenges generated by the apex of the smaller arch. The tracery is very powerful; the outer arch frame is insignificant; the design is a tracery infill in a wall cut-out.

An alternate entry into the west end of the church is provided through a portal in the north side of the westernmost bay of the nave. This portal consists of a cusped-arched doorway in what appears, at first glance, to be a shallow-gabled porch. In reality the gable is an illusion Teulon makes by breaking up the projecting stone molding mentioned above into a point above the door. A blind tracery rondel is inserted in this false gable. The apex of the false gable touches a triangular window placed in the true gable above.

Each bay of the nave is articulated on the side facade by means of a gabled roof which is perpendicular to the main nave gable. These six gables create a tall, sheer, spiky north wall, unrelieved by buttresses. (The gables allow for the buttresses to be on the inside as at Bodley's Pendlebury church.)

The chancel is slightly narrower and slightly taller than the nave. Its roof breaks up above the nave roof. From the east the church appears to have a twelve-sided polygonal chancel with an independently hipped, very steep roof. Actually the roof is a gable with a hipped east end, but the space is so constricted on the sides of the church that the illusion of chancel as polygonal structure is not corrected or resolved for viewers. The chancel buttresses reinforce the polygonal character of the apse and help to camouflage its resolution into the side

Exterior Detail of the West Portal at the Church of the Holy Trinity, Hastings
Teulon's tracery is invariably original; rarely is it based directly on historical prototype.

walls of the chancel. The apse walls between the buttresses open completely to windows that flood the chancel with light. Unfortunately, Teulon's handsome east-end composition has been damaged severely by the addition, in 1892, of a lower, polygonal vestry, slightly off-set from the axis of the main body of the church.

Teulon intended for the church to have a tower with spire, located above the south porch. Although the tower was never built, the porch was fitted into the triangle of space between the east end of the aisle, the south wall of the chancel, and the street. It accepts the street direction and is angled in relation to the walls of the building. The junction is very awkward; it looks as if the porch is askew. In its present stumpy form, it is alien to the larger composition. If it had been completed, it would have been, however unusual its angular placement, a strong vertical element around which the other masses would have been organized and anchored. The portal of this porch is the reverse of the two described above. Instead of minimizing the frame, it exaggerates it by the bold projection of its arch and the heaviness of its tracery. Teulon felt that a portal in the base of a tower should appear to have great strength in order to withstand the weight of the mass above.

The exterior of Holy Trinity is, in its present incomplete and modified form, less than completely satisfactory. It is true that when seen from the east (the direction of the town center) the church with its tower and without its vestry would have made an admirable backdrop for the Albert Memorial and a

Interior View toward the Chancel at the Church of the Holy Trinity, Hastings handsome object at the end of the Robertson Street vista. It is also true that the church accommodates its difficult triangular site remarkably well. However, the massing of the existing church seems unorganized and chaotic; and the sheer facades adjacent to the streets on the north, west, and south sides are not pedestrian-friendly. The church is too complex in form for its constricted location. Only the interest that is generated by Teulon's surprising massing and details compensates for the unsatisfactory appearance of the church from all but the east prospect. (Teulon's unorthodox massing is most satisfactory when it can be perceived in the round, from some distance; it needs to interact with the surrounding space. The church at Huntley, described below, is a good example of the power Teulon's complex form-geometries develop when they have adequate space around them.)

Inside, Holy Trinity is much more successful, if equally unusual. The width and height of the aisle are so generous that it seems almost equal to the nave in size. The nave is lighted by huge windows in the north wall; the aisle is lighted by comparable windows in the south wall. The two spaces are divided by an arcade of large arches, with apexes as high as those of the windows, carried on round piers raised on high bases. Because this arcade is so open, it is more a symbolic than an actual division of space. The result is an extremely spacious interior. Both

Exterior View of the Church of the Holy Trinity, Hastings, from the Northeast
This is Teulon's original design complete with the tower (which was never built) and without the polygonal vestry added.

major spaces have steeply sloping timber roofs. The construction of the nave roof is much more complex and ornate than the aisle roof; its purlins and rafters are carried on arched trusses that are supported on brackets which have shafts that continue down onto the faces of the columns below. Cast-iron rondels are inserted in triangular truss openings. There is no medieval precedent for these details.

The easternmost bay of the aisle is filled with a most unusual chapel that is a miniature aisled basilica. The chapel's timber roof and stone arcades are completely independent of the fabric of the larger church. It is as dark as the larger church is bright. The space above it is filled with organ pipes. This chapel, as interesting as it is conceptually, is not an integral part of the larger design; in fact, in its heaviness and the way it interrupts the flow of space between nave and aisle, it is an alien element. Teulon's flaw as a designer is his failure to discipline his boundless creativity.

In contrast to the chapel, the chancel is a true work of genius. From the darker nave, it appears as a brilliantly lighted space. Its upper walls are completely opened to colored glass. The arches of the windows are incised to resemble white marble filigree; they are supported by clusters of extremely tall, slender colonnettes. The five facets of the apse wall directly behind the altar and below the windows are appliquéd with delicate white marble tracery carried on black marble colonnettes. The arches below receive paintings on metal; the interstices are filled with gold and colored glass mosaics. The cornice that

Interior Detail of the Polygonal Chancel at the Church of the Holy Trinity, Hastings

Interior Detail of the Door Leading from Chancel to Chapel at Holy Trinity, Hastings caps the wall surfaces is marble filigree. The solid walls of the chancel are veneered with richly veined marble decorated with gold mosaic inlay.

The apsidal chancel is roofed with a series of radiating half-trusses that are a variation of those in the nave. White plaster ceiling surfaces can be seen through the dark lattice made by beams, purlins, and rafters.

The chancel is seen through the most delicate wooden rood screen imaginable. A magnificent pair of carved wooden angels decorates the gate in the rood screen and watches over the approach to the sanctuary. The chancel arch is gloriously carved white marble carried on colonnette clusters which have elaborately carved capitals recessed in the face of the wall.

The effect of the chancel is stunning. All details of the chancel are delicate, brightly or lightly colored, and rich, in contrast to the heavy, more sober design of the remainder of the church. The chancel gives the illusion of generating its own light and is symbolic of the glories of the heaven that awaits the faithful.

The design of the chancel details reveals Teulon at his most original. The door that leads from the chancel to the chapel is illustrative of the fanciful nature of the details. The door is rectangular except for cusped indentions of the frame at its upper corners. The frame is composed of a series of recessed moldings that make it appear to be an opening in a set of layered planes. The thickened upper frame, which is almost flush with the adjacent wall surface, supports a heavily carved projecting arch which has portrait busts as impost blocks. The tympanum is filled with a deeply cut relief of Christ as Good Shepherd. The composition demonstrates great mastery

over detail; it makes a basically two-dimensional design seem to be richly three-dimensional.

The Church of St. Thomas, Wells, Somerset

The Church of St. Thomas, Wells, was the idea of the Dean of Wells Cathedral, Richard Jenkyns, who felt that a church was needed to minister to the people in the slums which had developed on the east side of the city. Dean Jenkyns died before the church was built, but his wife had the church done during the years 1856–57 as a memorial to her husband. The new parish quickly outgrew its initial building; consequently the large south aisle was added in 1864. The capacity of the enlarged building is 592 persons.

Although Pevsner devotes only the briefest paragraph to St. Thomas, the church is one of Teulon's most interesting, most successful buildings. Its exterior is richly polychromatic; its exterior forms are complex, dramatic, and imaginative; and its interior spaces are open and spacious.

Although the church is much smaller than the Church of the Holy Trinity in Hasting and has little of Holy Trinity's rich decoration, it is similar in basic form. Both churches feature a nave and south aisle of almost equal size, each having its own steeply gabled roof structure. The twin gables are expressed in the west facade. Each of the four bays of the north aisle has its own gabled roof placed perpendicular to the main axis of the church. The second of these north facade gables receives a slightly lower, also gabled, entry porch with open, arcaded sides; the other three aisle gables have two-lancet, arched windows. The aisle gables are much lower at Wells than at Hastings, so the main nave roof, which can be seen behind them, remains the dominant three-dimensional element from the entrance side—a happier relationship of forms than at Hastings.

The rhythm of the aisle gables leads to and is terminated by a very powerful and handsomely proportioned tower and spire located at the east end of the north aisle. The tower is square and unperforated to the level of the main roof ridge, except for a single three-lancet pointed window near the base of the north wall. Buttresses placed on the diagonal brace its corners; a polygonal stair tower softens its connection to the apse wall. The belfry stage is slightly recessed from the square tower below. Its lower portion continues the square form of the tower, but its upper portion is octagonal. The transition from square to octagon is masked by pinnacles which rise from the corners of the square. Unusual flamboyant two-lancet cusped-arch grill openings are located on each side of the belfry; their heads rise into the narrow portion of the wall. Above the grills are steep triangular canopies with arched bottom chords; the canopies project, like dormers, from the base of the octagonal spire. These details reveal Teulon at his most unconventional and unorthodox. (The belfry and spire, together, are half again as tall as the square tower below.)

The main roof ridge of the nave continues, unbroken, over the chancel. The chancel terminates in a five-sided apse similar to that at Hastings. (Teulon liked this form particularly; most of his churches in-

Exterior View of the Church of St. Thomas, Wells, Somerset, from the Northeast

Exterior Detail of the West Facade of the Church of St. Thomas, Wells, from the Northwest
The twin gables on the west facade and the gabled north aisle bays are very similar to those at Holy Trinity, Hastings, but the combination of stone and brick in bands adds pattern richness that is absent at Hastings.

clude a polygonal sanctuary.) The south aisle block is not apparent from the street (the north side); consequently, the impression the church gives is of two major elements—the horizontal block of the nave and chancel and the vertical tower and spire—visually reinforced and decorated with small, low elements that serve to emphasize the strength and simplicity of the larger composition.

The three-dimensional composition of St. Thomas is unusually successful whereas that of Holy Trinity is not. The proportions of St. Thomas are more pleasing and the church is complete with its spire.

More important is the fact that it is a country church surrounded by green; it can be seen as an architectural sculpture while Hastings cannot. Both are built of fairly rough stone; the stone seems out of place in Hastings' urban situation but looks fine here. At St. Thomas, Teulon alternates three courses of stone and two courses of red-brown brick to create a polychromed, banded exterior wall. The bands continue unbroken through all forms, visually tying them together.

The interior of St. Thomas is extremely severe. Walls are smooth, beige stone; stone of a contrast-

Interior Detail of the Polygonal Apse at the
Church of St. Thomas, Wells
This is St. Thomas' most handsome interior
feature.

ing color is used only to emphasize the form of the
arches and to construct the cylindrical columns of
the arcades. Column capitals feature deeply carved,
naturalistic foliage. The nave and chancel are covered with steep arch-braced collar roofs. The faceted panels of the apse ceiling are elaborately stenciled; simpler patterns decorate other ceilings. The
junction of wall and roof is covered with a wood grill
that echoes the stone grill used as a cornice on the
exterior eave of the chancel roof. Slender shafts
resting on carved angel brackets support the ends
of the timber trusses in the apse. Clustered shafts
carry a filigreed cornice that caps the apse wainscot

and functions as a sill for the windows; very slender
canopied panels and broad inlaid panels alternate in
the wainscot. Window tracery is attenuated and elegant. Decorative effort in this small, simple church
is concentrated upon the sanctuary. The result is
very pleasing.

The only unsatisfactory element in the church is
the bleak termination of the south aisle in a large
square chapel with plain plaster wall surfaces. This
chapel, in scale, proportion, and decoration, is out of
character with the remainder of the church. This area
was renovated in 1930 and again in 1979; Teulon cannot be held accountable for its present appearance.

277

The Church of St. John the Baptist, Huntley, Gloucestershire

Exterior View of the Church of St. John the Baptist, Huntley, Gloucestershire, from the Northeast
This shows the complex composition of north aisle, chancel, vestry, and turreted northeast vestry entrance.

The Church of St. John the Baptist, Huntley, was built in 1861 through 1863. It replaced a twelfth-century church which was demolished, except for its tower, to make way for the new building. (Teulon integrated the old tower into his new church and added to it a spire equal in height to the tower below.) The old church was built of red sandstone; Teulon used the same stone for the new building, except that he dressed it liberally (and constructed the new spire) with white Painswick stone. The red sandstone walls are laid in an extremely rough, tight, ashlar pattern; the walls almost have the appearance of dry stone masonry. The white stone dressings of the buttresses at all the corners intersect the walls in a random, "crazy-quilt" pattern.

The church has many similarities to Teulon's earlier church, Holy Trinity, in Hastings. Like Holy Trinity, St. John the Baptist has a single aisle (a north aisle in this instance) that is almost as wide as the nave and is roofed with its own gabled roof structure, so that the main body of the church consists of two parallel blocks. The massing of the church is complicated by the addition of a gabled south transept, a vestry with a shed roof and a fanciful turreted entrance in the northeast corner of the building, a chancel roof slightly lower than the nave roof, and the extension of the aisle to a point halfway to the end of the chancel. The main entry is

Exterior View of the Church of St. John the Baptist, Huntley, from the Southeast

Note the heavy corner buttresses dressed in white stone and the unusual fenestration of the south transept.

Exterior Detail of the South Transept Tracery at the Church of St. John the Baptist, Huntley

strength. This work is an extreme example of the muscular Gothic style. The buttresses more than anything contribute to this strong effect. They are not only wildly checkered in appearance; they are dramatically overscaled. They are what is noticed first about this church.

Teulon's tracery designs are equally unusual. The south transept window is particularly strange. It is emphatically divided by a projecting molding that runs continuously across the face of the wall from buttress to buttress. The lower portion, approximately one-third of the height of the window, is a rectangular blind panel filled with a delicately carved geometric pattern, over which is layered a richly sculptural arcade of ogee arches supported by short shafts. The upper portion is roughly triangular and consists of a cusped arch that contains flamboyant tracery in an iris pattern. Two compartments are blind and filled with bas-relief sculpture; sculpted animals are used for impost blocks. The entire composition has a decidedly Moorish quality.

The color scheme inside is a reverse of the exterior color scheme; the dominant wall material is white stone, but it is banded and decorated with red stone. Arches are made of alternating red and white voussoirs. Clusters of polished red marble shafts around white stone columns support the arches in the arcade between nave and aisle. Their capitals consist of deeply carved foliage. (The sculptor was Thomas Earp, a gifted artist who worked for Street, Scott, and many other High Victorian architects.) Sculpture plays an important part in the effect here. The arched timber roof beams are supported on brackets that take the forms of the symbols of the Evangelists. Busts of the Evangelists fill rondels in the arch spandrels. Sculpted prophets and kings are

not through the tower, which is centered on the west facade, but through a south porch.

The masses are arranged in a picturesque manner that seems arbitrary. Eave lines are not continuous; buttresses are not the same size on either side of corners; the double pitch of chancel and vestry is extremely casual; yet the ensemble has great

Interior Detail of the Nave Arcade and Aisle Wall at the Church of St. John the Baptist, Huntley, Showing Teulon's Imaginative Use of Constructional Polychromy

Interior View toward the Chancel at the
Church of St. John the Baptist, Huntley
Teulon's delicate chancel detail stands in
stark contrast to the bold, muscular detail
of the nave design.

placed at the bases of arch moldings. An elaborately carved triptych forms a reredos behind the altar.

Teulon was uniquely gifted in being able to combine bold, muscular forms with delicate, feminine detail. The chancel at St. John the Baptist is a good illustration of this ability. The arch in the chancel wall is simple and massive, though richly decorated. Beyond it, one seems to be looking through a delicate arched lattice toward the altar and east window. The tracery of the east window echoes the delicate geometric patterns of the wood arch concentric to it. Although much smaller and simpler than the chancel at Hastings, the chancel at St. John the Baptist has a similar jewel-like quality.

The Church of St. Stephen, Rosslyn Hill, Hampstead, London

Time has been unkind to Teulon. Most of his churches in the London area are derelict or have been demolished. His masterpiece, the Church of St. Stephen, Rosslyn Hill, has been declared redundant and is boarded up and fenced in, inaccessible to the public. Structural damage to the building caused by settlement and slippage was repaired in the early 1980s so that the fabric is sound once again. It sits vacant, abandoned, and forlorn, waiting for an appropriate use for it to be found.

St. Stephen is the offspring of the Chapel of St. John, Downshire Hill—the architect, principle benefactor, first minister, and many of the initial parishioners were drawn from it. A beautiful plot on Hampstead Green was offered as a site for a new parish church in July 1864. Shortly thereafter a subscription drive was begun to raise funds for the building. Both Teulon and Ewan Christian were members of the congregation; Christian was offered the commission but declined it in Teulon's favor. (Teulon lived across the street from the site, enabling him to visit the work in progress daily, and allowing the congregation to construct the church without employing a contractor.) The funds for the church—7,500 pounds—were raised quickly, mostly through small donations from parishioners; very few large contributions were received. Work began on the church in January 1869; although the church was consecrated on the last day of that year, work continued through 1873.

St. Stephen is a very large church. It was designed to seat nine hundred worshippers; the total area of the nave plus the aisles is ninety feet long by fifty-eight feet wide. A tower, nearly 130 feet tall, rises above the crossing; its twenty-one-foot square plan unit contains the choir. An apsidal sanctuary extends the longitudinal axis eighteen feet to the east, and an entrance porch adds eleven feet to the west. Identical north and south entrance porches create a cross-aisle in the second of the nave's six bays.

The exterior of the church has none of the form complexity that characterizes Teulon's churches at Hastings and Wells. It has a fairly traditional composition of simple geometrical forms that build up on all sides to form a base for the dominant tower mass. Teulon felt that the size of the church was enough to give it interest and power; form complexity would distract rather than add to its great impression of strength and weight.

The style of St. Stephen is French thirteenth-century Gothic transformed into uniquely High Victorian muscular style. The forms of the church create a superb three-dimensional composition that balances the long horizontal mass of the nave and aisles with an equally dynamic vertical composition of transepts, apse, and tower. The clerestory adjacent to the tower breaks up on either side of the church to form gables which echo the gables of the transepts at smaller scale. These gables not only allow for the provision of large windows to light the chancel wall and pull the worshipper toward the chancel but they also provide a linking mechanism that softens the intersection of the powerful horizontal and vertical three-dimensional forms.

The great square tower is capped by a steep pyramidal roof. (All roofs, except those over the aisles, have a sixty degree pitch.) A circular stair tower engages the full height of the tower at its southeast corner; the cornice of the great square tower moves out and around the stair tower at the same level. The slender form of the stair tower adds a picturesque, softening element to the ponderous tower mass. A similar shorter stair tower is located at the southwest junction between the nave, porch, and aisle.

Exterior View of the Church of St. Stephen, Rosslyn Hill, Hampstead, London, from the Southeast
The massing of the church is similar to that used by Street in Oxford and by Pearson at Daylesford, except that Teulon's forms are rounder, heavier, and more sculptural in character.

The dominant exterior material is brick that varied from pale gray to dark red dressed, sparingly, with cream stone and granite. (Unfortunately the brick has aged to a fairly uniform dark red-purple.)

The church sits on a site that has a considerable slope down from west to east. This slope enabled Teulon to add a chapel for weekday services in a crypt below the apse. It also emphasizes the weight and power of the vertical composition of the east end.

Teulon stresses the visual weight of the church and the vertical build-up of the composition by using heavy stepped buttresses at all the corners and along the aisle walls. The buttresses are particularly effective on the west facade where they are used to bracket and contain the porch.

Although the exterior of the Church of St. Stephen is an example of Teulon at his least "roguish," it does have some surprising details. Wisely, because they emphasize the strong horizontal character of the aisle forms, the aisle windows receive square heads instead of pointed ones; they seem to be the bottoms of the rather short arched clerestory windows moved out into a parallel plane. The north and south transepts are not identical; the south transept is the full height of the nave while the north transept is only the height of the aisle. Consequently, the views of the church one receives when walking around it are not predictable.

Inside, the church seems particularly spacious. It is well-proportioned and well-lighted. Its nave is tall and gives the impression that it is barrel-vaulted because the bottom chords of the massive timber trusses are semi-circular in form. The nave opens to the chancel through a pointed arch that is distinctly Moorish in form; its apex is at the same level as the apexes of the large clerestory arches that flank it on either side. The impressive brick vault of the chancel is clearly visible from the nave. The choir, the space directly beneath the tower, is lighted on the north by a rose window; an oculus of the same size penetrates the wall between the choir and south transept.

The nave arcades are carried on cylindrical sandstone columns with boldly carved capitals featuring naturalistic foliage. The wide pointed arches are decorated with notched and chamfered brickwork of complex design. A projecting band separates the arcade spandrels from the clerestory wall and functions as a sill for the clerestory windows; this band breaks up at the bay adjacent to the chancel arch where the clerestory windows are larger and placed higher in the wall, adding to the emphasis upon the chancel. The western gallery located above the entrance porch opens to the nave through a three-bay

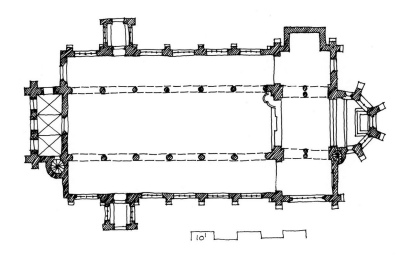

Plan of the Church of St. Stephen, Rosslyn Green
The simplicity of the plan gives no clue to the church's rich sculptural form.

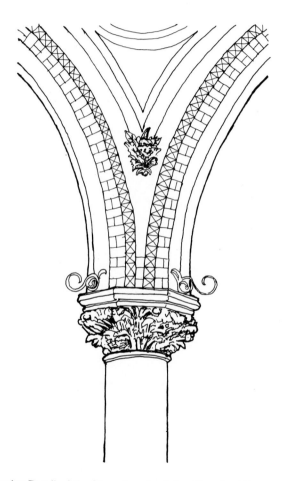

Interior View toward the Chancel at the Church of St. Stephen, Rosslyn Green
Height and mass combine to produce a majestic interior.

Interior Detail of the Nave Arcade at the Church of St. Stephen, Rosslyn Green, Showing the Notched and Chamfered Brickwork

arcade of segmental arches connected by rondels filled with gilt mosaic—a very unconventional design device.

Polychromy plays a large part in the success of the interior. Interior walls are faced with gray, yellow, and white brick laid in stripes and panels. The mosaics in the choir rondels and the alabaster reredos are by Salviati. (The reredos at St. Stephen is actually a wainscot from the floor level to the sill of the windows that fill the apse wall facets.) The overall interior effect, because of the color, patterns, and shapes, and the proportions of the space, is really more Romanesque in feeling than Gothic, and more Italian than English, or even French. Teulon himself described it as "Teulonesque"; perhaps that describes it better than any other term.

NOTES

1. Charles L. Eastlake, *A History of the Gothic Revival* (New York: Humanities Press, 1872; Leicester: Leicester University Press, 1970), 289.

2. Reginald Turnor, *Nineteenth Century Architecture in Britain* (London; New York: Batsford, 1950), 89.

3. Stefan Muthesius, *The High Victorian Movement in Architecture 1850–1870* (London and Boston: Routledge & Kegan Paul, 1972), 54.

4. The Church of St. Stephen, Rosslyn Hill, Hampstead (Greater London Council: Historic Buildings Paper No. 1, 1980), 3.

Teulon, Webb, and Lamb locator:

1. Holy Trinity, Robertson Street, Hastings
2. St. Thomas, Wells, Somerset
3. St. John the Baptist, Huntley, Gloucestershire
4. St. Stephen, Rosslyn Hill, Hampstead, London
5. St. Martin, Brampton, Cumbria
6. All Saints, Thirkleby, Yorkshire
7. Christ Church, West Hartlepool, County Durham
8. St. Simon and St. Jude, Englefield Green, Surrey
9. St. Martin, Vicar's Road, Gospel Oak, London
10. St. Mary Magdalen, Addiscombe, Croydon

CONCLUSION

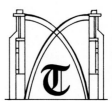his book has focused on the use of an eclectic architectural style, Muscular Gothic, the Neo-Gothic style of the third quarter of the nineteenth century in Britain, by a group of gifted architects to express in a uniquely appropriate way the attitudes and beliefs of the upper class Victorian society of the day.

In many ways the age was a paradoxical one. It was characterized by great confidence and by great doubt. On the one hand, it reveled in the glories of empire, the wealth accrued from industrial and agricultural progress, and the conviction that nothing was impossible for a man, a church, or a nation armed with strength, determination, and moral and religious certainty. On the other hand, the age was troubled by social injustice, the proliferation of urban slums filled with desperate people with little hope, and a church divided between those determined to revitalize the beauty and mystery of the Anglo-Catholic tradition and those committed to the personal, emotional Evangelical and Low Church movements.

High Victorian architects, and the patrons they served, attempted to create an architectural style that would be appropriate to the realities of the modern world but would also perpetuate the best of a glorious if highly romanticized past. In their nationalistic fervor they turned away from the "foreign and pagan" classical and Italianate styles that had been dominant in Great Britain since the early seventeenth century to a revival of Gothic architecture—a style that was truly Christian, that had flowered on northern, particularly English, soil, and that fostered memories of the age of chivalry when life was simple and good was triumphant.

High Victorian Neo-Gothic architects pretended they were continuing the development of their native medieval style, picking it up at the point at which it had been interrupted by the Renaissance. (This attitude was a conceit of course. The architecture they admired and revived was not the English Perpendicular Gothic of the late Middle Ages, but the Decorated Gothic of the period that had preceded it, tempered with forms borrowed from Italy, France, and Germany.) Because they were seeking an architecture uniquely appropriate to their age, they were not interested in simply replicating buildings of the past. They were trying to create an architecture that would accommodate new building types and new materials and construction techniques but would also express a direct connection with those aspects of the past that were most valued in Victorian society. In this effort they were remarkably successful. The Muscular Gothic style that they produced spoke boldly of the strength, power, wealth, and optimism of the day, legitimized by allusion to a glorious past.

High Victorian architects indulged in eclectic borrowings of forms and details from various medieval national styles and periods which they proceeded to rework or revise and to synthesize into their new style to add symbolic meaning to their architecture. They believed that architectural forms had associated meaning, that buildings told stories, and that societal values could be perpetuated through architectural language. They were romantics who desired buildings that would fascinate and enchant the eye, but they were also pragmatists who demanded that silhouette result from articulation of functional plan relationships. They never abandoned the classical belief as reaffirmed by Renaissance architectural theorists that architecture involved three considerations—commodity, firmness, and delight (or function, construction, and beauty, to use a more contemporary parlance). In fact, led by Ruskin, they placed such stress on beauty that they were willing to assert that ornament is the element that elevates building to the art that is architecture. Their concern for "truth and honesty" in function and use of materials combined with their fascination with color, pattern, and texture led to the development of ornament intrinsic to building design and construction—constructional polychromy. Their admiration of strongly masculine qualities led them to produce an architecture expressive of strength and power characterized by an emphasis on mass and weight.

These characteristics that distinguish High Victorian architecture, and to a lesser degree the other eclectic styles of the nineteenth century, were banished from progressive architectural thought by the rise of Utopian Modernism following World War I. Utopian Modernism, a stylistic designation synonymous with "Modern Architecture" or the "International Style," terms most often used today, dominated the period from the 1920s through the 1960s. It abandoned the traditional commitment to commodity, firmness, and delight with a new credo described by Gavin Macrae-Gibson as having three different themes—memory, expression, and morality.[1]

1. Memory. Utopian Modernists believed that great epochs of past architecture could be "emulated in their essence without imitating their surface."[2] They eschewed ornament of all kinds and were disparaging of both abstract/ideal and anthropomorphic proportioning systems. They were convinced that handsome form could only result from the pure expression of function, material, and technology. Macrae-Gibson says that the

Utopian Modernists "gave up pursuit of form altogether by seeking refuge in the doctrine of functionalism."[3]

2. Expression. Utopian Modernists believed that building form should be independent of past tradition; they thought it should be generated by the sum total of the superstitions and prejudices that comprise the "spirit of the day." They believed this spirit operated through the designer's intuition; if he were attuned to the time, his building would be appropriate to the time as well. (As a result of this attitude designers were forced to rediscover the wheel time after time. Past lessons learned were discarded in the search for appropriate new solutions.)

3. Morality. Forms developed in the past were considered inappropriate and, in fact, immoral for replication in the new age. Only novel abstract forms were sanctioned as expressions of the spirit; these were championed at the expense of symbolism, language, and meaning connected with place and the artistic traditions of the relationship between history and morality.[4]

Macrae-Gibson, Charles Jencks, Robert Venturi, and a host of other architects and architectural theorists who advocate a return to an architectural tradition that is inclusive rather than exclusive of lessons mined from past experience maintain that Utopian Modernism has collapsed under the weight of its own logical and spiritual inadequacies. They espouse a new style, most appropriately called Lyric Modernism, that returns consideration of aesthetic purpose (and all that that implies—historic allusion, a recognition of the relationship between meaning and style, ornament, proportion, etc.) as a valid and equal concern of architects along with function and construction. (The term "Post Modern," which is often used to describe the new style, is, in fact, a

misnomer and will not be used here; Lyric Modern does not replace Utopian Modern but is a development or enrichment of it. It retains those canons of modern architecture that relate to function and construction in an industrial society, but it allows them to be humanized by elements that have an exclusively aesthetic or cultural purpose. Macrae-Gibson used the term Lyric Modernism to suggest "songs sung in architecture about the search for value and meaning in a materialistic world.")[5]

Lyric Modernists are ascendent. Architects whose architecture is replete with historical references relevant to the present dominate the decade. The influence of the Lyric Modern works of architects such as James Stirling, Michael Graves, Ricardo Bofill, Philip Johnson, Charles Moore, Arata Isozaki, Robert Stern, Robert Venturi, Hans Hollein, Aldo Rossi, and Leon Krier is felt worldwide. Lyric Modern projects compete for a place with Late Modern ones in the pages of every architectural publication and can be found in built form in cities and towns everywhere.

These architects, and countless others like them, are turning to history to reveal truth that would not otherwise be apparent. They demand that we abandon the idea that there is but one legitimate style; they have returned to the conviction that design requires the conjunction of type and style, empathy and association, physical and intellectual meaning. They allow a new eclecticism that accommodates the replication of images or includes stylistic references to past cultures so long as these devices contribute to the contemporary meaning or significance of the work at hand. Their emphasis is upon the representation of culture through form rather than, as with Utopian Modernists, the abstraction of essence from form.

But what does Lyric Modernism have to do with the Muscular Gothic style of the High Victorian period of English architecture? Simply this: High Victorian architects were masters of representing culture through form. Their design approaches and the buildings they built have countless lessons to teach contemporary architects who are equally interested in representing culture through architectural form.

High Victorian architects were extremely knowledgeable about the ways in which visible objects affect viewers both by means of their instincts through their senses and by means of their minds through their perception. They codified pleasurable effects obtainable from architecture as being of two types, the Sublime and the Beautiful. Sublimity was viewed as associated with majesty and awe or pain and danger. It could result from great size or scale, magnificence, or infinity; but it could also result from obscurity, difficulty, emptiness, solitude, or anything that had potential to produce pain or danger. (Peter Eisenman espouses, half seriously, half tongue-in-cheek, that architecture should somehow relate to man's fascination with the safely bizarre, horrible, or dangerous and cites as justification our preoccupation with horror movies, roller coasters, drag races, and all types of sin.) Although High Victorian Muscular Gothic architects did not borrow the neoclassical forms utilized by such eighteenth- and nineteenth-century masters as Piranesi, Ledoux, and Boullee, they were influenced by the scale, weight, and mass of their projects and utilized these characteristics in their work. Such contemporary projects as Graves' Portland and Louisville office buildings, Richard Bofill's "Echelles du Baroque," and Rossi's Modena cemetery reflect a similar appreciation for the appeal of the Sublime and a sure understanding of the means to its creation. Work of this type rarely features ideal classical unity; instead it fragments, revises, and recombines classical elements in new ways to create meanings that relate to past culture but are also fresh and new. The success of its utilization of classical sources depends upon the action of empathetic forces, the associations with classical precedent, and the quest for the ideal values the classical embodies.[6] The techniques involved are much the same as those employed by Butterfield, Street, and others in their revision and utilization of Gothic designs.

Beauty was associated with passions that cause love or affection or with images that evoke pleasant memories or moods. High Victorian designers developed a picturesque standard of beauty that was richly scenographic and emotional. It featured movement, texture, color, effects of light and shade, occult balance, and surprising effects of mass and silhouette. It depended for its success not so much upon visual devices as upon associations engendered to the experiences of the past. Gavin Macrae-Gibson's analysis of Robert Stern's Bozzi House describes an extremely sensitive application of picturesque design principles to a modern commission.[7] The house composes differently from every vantage point; it evokes the pleasure, wealth, and serenity of summers in nineteenth-century beach resorts; its playfulness is a commentary on holidays and the informality of the contemporary lifestyle. Its effect upon the viewer is emotional rather than intellectual, although it demands an educated observer with the background and insight to understand the allusions made by the architecture. High Victorian Muscular Gothic architecture played the picturesque game superbly; it has much to teach the contemporary designer who wants to compete in the same arena.

Lyric Modern architects, in their efforts to add culture and meaning to modern architecture, have returned to a consideration of those factors that create sublimity or the picturesque. They are also aware, as were the High Victorian architects of a century ago, that ornament can be the handmaiden of meaning. They have abandoned the exclusivist and monostylistic characteristics of the Modern Movement in favor of an inclusivist and pluralistic view of architecture. Charles Jencks attributes this change to the visual dullness of Utopian Modernism; he credits the new style with attempting to enrich modern architecture by combining its language with another, often traditional, one.[8] Jencks is quick to point out, however, that Lyric Modernism is not a return to neoclassicism even though it uses such neoclassic tropes as colonnades, square windows, sconces, swags, sculptural groups, keystones, columns, capitals, arches, moldings, and polychromy. It is, instead, an *eclectic* effort to communicate with the many cultures that compose society; it reaches out to a variety of architectural languages in order to be broadly based. Moreover, it is non-canonical; it does not seek the integration, consistency, and propriety of classicism to the expense of the caprice, surprise, and informality of the picturesque. It makes eclectic choices depending upon the nature of the project at hand and the particular meanings the designer wishes to convey.

Architectural eclecticism has historically been of different types. Carroll L. V. Meeks categorizes eclecticism as *symbolic, synthetic, or creative.*[9] He defines symbolic eclecticism as having the literal forms of the past juxtaposed for symbolic and associative reasons (as in the re-creation of Colonial Williamsburg), synthetic eclecticism as having ele-

ments from the past combined to suit new needs and new purposes (as in Street's Law Courts), and creative eclecticism as having elements from the past utilized to create something original.

Symbolic eclecticism is of little interest to us; our society has scant interest in archaeological replication of historic buildings, although it has developed a refreshing concern for the preservation and/or adaptive reuse of existing historic buildings of quality. Similarly, little synthetic eclectic work is being produced; we no longer attempt to fit train stations into Roman baths or law courts into medieval town halls. However, creative eclecticism is of vital concern because it embraces Lyric Modern architecture—a style that accepts and builds upon Scott's comment that "Eclecticism is a principle of the highest value in the sense of borrowing elements wherewith to enrich, amplify, and make more perfect."[10]

The challenge to Lyric Modernists is to learn to use eclectic reference—historic allusion—sensitively and perceptively to add culture and meaning to their design language; it is defensible only if it truly enriches, amplifies, and makes more perfect. It is indefensible (except perhaps in amusement parks) if it is used only to impress, shock, titillate, or satisfy shallow nostalgic interests.

Meeks goes on to establish criteria for the evaluation of creative eclectic buildings that have application to Lyric Modern works:

> A creative eclectic building should be judged; *first,* as to whether it adhered to the constructive principle involved; *second,* whether the exterior was an expression of the interior, in either an 'ideal' or 'literal' sense; *third,* whether the forms were employed with freedom and independence rather than literal exact-

ness; *fourth,* whether the reminiscences were wisely coordinated and placed in perfect agreement with each other; *fifth,* whether it served the conditions and used the materials dictated by the age; *sixth,* whether the result was simple and comprehensible.[11]

Although there is substantial disagreement currently about criterion two—many contemporary designers no longer feel compelled to express the interior on the exterior or to have the building form articulate the building function—and there has been some diminution to the importance given to criterion one, these criteria are valuable to us in evaluating the accomplishments of both High Victorian Muscular Gothic architects and the Lyric Modernists of the 1970s and 1980s. The analysis of the nineteenth-century churches that constitutes the body of this book demonstrates that High Victorian Neo-Gothic architects were masters of creative eclecticism, sensitively applying these criteria in their work. Their example has much to teach those contemporary architects who are equally interested in achieving similar culture and meaning through creative eclectic means.

2. Henry-Russell Hitchcock and Philip Johnson, *The International Style* (New York: W. W. Norton & Co., 1966), 19.

3. Macrae-Gibson, XIII.

4. Macrae-Gibson, XIV.

5. Macrae-Gibson, XIV.

6. Macrae-Gibson, 120.

7. Macrae-Gibson, 100.

8. Charles Jencks, *Current Architecture* (London: Academy Editions, 1982), 13.

9. Carroll L. V. Meeks, "Creative Eclecticism," *Journal of the Society of Architectural Historians*, XII, 4 : 16.

10. Meeks, 16.

11. Meeks, 16, 17.

NOTES

1. Gavin Macrae-Gibson, *The Secret Life of Buildings* (Cambridge and London: M.I.T. Press, 1985), XIII.

LIST OF ILLUSTRATIONS

INTRODUCTION

PART I: *The Form Givers*

BUTTERFIELD, WILLIAM

PEARSON, JOHN LOUGHBOROUGH

BURGES, WILLIAM

PART II: *The Followers*

WOODYER, HENRY

PART III: *The Non-Conformists*

WEBB, PHILIP

LAMB, EDWARD BUCKTON

TEULON, SAMUEL SAUNDERS

INDEX